The Art of
Emotional Resilience

Chris —

Thank you for your
mentorship. This book
is real in large part
due to our time together.
Thanks for believing
in me!
Here's to the Resilient
life.

♡ Milly

ALSO BY MOLLY DAHL

YOUTH POSITIVE: Exploring the Unique
Genius of Every 21st Century Adolescent

YOUTH Positive Middle School Workbook

YOUTH Positive Teacher's Guide: A Deep Dive into
Mindfulness, Positive Education, and SEL

The Art of Emotional Resilience

An Everyday Guide to Resisting Reaction, Cultivating
Compassion, and Gracefully Managing Yourself

Molly Dahl

THE ART OF EMOTIONAL RESILIENCE
AN EVERYDAY GUIDE TO RESISTING REACTION, CULTIVATING COMPASSION, AND GRACEFULLY MANAGING YOURSELF

iUniverse books may be ordered through booksellers or by contacting:

iUniverse
1663 Liberty Drive
Bloomington, IN 47403
www.iuniverse.com
844-349-9409

Because of the dynamic nature of the Internet, any web addresses or links contained in
this book may have changed since publication and may no longer be valid. The views
expressed in this work are solely those of the author and do not necessarily reflect the
views of the publisher, and the publisher hereby disclaims any responsibility for them.

Any people depicted in stock imagery provided by Getty Images are models,
and such images are being used for illustrative purposes only.
Certain stock imagery © Getty Images.

ISBN: 978-1-6632-0983-2 (sc)
ISBN: 978-1-6632-0982-5 (e)

Library of Congress Control Number: 2021905697

Print information available on the last page.

iUniverse rev. date: 03/29/2021

NOTE TO READERS
Names of all the people portrayed in this book
(except my husband, with his permission)
have been changed.

To my mom,
for her extreme patience and for being my first and best teacher.
Thank you, Mom. I love you.

To all who have shown resilience in the tough circumstances of life and
all who continually work at it.

True happiness is to enjoy the present, without anxious dependence upon the future, not to amuse ourselves with either hopes or fears but to rest satisfied with what we have, which is sufficient, for he that is so wants nothing. The greatest blessings of mankind are within us and within our reach. A wise man is content with his lot, whatever it may be, without wishing for what he has not.

~Seneca

Contents

Preface

All eyes in the lecture hall were locked on our professor, Dr. Tal Ben-Shahar. I was on spring break from teaching high school Spanish in 2013, and excited to be starting this highly regarded positive psychology certification program with the WholeBeing Institute.

Throughout my thirteen years in the classroom, I had pursued studies in adolescent brain development, pedagogy and learning sciences, human interaction, relationship theory and practice, as well as Indo-Tibetan Buddhist studies. I had arrived at the intersection of science and spiritual studies, and I sensed that this program would offer a bridge to connect these two disciplines. I was hopeful that the teachings of these many areas of study could be woven into a useful net of practices, something that could support me during the big life transitions I was passing through.

Dr. Tal's introductory class on the history, overview, and lineage of positive psychology—the scientific approach to creating a life of thriving and flourishing with a focus on the positive elements and facets of human experience—was engrossing. I felt like I was taking the first step toward a comprehensive understanding of how to live my full potential.

He began our lecture that day by sharing a story about one of his teaching colleagues at Harvard.

On the first day of the semester, that esteemed Harvard professor of psychology was standing in front of a large, packed lecture hall, facing his three hundred eager freshmen. He carefully outlined the syllabus, covered the expansive reading list, detailed the writing assignments, emphasized the test dates, and made sure those freshmen knew exactly what their academic responsibilities were.

Being the seasoned professor that he was, he instilled in his new students the unmistakable certainty that they were now in charge of their own lives—not just their academic progress and success, but the day-to-day managing of time, tasks, money, relationships, and everything else that made up their lives.

Then he leaned toward his students, stretching up and out before him, and said clearly and firmly, "No one is coming."

A hush fell over the class, all eyes riveted on the professor. The silence lasted. And lasted. And then, one skinny, timid freshman near the front of the room cautiously raised a hand.

"Yes?"

"But Professor. *You* came. *You're* here."

The silence thickened. The tension mounted.

The esteemed professor peered at this outlaw, looked up at the other students, then back to the questioner.

"Yes. And I came to tell you that *no one is coming.*"

Back in our lecture hall, Dr. Tal stopped to let those words sink in. There we sat, three hundred plus adult professionals from around the world, all of us eager new students of Positive Psychology. A deep, shocked silence descended over the room as each one of us snapped into focused attention.

The inquiring edges of my mind felt like the tentacles of a sea anemone when the water is disturbed by a slight touch—stimulated, curious, on high alert. This wasn't a phrase I had imagined I would hear in our Intro to Positive Psychology lecture.

We collectively caught our breath, one body of stunned, reeling novices. No matter our current profession, our age, our life experience, the number of years spent in our chosen careers, we all felt the staggering power of that statement.

No one is coming.

This was radical. And frightening.

Each of us, in our own way, mentally processed this story, trying to reconcile it with our life experiences. Along with every other person in that room, I flashed through memories from childhood, from adulthood. The difficult and negative ones quickly surfaced. And, as the moments passed, each of us understood and absorbed the personal yet universal truth of this phrase.

No one is coming. All our challenges, all our heartaches and suffering, all our turmoil and grief, are things we ultimately manage alone.

Perhaps we have had shoulders to lean on, and reassuring words offered at just the right time. Maybe we were blessed with support from loved ones and therapists. But the work we have done to move past the struggles has been our own. And we know this, deep inside.

No one can live for us. No one else can do this inner work—it's up to us. No one can pull us up out of the depths of despair. And no one can fully enjoy the subtle, inner nuances of our joys and our successes. Except *us*.

Dr. Tal's story and its impact on my heart and mind was the clincher for me; this phrase would become the anchor of all my positive psychology studies and a guiding principle for the tricky times of my life that required careful decisions. Instead of taking an occasional swim in the waters of self-reliance, self-responsibility, and emotional ownership, it forced me to take a running leap and do a full cannonball into the deep waters of personal responsibility.

Total and complete accountability may not sound like a picnic, and many times, it's not. That's why so few people sign up for it. But I believe you'll discover, through the course of this book, that it is the key to your freedom and your happiness.

Personal responsibility is the foundation of emotional resilience. Yes, you can learn to "manage" your emotions better using many of the techniques and approaches I'll share here. But *mastering* the art of emotional resilience is the direct result of your commitment to personal responsibility.

Let's agree, here and now, that no one is coming. No one is coming to make your life easier. No one is coming to excuse you from the hard parts. No one is coming to rescue you. And just as importantly, it is not your responsibility to rescue anyone else.

With that in mind, let's begin our exploration of the art of emotional resilience with a little trip to the office.

CHAPTER 1

Showing Up

You walk into the building twenty minutes late for work. Things were chaos this morning: spilled milk, misplaced backpacks, two early phone calls, traffic. (Is there ever a day without a traffic backup?)

You drop your bag beside your chair, set your coffee cup down on your desk, reach to turn on your computer, and finally sit down, taking a deep breath. You mentally review your day's schedule and all you have to do. As your email inbox flickers to life on the screen, you catch sight of your boss's name in the queue of new emails. Your eyes lock on the subject line: "Present yourself in my office at . . ."

Your heart goes cold. Your cheeks grow warm. Blood races to your limbs. You feel your muscles tighten in anxiety and a pit opens in your stomach. Adrenaline flows as you prepare to defend yourself, but you don't know against what—or whom.

"Present yourself in my office." *Who says that?*

My boss doesn't talk like that, you think. *What's up? Have I done something wrong? Did she hear about the aggressive conversation between me and my coworker yesterday? Am I in trouble?*

Hands trembling, you click open the email and see that you are to be present in the boss's office in ten minutes. She would like to speak to you about a concern she has. Yikes! Your anxiety grows, and your internal questioning escalates to worst-case scenario.

Am I going to get fired? Yelled at? Am I getting a pay cut?

Breath coming in shallow puffs, you mentally dig up every possible thing that could have "gone wrong" in the last couple of days. You prepare your opening statement of self-defense: "Look, there's been a misunderstanding. I can explain." But your mind cannot find anything to explain. It does not land on any event that warrants a visit to her office.

Walking down the hall, your palms begin to sweat, your nerves are a mess, your face is tight with fear and uncertainty, your steps are shorts and measured. You avoid eye contact as you pass your coworkers' cubes. You wonder if anyone else knows what's going on. Are they watching your walk of shame, or blame, or whatever it is?

As you tap lightly on the boss's door, you realize you have barely breathed since opening that email. You release a long exhale and try once more to convince yourself, even though your heart is pounding, your blood is racing, and your mind is still searching, that it will be okay. But your conviction is weak-hearted. Your confidence will not come out of hiding.

Your boss invites you to come in, and as you push through the door, your inner resolve melts. You give into the fear. You stand before her desk like a third grader in the principal's office, sure that horrible punishment will come. You look past her face, at the picture hanging on the wall behind her head. You cannot meet her eyes. Your mind is a jumble of confusion.

Addressing you by name, and pausing until you turn your gaze to hers, she seems more threatening than ever. Somehow, by some horrible trick of neurobiology, your fear has given her tremendous power over you. Time extends, you glance nervously away.

She breathes audibly, looks down at her desk, and crosses her hands in front of her.

"Listen, there's something I need a little bit of help with," she says. "And I knew you were the right person to talk to."

Your breath catches. Your gaze immediately finds her eyes. You now see not a threat, but simply a human being, your boss, who needs your help. And to your surprise, she has been vulnerable enough to ask for it.

"Of course," you say, the imagined story melting away as the adrenaline and cortisol levels dramatically drop. With an open palm, she motions you to sit down. You settle in the chair opposite her with a silent, deep exhale of relief and the conversation opens with kindness.

How many times have you created a mountain out of a molehill, or built up a story about something that doesn't actually exist? How many times have you verbally "shot first, and asked questions later"? Or learned that you completely misread a situation, even though you were so certain you knew what it meant?

When we are overpowered by strong negative emotions, we can create whole stories and scenes that are complete fabrications. These concocted scenes take vivid and dramatic shape on the stage of the mind. Our neurobiology responds as if the story were true. We get sweaty palms, our heart rate rises, our respiratory rate increases, and our chest gets tights, all in response to a phantom.

We've all been there. Most people presume that these situations are just an inevitable side effect of being only human. But there is an alternative.

Emotional resilience enables us to push back against the narrative, to avoid getting wound up around something that might not be real, or true. When you practice the art of emotional resilience, you will be able to slow down, to take perspective, to pause before you start imagining the worst. And when you do end up in a difficult meeting, or a misunderstanding with a loved one, or even when someone cuts you off in traffic, you will be able to be present and available in the moment. You can use the logical, reasoning, questioning part of your mind, and get more of the story before responding.

In this book, we'll briefly explore the science of emotions so we can understand what's actually happening on the inside. I'll share insights from the discipline of positive psychology about the way positivity can counteract the negative emotions we experience. I offer a framework for cultivating emotional balance—a "palette" of skills, practices, and perspectives that, with steady and consistent effort, will help you master the art of emotional resilience.

When you employ these skills, you'll be able to avoid what I call *unfortunate emotional incidents*. You might have an immediate response to this phrase and know all too well the disaster that can happen when you don't, or can't, control your strong emotions. If you've ever been in a verbal blowup, regretted your choice of words, or "melted down," you've been there.

So that we have a common understanding of this term as it relates to the actual incident, let's break down the process of an unfortunate emotional incident:

1. We experience and assess a situation—this assessment often happens at a level of awareness just prior to our conscious awareness.
2. Our instinctual, automatic, and learned reactive behaviors kick in.
3. Our thinking brain is overpowered by our emotions and we end up on autopilot, reacting without fully processing the situation or the emotion.
4. We respond in an inappropriate or harmful manner.

These unfortunate emotional incidents can lead to feelings of humiliation, embarrassment, shame, guilt, regret, and even isolation from others.

Several defining characteristics help us realize that these unfortunate events occur in the outer world, with others:

- **The emotion is inappropriate to the situation at hand**. For example, you might make a joke or laugh at a funeral service, turn and walk out of the room when asked a question that makes you uncomfortable (a fear response), feel ashamed for expressing sadness, or feel guilty for feeling or getting angry.

- **The demonstrated level of emotional or behavioral intensity is incongruous or disproportionate to the actual event.** You might succumb to road rage and yell at the top of your lungs at the driver in front of you, or demonstrate apathy upon hearing the news you've just received a substantial pay raise, or withdraw from family members over a minor upset.
- **The engagement is harmful or damaging, either with words or actions, or both.** For example, you might stoop to name calling as you insult a person you disagree with, use sarcasm with your child, or in an extreme instance, use physical force against a person you're angry with.

Few of us can quickly move past an unfortunate emotional incident. We may re-play these episodes in our mind over and over, even to the point of obsession. The Indo-Tibetan texts identify this tendency to re-live an event as *ruminating* and *imagining*. These internal mental events of ruminating and imagining represent a "you vs. you" scenario, where you might even re-play the event including "I should have done..." or "I should have said..." creative options to the narrative.

Ruminating and imagining can be addictive. Yet they are irritating and distracting, even debilitating and destructive. In Buddhist teachings, they are referred to as mental afflictions, "anything that disturbs your peace of mind."[1] Practicing emotional resilience will free you from these, too.

In summary, the unfortunate emotional incident is an outer occurrence that happens in relationship with one or more other people. It comprises inappropriate and unacceptable, or humiliating and embarrassing, behavior—behavior that stems from strong, negative emotions. And though the inner mental preoccupation with rumination and imagining is not necessarily unfortunate, it can *become* unfortunate or regrettable when it causes reactive behavior that is damaging, to self and/or others.

What Is Emotional Resilience?

Resilience is generally understood as the capacity to recover or bounce back, from stress, trauma, or difficulty. Emotional resilience is that same ability applied to an episode where our strong emotions get the better of us. We've all had emotional incidents that have left us chagrined, exhausted, or downright humiliated. Being able to learn something positive from these events, which we can later apply to help lessen or prevent altogether another unfortunate emotional episode, is what we'll be exploring together as emotional resilience. It is not something that just happens to you. In many respects, it doesn't come naturally to human beings. Emotional resilience is something that we must learn—and cultivate.

There is nothing exotic, esoteric, or mysterious about the art of emotional resilience. It is not a religious or spiritual practice, yet every great wisdom tradition contains its seeds. The skills, the insights, and the tools are available to us all—if we take the time to discover them, and learn to use them. Every happy, fully-realized, flourishing human being practices this art.

A participant in one of my courses summed it up like this:

> *Lightness. A lightheartedness is what I feel about life now. I can get out of bed excited for the day. The heaviness of doubt and pressure are gone. The heaviness from clinging to my past has dissolved. I have been able to lay down the burden of negativity.*

Emotional resilience awakens a sense of deep ownership and autonomy: you become the owner of yourself and your life; you fully own your responses to the events of your life and the way you show up, day after day.

Think of this sense of ownership as *sovereignty*. As a sovereign being, you are independent and self-governed. You are in control—not your survival brain; not your strong emotions; not your habits; not your old, worn-out behavior patterns. You, as a conscious being with a conscience, acting from your inner goodness according to your values and strengths, will find the emotional freedom that creates this extraordinary lightness of being.

Big promises, you may think. And they are.

As I understand it, positive psychology promotes the development of emotional resilience as one of the defining characteristics of an individual who can thrive and flourish in difficult circumstances.

For our purposes in this book, let's establish our common understanding of emotional resilience in the following way:

- The ability to transform an undesirable emotion(s) and the automatic patterned reaction from a potentially unfortunate incident into an exceptional experience of personal growth
- The capability of an individual to recover or return to stability, balance, and contentment after an emotional difficulty, problem, or challenge has occurred
- The capacity of an individual to manage high levels of emotional challenge or stress over an extended period of time, with maximum efficiency
- The ability of an individual to be present, nimble, and resourceful during the ever-changing emotional events of life

All of these are the results of the emotionally resilient individual's exceptional self-management skills.

Emotional resilience is neither the beginning nor the end of our quest for a life of thriving and flourishing, but a necessary attribute, or characteristic, of the maturing-to-mature adult human. You might think of it as the useful mental equipment necessary to accomplish this task. It fills the inner reservoirs of positivity, courage, clarity, confidence, and personal integrity. When you are supplied with ample measure of these qualities, you become available to life and all its rich goodness.

Emotional resilience enables us to see that the sky is always blue behind the clouds. You are the sky; the clouds that arise and then pass are your trials and sufferings, anxieties and stresses, resentments and jealousies, and your annoyances and upsets.

But emotional resilience is much more than a positive attitude.

The practices of emotional resilience provide a flexible structure of meaning that supports you on your unique journey of growth and maturation. These skills are not the product of the latest trends, but authentic ways of being and living that have been proven through the ages.

I've gathered them here as a collection of easily accessible, go-to ideas and practices that will support you in the daily work of living your vision of your best self. Exploring, uncovering, and living what I call your Unique Genius requires some tools. Power tools, actually.

Our lives are composed of a series of problems and challenges to be worked through, interspersed with events that bring us joy and happiness. We can learn a tremendous amount about ourselves from the difficult situations. Many times what we learn is how we never, ever want to behave or speak again. (We'll discuss those unfortunate emotional incidents in much more detail later.) Emotional resilience enables us to respond to life's inevitable problems and challenges from a place of graceful self-awareness and self-control, and importantly, a place of compassion.

When we're not operating from stress, denial, or pain, we have space in our heart and mind to see the good and to see possibilities. But the pain and the negative darken and narrow our vision—with reason, and by design. When we are suffering or threatened, we need to be able to fix things, to quickly course-correct, so we're able to get on with life. Nature has equipped us this way. When our vision is narrowed by fear or anger, we have a better chance of staying on task until the problem is solved, or the danger averted. In short, we have a better chance of surviving.

This survival system enables us to face a threat, deal with it, then come up for air, and hopefully live in contentment for a while (rinse, repeat). But in today's world, it doesn't always work this way. Nowadays, many of us stay in a state of stress and chaos for days at a time, sometimes months. This chronic stress doesn't allow us to narrow in on one problem, solve it, and move on. Instead, it puts us into a state of overwhelm.

Once in overwhelm, we end up not being able to resolve any of our troubles. Instead, we drag them around with us, struggling just to get from one point to the next in our busy, busy lives. There is no coming up for air. There is no restful period of contentment. Our hyper-vigilant brain is stuck in high gear, responding to almost anything stressful with the same fight-flight-freeze response.

Emotional resilience allows us to manage the unavoidable stresses and trials of life so we spend less and less time in a state of overwhelm. When we can gracefully navigate the challenges we face on a daily basis, not allowing things to pile up and create emotional gridlock, we are better able to see the goodness of life. And we are much more likely to enjoy it.

Being emotionally resilient can be summed up in this way: being emotionally and mentally nimble during the rising up, and in the moment of, a potentially destructive emotion.

How I Became a Teacher of Emotional Resilience

I grew up in the high desert of Northern Nevada, grounded in a rural-family ethos of self-responsibility and hard work. We Dahls have a lust for life and living it big, for doing as much as we possibly can—to learn as much, to experience as much, to share as much, and to give as much as possible. I see this reflected in my siblings to this day.

My full-contact, rough-and-tumble outdoor childhood as one of six kids instilled in me a passion for experiential learning and adventure. My path through the world of higher education was extended by my thirst for powerful real-life experiences, including travel, as well as my love of challenging academic study. I attended two colleges and three universities, in two different countries, over eleven years, before finally graduating with a BA in Spanish Language and Literature. I then attended two more universities to achieve my three-year master's degree. Seventeen years after graduating from high school—years filled with many, many grand adventures—I earned my master's degree in Educational Leadership.

More than fifteen years at the helm of a high school Spanish classroom gave me a deep appreciation for young people, and how they learn to navigate life. Spending so much time with teenagers at the crucial developmental crossroads of adolescence and adulthood made me especially aware of the forces that shaped them—for better, and for worse. Their unquenchable desire to understand life mirrored and even deepened my own.

It seemed that every new avenue of personal growth fed my instinctive drive to share these discoveries, drawing me toward deeper study as preparation to be a better, more versatile teacher. I completed a yoga teacher training program, a meditation teacher certification program, a year-long Certificate of Applied Positive Psychology program, and a teacher certification program in Cultivating Emotional Balance. To nourish my own spiritual growth, I attended dozens of meditation and philosophical-studies deep retreats.

I loved learning, but I also loved doing and applying what I had learned. My life's signature pattern has turned out to be *experience, learn, practice, serve, and share.*

In 2016, I developed a positive psychology curriculum for teenagers, *YOUTH Positive, Exploring the Unique Genius of Every 21ˢᵗ Century Adolescent*, as well as a teacher training program. This coincided with the nascent educational movement to include Social Emotional Learning (SEL) in school curricula. I began to share *YOUTH Positive* with school districts from the Bay Area to Boston. But I discovered that something was missing.

As much as kids needed and were hungry for this important information, I learned that I also had to reach the adults in their lives: their teachers and their parents. As students were gaining the skills of emotional literacy, resilience, and communication, they would often go to other classrooms or home to situations that lacked a supportive environment, or in some instances, were toxic environments. Many students went away from school to places that reverberated with harsh words and unkind behaviors, making it extremely difficult to find the support necessary, especially at that stage of life, to cultivate their budding emotional resilience. My own experiences with the "adult world" painted a clear picture that not everyone had had opportunities to learn the essential skills of emotional literacy and resilience.

As I worked to share this information with the adults in the education profession through teacher training programs, and with parents through workshops and presentations, I co-created an educational non-profit, Mindful SEAD (Social Emotional Academic Development) to facilitate adult social-emotional learning. And, because we can all find such personal power and freedom in gracefully navigating the inner emotional world, I decided to move beyond the realm of education and go big, into the adult world at large. You now hold in your hands a book designed to share "the classroom" of social and emotional skills, all of which can be learned.

Awareness: The Key to Emotional Resilience

Awareness is paramount to cultivating emotional resilience. Self-awareness is the key to all other awarenesses. It includes several components of awareness: your breathing, your physical body and its sensations, what emotion(s) you're feeling, the degree of emotional intensity you're experiencing, and your thoughts. And even more importantly, your self-awareness is a pervasive sense of knowing who you are, your intrinsic worth, and what you have to offer. It is your sense of connectedness to others, to nature and the natural world, and to life in general. It can be summarized as the sense of knowing the self and the presence you bring to life, the presence you are. It is more than knowing you are a stack of bones held up by muscle strength and tendon and ligament support. It is more than knowing how you feel and what you think. It is the expansive sense of knowing that you belong on this Earth, that it is your home. Self-awareness enables you to bring all your finest qualities to the world around you, even as you are aware of and work on your areas of growth.

Self-awareness guides you in the cultivation of managing runaway emotions as well as erroneous thoughts, both of which cause stress, distress, and suffering. As you move deeper into knowing yourself, you will become more and more clear on how your thoughts play a foundational role in creating your inner narrative, and thus your outer life.

It's useful to observe, and then to know from your own observations, that although your thoughts are powerful enough to create your outer reality, they often do not create your emotions. You can mentally recall a past experience and begin to feel emotions that were felt during that original experience. These emotions can build to the same intensity that was initially felt. They may arise in a heartbeat and can have the power to totally consume you, blocking your thinking mind from participating in any way. Even as your emotions can be generated from your thoughts, they are also independent of your thinking mind. Your emotions sometimes naturally arise without any intercession from your cognitive brain centers. They are automatic and instinctual.

> Your emotions are an automatic
> and instinctual process.

This information is not only useful but can also be extremely powerful. As we will discuss in more depth later, you can recreate emotions by conjuring up a past event. You can also bring emotions to life by imagining a future event.

For many of us, the thinking mind is where we find our self-awareness. It is how we process life's events and how we make personal meaning of those events. Our thoughts can have tremendous power to affect our mood and our attitude, our sense of well-being or lack of it. Our thoughts are an important ingredient in how we see the world around us and our place in it.

Your thinking ultimately creates your reality.

For example, the distracted driver that plowed into Jamal's car was not created in his head, of course. But the thoughts that he had about that experience were. The immediate upset might have been purely emotional. But the meaning he added to it: "That jerk should have stopped!" or "Why does this stuff always happen to me?" definitely came from his thought processing.

Emotional resilience offers you a way to respond to the events and occurrences of your life, good and bad, in a way that supports your personal growth and long-term well-being. As you become aware of your thought processes, you can choose to manage your inner dialogue differently. Consequently, you can choose to respond differently. In this way you cultivate your sovereignty. This is how the art of emotional resilience enables you to create a different reality.

What Emotional Resilience Is Not

We probably all have a pretty clear idea of how a person who lacks emotional resilience behaves. We can probably all remember that last time we lost it. It's not an enjoyable experience!

Think back to the last time you were with someone, or even a group of people—coworkers, employees, high-level managers or C-suite leaders, and someone raised their voice, maybe even to the point of shouting.

What was the general shift in feeling, the energy of the room? How much respect did you lose for that person? On the collective level, how much respect did the whole group lose? We know how bad it feels to be yelled at. We know that the yeller has lost control.

What we might not realize is that often, the yeller has an unconscious belief or idea that he or she will gain control by being louder. Yelling in a tricky emotional situation, usually, but not always, is because the person doesn't feel heard. When we don't feel heard, we don't feel validated. That means that we don't feel valued, and ultimately, that we are valueless.

So the voice rises to yelling or screaming.

"You will hear me!" or "I need to be heard," is the inner script of the person struggling to make their point, to be right, or to gain worth. And tragically, that yelling has exactly the opposite of the desired effect. We lose respect in the eyes of others when we lose our ability to modulate our voice, which of course is the loss of the ability to self-regulate and self-manage.

As we slide backward into emotional regression, our Inner Two-Year Old crashes in on the scene, believing that throwing a fit will get us what we want. The fit-throwing is part of an old patterned behavior, bereft of the rational, thinking mind that helps us make beneficial decisions. The yeller is most likely not *thinking,* but rather reacting from this old pattern, which, coupled with the powerful negative emotion, reduces the thinking mind to almost nothing.

There will be people in that audience, or in that meeting, who will understand the yeller's struggle. They may tuck their top lip inside their bottom one, and avert or lower their gaze, perhaps reminded of their own previous emotional outbursts and the embarrassment and pain sure to follow. They will wish for the speaker to just stop it, to be still, to breathe, to *get it together.*

Don't ruin this for yourself, they think, with tolerance born of personal experience.

And then there will be those in the room with no tolerance for this lack of self-discipline and control. They will lean back, wearing a mask of social disgust and scorn for this infantile creature, behaving so poorly in a public space. Some of them will have just enough inner *oomph* to find a vocal expression of their disgust.

"Please get a hold of yourself. Remember where you are," they may have the spine to admonish the fit-thrower. But many won't bother to push back; they will simply write off the offending yeller as someone who can't be trusted to behave like an adult.

And what if it's the person in charge who is the offensive yeller? What happens then? Complete loss of respect for that leader, boss, teacher, parent. And when the loss of respect happens—what then?

It exacts a heavy toll.

Loss of productivity, loss of engagement, loss of trust, loss of wanting to be there and of wanting to participate. Showing up out of necessity. Listening, but being checked out. Biding time until the resume can be updated and pulled together. Aggressively planning life after graduation—moving out and getting the heck away from home.

And of course, yelling is not the only violent form of communication. Sarcasm or ridicule can be equally as destructive.

No matter our habits, our upbringing, or our background, we must practice self-discipline, self-respect, and emotional self-management. Without the ability to govern the self, we won't be able to trust ourselves. All positive and supportive relationships are built on trust. If we can't demonstrate trust-worthy behavior, it will be hard, if not impossible, for others to trust us.

If we don't observe trust-worthy behavior in others, we will struggle to trust them, too. We cannot learn from people we do not trust. We cannot work effectively and productively with or for people we do not trust. We will not go the extra mile, or make the extra effort for a leader who doesn't instill trust. We will not weather the inevitable challenges of our job, or school, or family relationships when there is no trust. Employees will quit, students will drop out, spouses will end their marriages, friends will stop speaking to one another.

The root of all we want and hope to get in our relationships with others comes from the quality of relationship we have with the self. If we yell at others, it's probably a good sign that we're critical and judgmental toward our self. If we can find our patience and speak kindly, it might be an indicator that we can give ourselves permission to be fully human, allowing that we don't know it all, that we make mistakes, and that we can learn from others. What we are on the inside must show up on the outside; it must show up as our words and our behaviors to others. To paraphrase, *garbage inside, garbage outside.*

The Benefits of Cultivating Emotional Resilience

Let's take a moment to survey the myriad benefits of this practice. The list is long: some skeptics might even accuse me of over-promising. Please take your time as you read through them. Note the ones that speak to you the most—and also the ones that make you raise a doubtful eyebrow. These are often the ones where we have the most potential for growth.

Benefits occur on many levels, both inner and outer. For simplicity's sake, I'll list them in two categories:

Inner Benefits

- Authentic self-awareness—freedom from false perceptions of the self
- Positive self-talk
- A growth mindset, cultivated through perspective-taking
- Freedom from a judgmental, critical attitude toward self and others
- Effective self-management and self-discipline
- Beneficial, more objective and effective decision-making
- The ability to witness suffering without becoming its victim
- Reduced anxiety and stress, and decreased chronic stress and anxiety
- The ability to stand in your own shoes, with a sense of self-ownership, humble pride, and joy for all that you are
- Dissolution of fear and doubt

Outer Benefits

- Freedom from impression management (seeking to influence how others perceive you)

- The ability to demonstrate genuine empathy and compassion for self and others
- Clear, authentic, and non-damaging honest communication
- The ability to disarm and eventually avoid conflict
- A reduction in the intensity and frequency of, and ultimately elimination of, unfortunate emotional incidents
- An ability to cultivate positive, supportive relationships of trust
- Power to effectively navigate and overcome the challenges of life
- The capacity to enjoy yourself and all that life brings your way
- More laughter, more fun, and not sweating the small stuff
- Positive social awareness, behaviors, and interactions—civil discourse, manners, kindness, politeness, following the rules of traffic, etc.
- The ability to maintain equanimity and not take offense at the comments and behaviors of others

An impressive list, isn't it? What would you be willing to pay for a magic pill that promised all these things (and offered only good side effects)? Probably a lot. This is all available to you, now, for the price of reflection and your consistent personal effort.

Some of the benefits of cultivating emotional resilience that you see here are also the *ingredients* of emotional resilience. For example, *positive self-talk* comes from being able to take perspective, to step back in order to see more broadly the situation at hand, and to tell yourself, "No, I am not an angry person. But this situation does make me feel angry." As an ingredient, you can see how talking yourself through your emotional *experience*, as separate and distinct from your *identity*, can help you take perspective of the situation and not immediately fly off the handle. These benefits feed the virtuous cycle of both *becoming* emotionally resilient and *experiencing* emotional resilience. The more you practice it, the more of it you will have, and the more of it you will demonstrate.

But becoming an emotional resilience artist is a *process*, and a life-long one at that. Emotional resilience is not a one-off event. It doesn't happen overnight. It requires you to show up self-aware, self-determined, with your intention fully formed in your mind. It will require you to be—consistently, over time, without ceasing—your unique genius.

Hard work is a given.

But don't let that deter you. On the other side of that hard work is freedom: freedom from life feeling hard, from life being too much, or from life seeming unfair.

You can't just imagine or say that you are emotionally resilient, any more than just *saying* you're a concert pianist will make it so. You actually have to demonstrate it, and when you do, you will find emotional resilience is your ally in the fight for a good life. It is the only way to fully live your unique genius. And it is the single most fundamental skill in ensuring your overall well-being.

If you are deterred or dismayed by the prospect of the hard work, the commitment, and the letting go required for emotional self-mastery, there is an alternative: being flung from one unfortunate emotional incident to another, with barely enough time to catch your breath, and marinating in toxic emotions like anger, jealousy, resentment, fear, and anxiety.

We all know change is difficult. It requires serious work and effort. However deep your longing to live your ideal life, to make the changes you hope for, if you set off believing you can do that without emotional resilience, you're probably not going to get there. We know through our experience that things will most likely stay just as they are. Or they may get worse. We don't want worse!

We know that better is possible. So let's focus on that. Let's put our efforts toward better. And as my Buddhist teacher was fond of saying, "Better *for* others. Not better *than* others."

Freedom: Waiting in the Wings

If you're reading this book, it may be because you're going through a challenge. It may be because you're suffering. Or it may be that you crave a more meaningful existence and are ready for a life of thriving and flourishing. Practicing the art of emotional resilience will make these things easier. But unless you're an emotional resilience savant, you won't master these skills overnight. And that's okay.

As you set out on this grand adventure and begin your practice, your outer life may not look all too different. It will still have its peaks and its valleys. And as you know, *stuff* will still happen. Practicing emotional resilience will see you hiking those peaks and skidding down the steep trail into those valleys; it will have you trudging through the stuff. The struggle is real.

You will get knocked down, sometimes knocked down hard. You will still have doubts and questions and suffering. You will sometimes feel that life is unfair and hard and sucky. There may be moments that make you feel you can't go on.

There will be some days that you just wander through, numb and checked-out, simply getting by. You might languish in self-pity, craving comfort, escape, and answers. You'll wonder when you'll achieve freedom from your suffering, if ever.

Those answers, that freedom, will come. As surely as the sun comes out after a mighty storm, when you cultivate emotional resilience, calmness will come into your life. Sometimes, it will creep in in stocking feet, so stealthy you will barely notice it wrapping its soft tendrils around your tender heart. Sometimes it will wash over you like a wave, leaving you clean and clear and open. And other times, it will sneak in and kiss you on the cheek, only to flee like a timid lover.

But it will come.

Until then, we are at the whim of our emotions, tossed about by the fluctuations of our moods, our hormones, our likes, and our dislikes. When our emotions are at the wheel, we're basically suckers, having fallen for one of the oldest tricks in the book of survival. Learn to self-manage your emotions, and you'll call the shots.

If we don't pay attention, if we don't choose wisely, we can go through all these challenges and trials and potential growing experiences and come out on the other side as a cranky old geezer, a bitter cynic, or a woe-is-me-fatalist, not having learned a thing. We can be crushed by our difficulties and find ourselves left lying on the battleground of life, broken and bloodied and bawling, *Unfair! It's so unfair!*

It happens all the time. We see it everywhere. We have probably, at some point, been crying the loudest. Let's not do that again.

When we are emotionally resilient, we are able to see and understand that our life is about choices and taking perspective. We might find it useful to hold our expectations of life as we do our expectations of the sky or the ocean. The sky can deliver rain and sunshine; the ocean can float our boat and swamp it in waves. Yet it's our free will that enables us to *respond*. When the rain comes, we can choose to open an umbrella, or dig an irrigation ditch to water our garden. We can go out and play in it, enjoying the life it brings. Or we can let it soak us to the bone and give us hypothermia!

When it comes to choosing the way we treat other beings, we are wise to remember that what comes around goes around, that what we give we must get in return. It's sometimes so hard to keep that in mind, to allow that it is true and real.

In the good times, most of us praise the reciprocity of life: "I did that, I was generous, and I worked hard, so now I'm reaping my rewards." But when we get the short end of the stick, when things don't go our way, it's not so easy to recognize that golden axiom.

"What did I do to deserve this?" you might ask.

Would you prefer not to get the short end of the stick in your life? Would you prefer that life's upsets and storms were less frequent, less intense, and shorter when they do happen? Would you like calmness to be more and more the norm of your life?

If you do want the calmness a little sooner than later, I will introduce you to practices that will speed it along its way to your mind and your heart.

Begin Where You Are

Like any art form, you may begin your exploration of the art of emotional resilience with some native talent, or you may start with very little. You might be the sort of person who can find humor in annoying or exasperating situations, or you might have a quick temper with a short fuse. You may get discouraged easily, or try hard to maintain an optimistic outlook. Whatever your starting point, like any art form, be it painting or music or dance, there are fundamental principles that will make you better. There are skills that you can learn.

I do not discount the additional emotional challenges faced by individuals who suffer from neurochemical imbalances and organic mood disorders, such as major depressive disorder, bipolar disorder, and anxiety disorders. I am not a mental health professional and this book is not intended to take the place of professional counseling and appropriate medical care. And the practices of emotional resilience can benefit even those who have a steeper "climb" to well-being.

Mastering the art of emotional resilience is not easy, but it is achievable. Like all artistic masterworks, it requires your effort and dedication and every ounce of your skill. It takes time and patience. It requires your energy and your commitment.

Finally, you must leave room for grace. Emotional resilience requires a deep sense of allowing and surrender. Like a watercolor, the art of emotional resilience is at its most beautiful when you embrace serendipities and accidents. If you're a watercolorist, the more you try to perfectly render a cloud, the less natural and easeful it appears. When you let the movement of the water happen, and allow the pigment to drift, unexpected and beautiful things take shape. But using the right brush, the right paper, enables you to have the *best* accidents.

As you work and you try-try-again, please soften around the edges of your insistence and allow the wisps of grace-given support to fill in where you lack, to bolster where you are still fragile. A touch of surrender is required to become the master of yourself.

What to Expect from This Book

In these pages you will find the story of how life's challenges make us who we are. I will share age-old wisdom about the causes of stress and anxiety and how our hard-wired survival behavior contributes to how we *react*, rather than *respond*. You'll learn how to take perspective and make personal meaning that supports your well-being and that of others.

We will explore the tiny space, the gap, that exists between the emotional experiences that happen at the physical and psychological level and your reactions or responses to them. This gap is where you will begin to create greater happiness, peace of mind, and well-being. Cultivating emotional resilience is first of all a process of developing awareness: awareness of the gap, awareness of your hard-wired scripts, and awareness of your habitual reactions.

But there is another, equally powerful and necessary component: when you get tired of thinking and contemplating, the art of emotional resilience becomes the art of letting go—surrendering yourself to the availability of the moment. When we reach those places, I will invite you to come into "current time," and simply let yourself be, with nowhere else to go and nothing else to do. Depending on the event that's happening for you in current time, the art of emotional resilience is something you'll both actively cultivate and gently allow.

You will also find encouragement to help you press on during those times when you just want to turn from your frustration and walk away. You will find cheerleading for when you just need to know it will get easier and things will be better. And you will also find a firm voice that tells you not to wimp out and not to try and cut a deal with your mental affliction, your Inner Critic, your negative emotions, or your seemingly insurmountable weaknesses.

Mental afflictions are a primary concept in Buddhist philosophy. This term is not to be confused with mental illness. Mental afflictions are what my Buddhist teacher calls "our real enemies," and "our internal enemies." He explains that a mental affliction is anything that disturbs our peace of mind, that obscures our happiness. Our mental afflictions are the causes of our distress and suffering. They are the non-helpful story we create around the events that happen in our lives.

Naturally, we humans would prefer the "easy" pill, a do-over button, or an emotional makeover. We would like the proper and necessary tools to magically show up, ready for our use. Of course, we don't really want anybody to tell us how to do things. We want to do things our way. And we're all familiar with the quote about insanity: doing the same thing and expecting a different result.

According to Dr. Tal Ben-Shahar, positive psychology is "the study of what works."[2] When we can model our lives on those individuals or organizations that have overcome challenges and hardships to become successful, we have a clear guide and pattern that we know works.

When you are living at the whim of your strong emotions and the resultant unfortunate emotional incidents, you are not living your best life. You are not living from the place of *what works* to create a life of thriving and flourishing.

You don't have to re-invent the wheel, but in this adventure, you will have to tailor things to fit your unique way of being. As you adapt and modify the practices of emotional resilience to fit you, you are taking the best of what works and making it work best for *you*.

In the chapters that come, we will explore and weave together:

- proven practices of cultivating emotional resilience
- the science of emotions and positive experiences
- the power of positive emotions
- the inner tools and resources those experiences create within us.

We'll delve into the art of emotional response, and then go even deeper into the practices that will allow you, slowly and progressively over time, to unfold the potential of the emotionally resilient artist hidden within.

How to Use This Book and the Exercises in It

As you read this book, please take your time. Please be patient. This is a process that cannot be rushed.

If you come across concepts that seem familiar, please consider them as you would when encountering them for the first time. My goal is to help you translate these ideas into practice, to make them a part of your daily life. Repetition and reinforcement will be key to your success.

Does something I'm suggesting sound so simple—or even simplistic—that you're tempted to breeze on past to the "meatier" stuff? Please don't. Give yourself the time to explore each concept with fresh eyes. Give yourself the space to consider how the concept might look in your life, as you tailor it to fit and then apply it in your practice.

At the end of each chapter, you will find a section titled Art Class. This is where you will apply information through practices or exercises. Please have fun in Art Class! Be creative with it.

Maybe, Maybe Not

You will occasionally come across the phrase "maybe, maybe not" in these pages. This is an opportunity for you to really consider the material being shared and see how it suits your own life. It is not meant to be wishy-washy, nor is it a sign that I'm unfamiliar with what I share.

"Maybe, maybe not," is my way of honoring that your process of discovery is uniquely yours. Your experiences are yours, and yours alone. You are free to accept or reject any suggestion, practice, or idea. When you do take the time to try them on for the best fit, you are tuning into and cultivating your unique genius. You are practicing how to more fully inhabit the unique being that you are and to share the unique gifts you have to offer.

When you come across "maybe, maybe not," it is an invitation to make your own best decision on how to proceed with the information being shared. In considering this phrase, you are also subtly and ever-so-gently training yourself to live in the uncertainty of life and all that it is. We have a need for certainty, but nothing is certain. Many things that seem certain often turn out to offer only false hope and security. When we can be comfortable in uncertainty, in not knowing, in not *having* to know, we move into a more authentic search for meaning and understanding, rather than seeking proof that something is right or wrong.

In allowing for uncertainty, we open to possibility. In possibility lies choice. And choice allows us to take what fits and use it, to ponder what *might* fit and have the courage to try it out, and to put back on the shelf what doesn't suit us. And remember, you can always take it off the shelf later. You never know how things in life will unfold, and what changes may occur down the road.

How Practicing the Art of Emotional Resilience Can Transform Your Life

As you learn to master your strong, negative emotions and become the artist of your own emotional resilience, your life will begin to feel more intentional, and less like a series of circumstances beyond your control. As you gain control of potentially destructive emotions, you will create a spacious awareness of life around you. As you leave behind useless rumination and imagining, as you stop wishing things were different, all that mind-space becomes available to see the ever-present goodness and beauty of life that *already* exists around you. You then become available to fully live each present moment; available to the potential magic held in each experience and in each relationship. You become available to savor the joys of life.

Emotional resilience will enable you to embrace the inner work that is required for these wonderful changes to unfold. It will ensure that you don't capitulate to fear or doubt. You will recognize and acknowledge the outer forces that play upon your life—without letting them overwhelm or even wreck you.

Emotional resilience creates a firm knowing in your heart and mind that things are the way they are, and probably the way they are meant to be. (My Buddhist teacher used to say, "It's like this now.") You will be able to move gracefully through whatever your life presents you at any given moment. You will enjoy expansiveness of mind to take perspective on the reality of your own life and live fully present in your experiences, each one of them whatever the circumstances.

When you practice the art of emotional resilience, you will also be able to see each person in your life, from your family members to your coworkers to the random strangers you encounter, for the human beings that they are. You will be able to take the time to hear their words and see their behaviors as a way of avoiding pain and/or seeking rewards. You will have the ability to hold in the space of your mind some of the possibilities that may be going through *his* or *her* mind, to see beyond the immediacy of the moment into others' wish to be happy.

Emotional resilience will soften the hard edges of judgment, criticism, and comparison. It will ease suspicion, envy, and jealousy. You will be a better leader, a better boss, a better employee, a better team member, a better family member, a better friend. Why? Because all relationships are emotional in nature, and in having ownership over your own emotions, you will have power to shape the quality of your relationships.

> All relationships are
> emotional in nature.

Though practicing the art of emotional resilience will enable you to feel better, to have better days, and to have better relationships, there is another important mission at hand.

Your life is meant to be good and useful. You are meant to uncover your true, unlimited potential and live the full measure of your creation. Anything less than your best will leave you unsatisfied and hungry for experiences that allow you to truly live, to get your hands dirty in the rich soil of life. Your desire to be good and to do good are shared by most of your fellow human beings. The human story is one story, with myriad points of entry. Just as an ocean that is made from trillions upon trillions of drops, you are one lustrous, essential drop in the story of humanity.

What is your entry point into that great story? What unique genius do you offer, that only *you* can offer? If you fail to find it and live it, you will never be truly happy. So don't be afraid of the dark times that come your way. Don't be afraid to get up and try again. Don't be afraid of your light. And certainly, do not be afraid to share that light with others. We need it. We need you, in all your emotionally resilient grandeur. On "most days" (as my dental hygienist says), if every day feels like a bit too much.

As you prepare to embark on this exploration, stop for a moment and consider all that is at stake. Ask yourself—and write your answers, either here or in a journal if you use one:

- What is my deepest inner longing?
- How do I want my life to change?
- What does my ideal life look like?
- What would it mean for me to spend most days living my unique genius?

Art Class: Current Time

"Man must not allow the clock and the calendar to blind him to the fact that each moment of life is a miracle and a mystery." ~ H. G. Wells

Let's take the first step into this adventure of emotional resilience, the *art* of it, with one of the primary practices you will use to develop your skill as an artist of emotional resilience: coming into current time with yourself.

Current time means now, this ever-constant, eternal moment of right now. It is the place where the ever-changing *events* and the personal *experiences* of life happen. (For our purposes here, let's understand the event as the objective occurrence and the experience as your unique story of the event.) Most of us spend a great deal of our life *not* in current time. We worry about the future, we ruminate about events in the past, or we attempt to think about or do too many things at once (the dreaded multitasking—more on that later).

Coming into current time means re-connecting not only your mind and body, but also your thinking awareness to the many distinct layers of the self. Current time enables you to be attentive and perceptive to where you are now—physically, mentally and intellectually, emotionally, and spiritually. It is connecting these layers of the self to the reality of the physical world, interpreting the experience of your physical senses—the light around you, the temperature of the air on your skin, the sounds you can hear, the smells permeating the air, and anything you might be tasting—through your thinking process.

Now, not an imagined future or a remembered past, is the only place where emotional resilience can be created. Let's practice together.

- Feel yourself wherever you are seated, maybe on your couch or comfy armchair.
- Come into current time with yourself. Become aware of your breath. Feel your seat on the chair beneath you. Feel your feet on the floor, or tucked under you. Feel your spine, your hips, your shoulders, the expression on your face. Frown or smile?

- How is your physical self, your body, in current time?
- Come into the mental and intellectual layer of yourself in current time. How are you doing in the space of your mind? Right now, you're probably focused on reading these words. Maybe you still believe the myth of multitasking and are trying to watch a program on TV or send a text or scroll through social media. Let go of all else except these words.
- Now you are in current time intellectually and mentally. Doesn't it feel good to focus on just one thing? We'll be exploring this idea a lot together in these pages. Research tells us that we actually can't multitask.
- What about being in current time with your emotional self? Sometimes, that can be scary or yucky. Sometimes, it can be wonderful. Either way, what is your emotional "status" in this current moment? Without judging it as something good or bad, can you just be there, with whatever is happening emotionally in you? No judgment. No self-criticism.
- And now, I invite you to move deeper still, into the deepest layer of the self. Some call it the *soul*, or the *spirit*. Some like the words *divine self*, or *essence self*. Some like *Self* with a capital S.

> From here on out, *Self* will be used
> as separate and distinct from *self*.

Self, capital *S*, is the essential part of the self that on the best of days, inspires you to say to yourself, "I am really loving myself! I am good at this game of life. I have a lot to offer! And so many blessings to enjoy."

Deep self-awareness invites us to be in touch with that deep, sacred part of the self more often than not.

When you can come into current time in your own Sacred Heart, or Inner Knowing—the highest or most true part of you, a part worthy of respect or even devotion—you touch truth. Your Inner Knowing is something only you can identify and define. As you explore what the phrases *Sacred Heart* or *Inner Knowing* bring up for you, you may eventually find yourself connecting to a sense of awe and wonder for all you are, for all you are becoming, and for all you can become. Can you connect to that now? If you find even the tiniest speck of light or love or hope, you can be assured that you are on the right track.

So then, let's return to our practice together.

Art Class: Breathing

Everything begins the breath. Breathing will be your foundational tool for practicing the art of emotional resilience. You'll breathe intentionally to calm yourself and move away from the brink of a disastrous emotional outburst or an agonizing inner meltdown.

Though we breathe all our life, we actually need to learn some new skills to take full advantage of an extraordinary but simple practice called diaphragmatic breathing—allowing the belly to expand on the inhale and to soften on the exhale. You use your diaphragm, rather than the intercostal muscles between your ribs. This is how you were actually designed to breathe.

When you breathe using the intercostal muscles, especially up high above the heart, you are signaling to your body to either move in to, or stay in, fight-or-flight response. You can create anxiety and stress through high chest breathing. Your sympathetic nervous system is in charge of your safety and survival and this shallow, rapid breathing tells your system to move blood to the extremities and away from the thinking cortex of the brain, preparing for fight-or-flight. (In this work, we'll focus on fight or flight, without including freeze. Although we commonly understand the freeze part of fight/flight/freeze to be the "deer in the headlight" response, it is more complicated than that. Briefly, when the fight or flight escalates to freeze, we've moved into a place where the body assesses a real and very serious threat to life. The nervous system is in extreme overload and is either awaiting a chance to escape or preparing to die.[3]) Chest breathing doesn't facilitate sound decision making but propels you toward a habituated, automatic reaction to the situation at hand.

Especially under adverse circumstances when you begin to feel the first flush of emotional upset, exhale long and slowly, pulling your belly in toward your spine, releasing the air through a slightly open mouth, keeping the lips soft. A long, slow exhale can begin to dissipate the chemical cascade of stress and anxiety that your nervous system sends out as an "all systems go" to keep you alive. Inhale through the nose, with lips lightly closed. This breathing is calming and steadying to your whole being.

If you find yourself in pain, you are probably holding your breath. This tightening up and restriction during pain is something we do naturally. Somehow, when in pain, we have an instinctual awareness that holding the breath will hold off the pain. When you catch yourself here, by all means, breathe! Again, exhale long and slowly, regaining awareness of the present moment.

Diaphragmatic breathing moves us into a *rest and relax*, or *rest and rejuvenate* state.

Diaphragmatic Breathing

- Sit or stand up tall. Allow your spine to lift without becoming rigid. A tall spine helps open the rib cage, allowing maximum expansion in the lungs.
- Relax the shoulders, face, and jaw. Lips together. Teeth apart.
- Soften the belly, letting it extend, big and round, as you inhale through the nose. Inhale all the way to completion, where you can't take in any more air.
- As you exhale through the nose, slowly draw the belly back in toward the spine. Please don't exhale a big gush of air. You would like your exhale to be the same length as your inhale, if not slightly longer.
- Repeat for at least three breaths.

```
┌─────────────────────────────────────────────┐
│                                               │
│   Cycle of Breath = Inhale and Exhale         │
│                                               │
└─────────────────────────────────────────────┘

┌─────────────────────────────────────────────┐
│                                               │
│        Five-seven count breathing             │
│                                               │
│   •  Inhale slowly, counting to five.         │
│   •  Pause.                                    │
│   •  Exhale slowly, counting to seven.         │
│                                               │
└─────────────────────────────────────────────┘
```

You can try this **five-seven count breathing** to help you get the hang of a slow, steady exhale.

- Find your breath. Exhale.
- Inhale through the nose, counting to five at a steady pace. Pause.
- Exhale softly through the nose, counting to seven at the same steady pace.
- Repeat for at least three more cycles of breath. (Each cycle is an inhale and exhale.)
- After your last exhale, let the breath breathe itself, finding its own steady rhythm.

If you're on a roll and like how this feels, do three more cycles of five-seven count breathing. Practice this several times a day. A great place to practice this one is in traffic, especially at red lights, or on the train or metro. If it feels like a useful idea, set a chime on your phone on the hour to remind you to stop and breathe your deep, five-seven count breathing. Slowly, over a week or so, work your way up to about fifteen cycles of breath.

- If you are feeling rather good about your smooth, rhythmic fifteen-cycle practice, try lengthening your inhale to seven counts and your exhale to eleven, the **seven-eleven breath.** If you run short on your exhale, try a pace of six-nine: a six-count inhale and nine-count exhale.

- As you practice, notice your mind and emotional energy. Does anything happen for you? How do you feel? There is no right answer, but usually you will feel noticeably more calm.

Current time is now your paint and your breath is your brush. This is the essential daily practice that will enable you to become an artist who creates emotional resilience with one or two masterful strokes, using the breath as your primary tool.

CHAPTER **2**

The Power of Intention

"Why Am I Here?"

Life during my early post-high school years was fraught with many moments of uncertainty and self-doubt. I had planned on enrolling at University of Nevada, Reno, an hour's drive away from home, right after I completed high school. Neither of my parents graduated from college and had not been actively involved in helping me choose the direction of my life after graduation.

I had received a $700 scholarship and was excited enough about enrolling for my first semester. I made the necessary phone call to register myself for classes (this was long before the internet) and wrote a page full of notes and the list of the courses I needed to take. A few days later, I drove all by myself up to the university registrar's office.

When I arrived and finally found that office, they had no record of me. Nothing. Not my name. Not the list of classes that I'd registered for by phone. Not a thing.

I was at a loss. With a deep sense of discouragement and invisibility, I slunk out of the musty basement office, back into the sunshine and blues skies and thought to myself, "Well, I guess I'm not university material."

And so began the rough days of looking at my own despondent reflection, wondering who I was, why I was here, and what I was doing. I didn't know what to do with my life. No one really offered suggestions or support. So I floundered around for a bit until I got my feet under me and enrolled in a program to be a Certified Travel Agent, to prepare for employment in the tourism industry.

I went to work in a brand-new hotel in Southern California as part of the opening team. It felt good and important. But it was OK only for a while. It didn't fulfill my inner desire to do something more, something bigger. I was still fairly young and at that point in life, had no idea that a personal *Why* even existed.

So for many, many years I wandered: through several colleges, universities, and countries. And through countless inquiries into the big Why of life. I ultimately came full circle and found myself again for the first time back at the University of Nevada, Reno. This time I was successful. I finally graduated with a Bachelor's Degree in Spanish Language and Literature. I had done of lot of introspective pondering and searching, a lot of academic studies and research, but I still didn't have my personal Why figured out.

What I did come to realize, however, was that life was my best teacher. I didn't like the confines of a classroom. And yes, I did learn many things in my college and university courses, from textbooks and lectures. But in the eleven years between high school graduation and earning my bachelor's degree, I learned more by simply paying attention, by falling and getting up, by letting life change me, and by not being afraid to try.

Resilience doesn't come from reading words printed on pages, no matter how poignant and inspirational the story. Self-worth doesn't come that way either. Neither does perseverance.

These inner traits must be cultivated through the felt-and-overcome experiences of adversity and challenge. As an educator, I've seen firsthand that many administrators, teachers, and parents think that adversity is a four-letter word, that we have to protect the children from any and all adversity—anything that might cause upset, or struggle, or challenge.

Adversity and failure get quashed at their slightest mention. They are seen as the enemy, the thing to avoid at all costs.

Hogwash.

We cannot develop resilience without something toward which to demonstrate resilience. The same goes for perseverance, and the other character traits required to experience a life of thriving and flourishing.

What does that mean for us, here together on these pages?

It means you are going to recognize that life sometimes does not go your way and that you are going to own your behavior when it doesn't. Emotional resilience starts with emotional ownership—and ownership starts with intention, which then guides your self-concordant goals and your quest for self-responsibility.

Pop the Question

An important positive habit of mind that the emotionally resilient artist develops is setting a daily intention. This may not be a new habit for you, but let's get really specific on how we set that intention.

Ask yourself, "Why am I here?"

Go inside the space of your Inner Knowing and quietly listen for an answer. Don't think. Be mentally silent and aware of what arises from within.

We have a strong habit of needing to think and produce with our cognition an answer to every question we ever receive. There is much freedom and connection to your self-awareness and your Self when you allow wisdom to arise from within, without forcing it. You may try letting your intention be something that brings you into partnership, on the inside, with your Inner Knowing, rather than be something you *think* you need to do or achieve.

Does the question, "Why am I here?" bring up some big, existential wonderings? Maybe you've already done this discovery process for yourself. But if you have gotten this far in life without deeply examining your Why, or if the Why you began with no longer feels compelling, it might be time for some deep contemplation—for a little change.

Imagine the last time you felt like your life was really a mess. I mean a big one—when you found yourself asking your crumpled face in the mirror, "What am I doing, and why I am here?"

You may have been in a dark-night-of-the-soul without recognizing it. You may have been asking your Inner Knowing for guidance and an intention to set your life straight.

At the end of this chapter, you'll find an exercise to set your intention through a powerful inquiry. You will also explore a set of questions to help you discover your own Why. As your Why is discovered, it becomes the motivating force behind your goals. In the world of positive psychology, goals are labeled "self-concordant" when they align with your deepest intentions and values, free from the pressure and influence of the outside world. When your values, intentions, and goals are aligned with your inner truth, you have a much better chance at actually accomplishing these goals.

In the process of establishing your self-concordant goals, please look inside and get clear on your values, your intention, and your personal Why. Are they aligned? Sometimes during this discovery process, you will notice that some inner part of you is uncooperative. You might realize that something you think or feel is really important, or *was* really important, no longer holds sway in your life.

Give yourself time to ponder and reflect. Journal and get your ideas out on the page. As you listen on the inside, and honor your Inner Knowing, you will have the courage to release beliefs, ideas, old patterns, or even once-cherished parts of the self that no longer resonate with who you are *now* and where you are going on your path of self-mastery, toward a life of thriving and flourishing.

Set Your Intention

When you know what you're doing and why you're doing it, when all your inner parts are aligned, don't you find that things are easier to manage—even fun to manage? Maybe it doesn't even feel like you're managing, but just *allowing* the serendipity. When you are living your life purpose by regularly working toward your highest goals and aspirations, you worry less, are less distracted by the negativities of life, and bounce back more quickly should you make a misstep.

Having clear intentions endows you with resilience. Being in alignment with your Self creates resilience. How? When you know in your heart and mind your big Why, it is easier to stay focused on the outcome and you are less likely to get distracted or waylaid by obstacles and emotional distractions as you press on toward the fulfillment of your self-concordant goals. When you set intentions, you increase the chance that you'll stay the course and endure to the end of a challenging path toward your goal. You might arrive at that goal gracefully, artistically—or just barely, crawling in on hands and knees. But you will arrive.

Intention matters. In our Western culture, we know the phrase "The road to hell is paved with good intentions." Maybe. But maybe it's not. Maybe our intentions really carry some positive power. If we have authentically set our *own* intentions and are not living by the *shoulds* of someone else, our intentions become our North Star. When we fail, they can guide us back to our centered alignment. If we begin to drift, they can help us course-correct. They can even allow us to recognize opportunities or paths we might not have expected or anticipated. But if we happen to be living the intentions of another, then maybe the phrase should read, "The road to hell is paved with other people's good intentions for me."

Knowing that intentions matter might help you be a little kinder to yourself. This knowledge can offer a sense of resting in your good intentions, while allowing for the sometimes-chaotic outer circumstances of life that keep us from acting on the intentions we hold in our heart. Your good heart is brimming with desire to do good in the world. Don't allow your intentions to become another reason to feel guilty that you're not doing enough or not being enough.

The intentions you hold in your heart, when resonantly aligned with your deepest truth, will ultimately guide you to embodying and living that truth. They don't necessarily need to be a conscious thought that you repeat to yourself every day, or even multiple times a day. They are different than affirmations. We can think of our intentions like the white lines painted on the side of the road. You know they are there. You know what they mean. You know they are a guide and a protection for you, keeping you in the safe zone inside the lines, indicating useful boundaries. You certainly don't need to re-paint them every day.

It can be useful to consider our intentions from the perspective of Dr. Wayne Dyer, who shared that "Intentions are not something you do, they are something you connect with."[4] They can be your strongest link between your Self and your self, guiding you to stay inside the lines of your values and your truths.

Whys vs. Shoulds

As I learned to navigate the many opportunities and challenges of my young life, I had to shed many expectations of others. When I was overburdened by what others thought I should be, and should be doing, my road was a bit hellish. My heart was miserable, my vision was clouded, and my life path was leading me who-knows-where. I wasn't sure I had a life path! As I was able to ponder, contemplate, and eventually find value in some of those expectations, I was able to decide which were worth keeping and have the courage to throw out those that didn't serve me. I could then authentically own as mine those intentions that I had consciously chosen to accept.

Taking the time to seriously evaluate what was important to me allowed me to silence the many outer voices and come deep into the place of my own Inner Knowing. A sense of guidance beyond my mind encouraged me to simplify, to identify one or two things that were of infinite worth to me and to place my focus there, as my guiding principles. As I did, I set a firm intention to stay quietly and inwardly focused. This enabled me to create a little buffer zone to hold at bay the busyness and allure of the outer world in its attempts to capture me with its flash and glitz. And I do love glitz! But knowing my intentions were the power to keep me from outward distractions and the power to achieve my goals, I found a new glitz and a new appeal in the quiet moments and in the beauty of a settled and still mind.

Just because we set an intention once doesn't mean that we won't need to revisit it every now and again. At different seasons of our lives, our needs and wants are different and might require situationally unique intentions.

And listen, when you do establish your intention, or a personal Why, that doesn't mean you are bound to that no matter what. If you outgrow it, you can change it. Or it if ends up feeling cliché or trendy and loses its appeal, by all means change it! Our intention and personal Why are never meant to bind us, to constrict us, or "keep us in line". Their purpose is to help us through the passageway of liberation to the state of freedom. If you need to walk that path for a while without intention, or without a Why, go for it. You do what you need to do to really live your unique genius—free to change your mind, or not. Free to be wishy washy if necessary. And free to be deeply committed if that's what's call to you.

Spoiler alert: You can't do it wrong.

During child-raising years, a big portion of our intention and energy is focused on family and children. What a beautiful way to spend time and energy! Children growing into teens, and teens growing into young adults, are some of the most amazing people on the planet. They are so vibrant, so full of life and questions and possibility, and unjaded by the hardships that can beset the average adult.

When the children leave home, a re-evaluation might be in order. If there are no children, or no children yet, your intention will have a very different flavor. If the opportunity, or harsh reality, of a career change, selling the home, death of a loved one, divorce, or any other of life's events call upon you to re-assess, a new intention might bubble right up from the center of your knowing heart.

Ask and You Shall Receive

When we quiet ourselves enough to ask—in deep introspection—we can come to understand what our Self wants our self to know. Indeed, Self will share the profound inner truths with great, loving immediacy. When we listen on the inside, the place where no "shoulds" interfere, we will know. And in knowing, we will have the resilience to overcome whatever it is that might obscure our path—strong emotions included.

I used to teach a yoga nidra class once a month. This yoga is known as yogic sleep, the yoga of deep relaxation. It is a practice that clears from the many layers of the self the noise, chaos, and stress of the outer world. It allows the truths held in the space of the inner heart to surface into conscious awareness.

Big things can happen as a result of a yoga nidra experience. One of my students, Heather, approached me after a class one night and told me that because of yoga nidra, she was getting divorced. My heart dropped. My eyes bugged out. As I quickly masked my surprise with a calm expression, not knowing if divorce was a good thing or a bad thing, I asked her how she felt about that.

"It's the best decision I've made in my whole life."

Relief flooded through me. "Would you share with me how you came to that decision?" I asked gently.

She briefly recounted that her intention was to know the best way to proceed with her relationship, so that she and her husband could both be happy and live their own truths. In the time of the nidra practice, she became so still and her mind so quiet that her heart shared with her that in order for her to be truly happy, and to live the life that was waiting for her, the current relationship was an obstacle. She felt a surge of courage and knew the best thing for all involved was to separate and go her own way and send her husband on his own path. She was so overwhelmed with love and hope that tears spilled from her eyes, her heart full and joyous.

"I heard my Self clearly. There's no denying it. And there's no way I cannot follow my inner guidance. I haven't felt this good in a very long time," Heather concluded.

She knew clearly what direction her life would take, based on her intention that all involved in the painful relationship find their way to freedom, happiness, and fulfillment.

As we learn to quietly come inward, listening to and feeling the way our Self communicates with us, we experience the wisdom of knowing—not sure *how* we know, but certain that we *do* know. And it can be oh-so-easy to trust that certain, inner knowing.

Weaving the Fabric of Our Life

As crucial as intentions are to living the life you want, they don't work in a vacuum. It's the synergy of intention and lived experience that provides us with the insights that enable us to create the life we want. Not everyone grows up knowing "what they want to be", though some do. For most, the discovery that occurs through life's experiences plays a huge role in shaping who we become.

Becoming a teacher of the art of emotional resilience has been my life's work, though I didn't recognize this until deep into the journey.

Early on my path through young-adulthood, my life experiences offered subtle suggestions of the topic, hints at what was to come. As I began my formal studies of positive psychology and emotion sciences, and I started to pay attention to those past experiences and could see them in a different light, I discovered that I was exactly where life wanted me to be at that point in time. I understood where I had arrived and how much each step had mattered. I recognized that the work I had done had been a remarkable teacher.

I learned a great deal from every job I had, and from the people who taught me those jobs. I worked in a florist shop and greenhouse. I spent time in the hotel industry. I worked as a telephone and a PBX operator and at fast-food and sit-down restaurants. I was a wildland/forest firefighter and a paralegal. I worked in a bakery and as a coffee shop manager and counter girl (long before the word *barista* became part of the American vocabulary). I was a school teacher, yoga teacher, and bookstore clerk. And I worked many of these jobs simultaneously. It was sometimes a struggle to pay the bills on a teacher's salary.

It would be easy to consider these many different jobs as a distraction or a detour from my real goals, but it was never my goal to be a school teacher. But, somehow I landed a job as a part-time high school English teacher—and I loved it! So much so that I stayed in the classroom as a Spanish teacher for fifteen years.

I later came to understand that all those varied work experiences are what made me a good teacher. As part of my *praxis*, putting theory and knowledge into action, I was able to take all of these rich experiences with me into the high school classroom. My diverse and rich life adventures enabled me to connect with my students on a real and personal level and helped me forge authentic relationships of trust. Those powerful bonds helped me create a dynamic, engaging, and healthy learning environment where almost all of my students were able to thrive, to flourish and of course, to learn.

The most important part of creating the life I want to live is cultivating the ability to integrate the experiences that I've had, to find value in each of them, and to give them a special place that beautifies the tapestry of my life. Nothing I've experienced has gone to waste, discarded as unimportant or extraneous. Some of these experiences are obvious in their effect on who I am and how I show up every day. Other experiences have had to pass through the refiner's fire to separate the dross and distill the useful bits.

Those experiences might not even be recognizable in their original form, but I've extracted the essential learning and knowledge and cast off what no longer serves any useful purpose.

I've come to recognize that I'm a weaver, taking the individual threads of my interests, studies, and adventures, and interlacing them. The warp threads are the powerful experiences and learnings of my childhood, which created the essential framework. Through these, I have woven the weft threads—the colorful, rich, and varied exploits, escapades, and accomplishments of my life as an independent woman.

I attribute this to the fundamental habit of my life: contemplation. Consideration. Pondering. Mulling things over. Key to this is putting my thoughts, ideas, beliefs, my questions, my wonderings, and my inquiries onto the pages of my journal. This brings them into the real and visible world, and ultimately enables me to move them from the page into my words, actions, and behaviors.

Each experience we have contains lessons, if we are willing and able to receive them. Sometimes they arrive as flashes of insight, but more often than not, life's lessons only reveal themselves after being processed through deep contemplation, reflection, and even a bit of alchemizing. I've let the impurities burn away in the crucible of my meditation practices and allowed the gold, the most valuable parts of each experience, to find a home in the story of myself.

Contemplation, or reflection, is a key skill in practicing the art of emotional resilience, but it has another mirror-image skill: the ability to connect with and use your intentions. Practiced together, intention and reflection create a vital rhythm for living your unique genius.

The concept of setting intentions gets a lot of attention in our popular culture. "Setting intentions" has often been presented and taught as a complete practice. *Set intentions, submit your wish list to the Universe, sit back, and watch them all manifest!*

In this chapter, we'll understand a different perspective on intentions and how they work as part of the art of emotional resilience. Setting intentions is like setting a course: you familiarize yourself with the territory, map out your path, and look for obstacles that will trip you up. As you get to know the lay of the land, you will have a general idea of what's coming. And even with that general idea, you still recognize and know that the territory is not the map. You still have to take the journey. You still have to get out there and start living your intention.

Your intention-discovery practice doesn't have to happen all at once, in one sitting. Sometimes it's really nice to ask yourself the big question, then give yourself the space of several days, or even a week or so. As you ask yourself "Why am I here?," you might not immediately know. And that's OK. Let that question roll around in your heart and mind. Be attentive to what surfaces, to the small inner nudges you receive, to the things that catch on the corner of your mind and won't let go. Allow for the process to unfold without forcing it. Like a flower, it will not open from bud to bloom until it is good and ready. You cannot pry the petals apart; you cannot coax the bud to open for you. You must patiently wait on Mother Nature. But wow! When it's ready, that flower is perfect and beautiful and right on time, just like your intention will be.

Your intention is just for you. No matter how much we may hope or want others to change, if we stop and think about it, we will realize that all change is self-change. Let others come to their own intention as you focus on yours.

Let your intention be short, positive, and powerful. Like the image that captures the thousand words, your short phrase of intention should hold deep and broad meaning that, as you speak it to yourself, fills you with peace, excitement, and an encompassing satisfaction that you're on the right track.

Enter Ms. Inner Wisdom

Growing up in the religious community that I did left some lasting impressions. It was a good upbringing, with many valuable practices and teachings. As I struggled to find my place there as a single woman, frustration mounted until I could no longer allow myself to be subject to the dictates of what it meant, from that perspective, to live a religious life. Not being married, not being a mother, meant failing as a woman. I tried desperately to find the husband I'd been told would make me happy, to have the children that would make my life complete. The biological time pressure was intense.

All that made me afraid; afraid that I wasn't good enough, that I'd never be good enough. Which then made me afraid that I wouldn't have enough— enough love, enough money, enough time, enough worth, enough pretty, enough youth, enough smarts—enough for someone else to love.

And all that fear made me a bit frantic. Then it made me angry. Then it made me mean.

I didn't like being angry and mean. I didn't like how I felt. Some big changes had to be made.

So they were, over the course of many years.

I eventually parted ways with the religion of my childhood, opting for a life of ignorant bliss. I felt free from the restrictions and requirements that had previously shaped my life. No one was pressuring me to get married and have babies. No one was judging or establishing my worth as a woman. But a hollow and empty space inside my heart began to grow. I felt far away, floaty, and untethered. I couldn't explain the far away feeling to anyone, even in conversations with trusted friends. But I knew that I needed an anchor.

A friend suggested I attend the annual Thanksgiving retreat at Lake Tahoe with a Tibetan Buddhist monk. Being relieved at not having religious dictates to govern my life, I wasn't sure I was ready for anything that involved monks. But I liked this guy friend, a lot, and thought it would be a great chance to spend time with him.

Well, I was in for something much, much different than I had expected.

I hated it.

The retreat "center" was a church summer camp for kids. It was rustic—to say the least. We retreatants stayed in the kids' dorms, (women on the north side, men on the south). The concrete block buildings had been built for summer residents, with no central heat and only cold water. The bunk beds were constructed of two by fours with plywood platforms. My borrowed sleeping bag was too short for my six-foot frame and the thin bag's lumps of feathers did little to protect me from the late-November chill in the Sierra, which dropped into the low 20s at night.

At sunrise each day, teeth chattering, I forced myself out into the icy morning air, and traipsed to the dining hall and the cup of hot coffee that promised to warm my bones. Breakfast was a silent affair, meant to invite a deep internal awareness to the waking moments of the day, uninterrupted by useless chatter praising the oatmeal or expressing dismay at the lack of real cream for our coffee.

I loved the silence. It reminded me of the rare moments of meditative stillness that I had experienced six years before, at my first yoga teacher training at an Ashram in rural Virginia. I also knew the silence was protecting me from my Inner Critic (or Internal Narrator), the big complainer who took center stage, dramatically and bitterly bellyaching about the cold and the lack of comfort—not to mention a missed Thanksgiving with my family: no homemade pumpkin pie, no family-tradition mashed potatoes. No turkey! There was no way I was buying into their Buddhist-vegetarian tofurkey nonsense. (Silence is sometimes such a saving grace!)

After breakfast, we met for teachings in the chapel, which had an astonishing view of the lake and the dramatic rise of the west-shore mountain peaks framed by an ancient, leaded-glass cathedral window. I wasn't really down with the teachings. I was too close to my recent exodus from organized religion. I most certainly was not down with a 280-pound monk in maroon and saffron robes telling me what to do, and what and how I needed to think, in order to live a spiritual life.

To escape, I sneaked down to the water's edge and threw stones into the cold November lake. The frigidity of the water reminded me of the rigidity of religious teachings. I wasn't sure I wanted to step back into a religion, with its required surrender and sacrifice. I pondered deeply, sitting on the damp sand, the wet-cold seeping into my bottom, the wind off the lake raising the color in my cheeks.

The guy (who, nine years later, ended up being my husband) I had come with wasn't very concerned about me; many of his friends who he had not seen since last year's retreat were there. I felt like an outsider. I really wanted to go home, but I had gotten a ride with him. I was stranded. Considering my options as I sat on that chilly shore, I decided that I just needed to get warm.

That afternoon, the teachings had been moved into the space where the yoga sessions were held. It was much warmer there and apparently I was not the only one suffering from the miserable cold. Huddled in a far corner, wrapped in a wool yoga blanket, I tried my best to stay focused on the teachings. Maybe there was a morsel that would do my heart good.

The 280-pound monk did have a pretty entertaining way of speaking. He was funny and surprisingly irreverent. At first, his irreverence for sacred things really got my goat. It was part of what made me skip out on the sessions in the chapel. But now, I began to wonder why he displayed such a cheeky attitude.

The more I listened, the more I appreciated his perspective. I realized that his irreverence wasn't really irreverent at all. It was the kind of teasing that happens when brothers and sisters are so close and know each other so well that they develop their own secret language. It was teasing that actually expressed endearment, filled with the same sort of knowing looks and private expressions.

The monk had previously been a university professor of comparative religions at several prestigious schools on both coasts of the US. I realized that he knew his religions so well and regarded them with such honor and love that he could find the joy and the lightness in each one.

I wondered if I too might one day come to appreciate the value of the teachings I had grown up with. And if I could ever learn to appreciate this new, unfamiliar, Eastern religion that I was now learning about.

And then he said something that made me sit bolt upright.

"If there is something in the teachings that doesn't click with you, something you struggle to fit into your mental processing and your existing belief structure, don't throw it away," he said. "Don't throw out the baby with the bathwater! Put it on the shelf. Let it rest. Give it time. When the time is right for your consciousness to process it, then take it down and contemplate. Put it into your meditations and see where and how it can add value to your life. Again, don't throw it out. Just set it down for now and don't worry about it."

My wandering mind had caught the edge of a truth that my deeper Self knew my doubtful and dismissive self needed to hear.

"Relax, already!" the monk concluded with his favorite phrase.

"Oh, thank you!" whispered my softened heart, glad at the prospect of choice. "Thank you," whispered the empty, hollow space inside that knew that I could not exist solely on the material goods, the external experiences, and the relationships of my "outer" life.

In those words of permission lay the release of all the frustration and angst I had had about religion and what it meant to live a religious life. In those words of permission lay my freedom.

And then and there, with those softly whispered thank yous, the voice of my Inner Critic died a quick and painless death on the floor of my wide-open mind. The voice of Ms. Inner Wisdom entered the scene, robed in splendor and light. She was sweet and lovely and oh-so-generous with authentic praise and kindness. She was everything the Inner Critic could never be, could never *have* been. Ms. Inner Wisdom reminded me that all my life experiences—the good, the bad, and the ugly—serve for my growth and development.

She confirmed that there was, there *is*, nothing wrong with me, that I am enough. She gently taught me that I am the source of my own goodness and that only I can block that goodness from flowing to the world.

I learned to trust Ms. Inner Wisdom, and came to understand she was the guide who would never steer me wrong.

The teachings at that Thanksgiving retreat, and the insights of Ms. Inner Wisdom, helped me understand that mental afflictions happen, not only in relationship to the inner voices, but often in relationship with others.

For example, we may be having a good conversation with our boss— perhaps it's our six-month evaluation. Then one tiny piece of constructive advice is offered, and it sets us off. We ruminate on that one sentence, even at the cost of all the positive points of the evaluation. We create a mental affliction because we get hooked by something we don't like, and rather than enjoying all the good of that conversation, we respond with negativity to the one tiny thing.

Sometimes, we obsess over that little point of advice so much that we fabricate a whole story that eventually strains what was once a positive relationship with our boss. However obsessive we might become, we can reverse direction and undo the false narrative. We can pause and take perspective and see that what the mind created around our hurt feelings is not always true. We can manage our obsessive compulsive delusional narrator and admit to ourselves that we are fixated on a mole hill.

As we learn to successfully manage our inner dialogue, we better negative potentially destructive emotions. Through the cultivation of our emotional resilience and balance, we find ourselves mostly free of the suffering and stress brought about by wrong thinking. When we can free ourselves of

Sell your books at
sellbackyourBook.com!

Go to sellbackyourBook.com
and get an instant price quote.
We even pay the shipping - see
what your old books are worth
today!

00035460842

this wrong thinking, we have won the fight for the good life. When we free ourselves from our mental afflictions and our Inner Critic, we befriend our Inner Wisdom.

Remember that battleground where we cried *"It's so unfair!"*? We won't find ourselves there anymore, for that battleground is the territory of the fixed or negative mindset and patterned reactions. When you find freedom from your mental afflictions, you step from that dark territory into a growth mindset that offers vision and insight. As you do, you can take perspective, recognize options, and make beneficial choices. And those choices create even more freedom.

Metamorphosis

The appearance of your Inner Wisdom on the scene of your mind will happen in a way personalized and unique to you. Keep your eye out—it might be very subtle and gradual. Or it might happen with a big *boom!* and a resounding "Hey! Listen up, will ya?!" Your Inner Wisdom knows the best way to get your attention. You Inner Wisdom speaks your language, and you will understand it. The more you listen and pay heed, the more trust you will have that your own Inner Wisdom will be a reliable guide for the rest of your life.

The transformation from Inner Critic, AKA the Delusional Narrator, to the Voice of Inner Wisdom is one of the fascinating and exciting possibilities that lie on the path of becoming the artist of emotional resilience. It is the process of developing self-awareness and then cultivating that deep awareness into self-knowledge, self-management, and self-regulation. It will happen for you in your own way, as unique to your experience as your own experiences of life are unique to you.

When the voice of your Inner Wisdom slays the Inner Critic dragon, things may shift radically for you. This is a transmutation that can leave your old life in the dust, as you step into your own unique genius and allow yourself to live it every day.

Once a caterpillar becomes a butterfly, it can never return to the cocoon, nor to the wormlike creature it once was. Learning to listen to and trust Inner Wisdom is the cocoon, or chrysalis, stage of your development. It's long. It can sometimes be unpleasant and uncomfortable. I wouldn't be surprised to learn that it hurts a caterpillar to do that whole metamorphosis thing. Such a transformation may be pretty painful. But the results are amazing. Breathtaking, even.

And so is the emergence of your voice of Inner Wisdom. You simply have to trust the process.

As my Ms. Inner Wisdom gained her strength and my trust, the deep sadness and unknowingness that resulted from the loss of the previous me continued to gently dissolve.

This dissolution process sometimes felt like an eternity. But the consequential deep quiet allowed new growth. Ms. Inner Wisdom encouraged a new sense of self to peek from the tiny pocket of ash that remained inside me. A tender shoot reached upward into the light and a determined root searched downward into the nutrients. And my occasional tears watered that growing plant of the new, unique me.

I finally was able to reach up and breathe into the light of a nascent, emergent, promising life.

That cold November day, and the resulting death of my old, angry, and fearful Inner Critic, proved a blessing. It most certainly did not feel like it at the time. And yet, there I was at the end of the Thanksgiving weekend retreat, after a couple of years of deep soul-searching, a new person in my same old body. I felt radiant and sure. Powerful. Sovereign.

My newfound sense of autonomy was exhilarating. Released from the bondage of the Inner Delusional Narrator, I felt like I was living as my true self for the first time in a long time. My controlling grip on life and my relationships eased. I began to see others for who they were and was able to meet them where they were. And it was just so much easier. All of it: my job, my students, my colleagues, and my personal relationships.

My concerns about living the should life—you *should* do this or you *should* do that—disappeared. The sense of sovereignty that results from being the artist of your own emotional resilience will help you come out from under the oppressive burden of *should*.

Lessons from Amber

As I was happily going about my post-Thanksgiving-retreat school days sharing the goodness of life and the Spanish language with my high school students, my principal recognized my change of attitude. She invited me to be the New Teacher Mentor at my school the following year.

The next August I met Amber. She was in her first year of teaching and so was enrolled in the New Teacher Mentor Program. That year, nineteen new teachers came to our once-a-week lunchtime meetings. New teachers have a lot of questions. We all had much to discuss during that short meet-and-eat in my classroom.

Amber was young, maybe the youngest of the group, and didn't have much life experience. She had many questions, and asked them in a loud, insistent voice—the squeaky wheel of the group. In our time together, I continually urged her to take perspective. It was a struggle for her to do so. She had graduated high school, gone straight to the university freshman summer program, graduated four years later with her teaching degree, and come right back to the high school classroom. Amber's whole life had been spent in a classroom.

Whatever her other life circumstances had been, they'd turned her into someone who was deeply afraid of not knowing something. But as a classroom teacher, she thought she could never admit to not knowing. To her, that was a sign of a bad teacher. So in her determination to know, and to know it all, she became the teacher the students called The Screamer. It broke my heart to hear kids talking about her in the hallways, sharing stories of how bad The Screamer had been that morning. Some of my students were in her class, too, and I heard hair-raising firsthand accounts from them.

In my efforts to be a good mentor, I invited her to come and sit together during one lunch period, just the two of us. I wanted to get to know her as a person and hoped to create a friendship that could be more supportive than formal mentorship. It was awkward. She smelled a non-existent rat, and didn't relax enough to create any sort of friendly dynamic. I simply encouraged her to be kind, to support her students, and to do her best.

During the next new teacher mentor meeting, as I spoke with the group, I got nothing but daggers from her. I was puzzled, thinking that our private lunch meeting couldn't possibly have produced such extravagant disdain.

The next day, I understood. It turned out that our vice principal had recommended, as part of her mentoring and growth program, that Amber observe my classroom, to see a positive dynamic between a teacher and her students.

I appreciated the confidence of the vice principal, but thought it would have been better if he had spoken with me first. They showed up together, unannounced yet welcomed, and sat side by side in a far corner of the room.

Every now and again, he would lean over and whisper commentary. "Did you see that? That is a great questioning technique," he pointed out. And, "That is how you can transition from one activity to the next without losing control and having to waste time getting your students back on task, and without raising your voice."

Forget the *Inner* Critic! Amber was hearing the Critic's voice out loud, confirming everything she feared.

I grew continually more nervous, seeing on Amber's face a deepening hatred marked by the narrowing and darkening of her eyes and the clench of her jaw. The rigidness of her heart space was a dead giveaway of her contempt and anger toward me. This was definitely not working as the vice principal had expected.

That afternoon, I went to talk with him. I expressed my concerns and wondered if maybe Amber might be better off with a different mentor. He said no. He wanted her experience with me to teach her how to work with difficult students and in difficult situations. He felt that since I knew what I was doing, and had studied the positive psychology of relationships, that I wouldn't take things personally. He was sure that I could create a space in which she would feel safe to learn and that I would be an advocate for her. Again, I felt a deep sense of gratitude for his confidence in me, and I trusted him, but I still wondered. He ended our conversation with a promise to support both me and her, to check in often, and not to let things ever get out of hand.

The year progressed, but Amber's classroom presence did not.

At my last mentor lunch meeting of the year, we had a little bit of a celebration. Each participant received a certificate of completion of the Mentor Program. I had created awards for Most Improved, Funniest Shared Story, Best Student Experience, and other light-hearted yet meaningful events during the year. It was hard for me to come up with something for Amber.

At a loss for ideas, I spoke with my vice principal to get an idea for an award to give her. He suggested Best Voice Projection in the Classroom. *Ooh.* I didn't know how that would go over. So I consulted with several of her students.

It was the biggest surprise of the year. Some of those students loved her. They felt supported by her in a way they didn't by any other adult at school. Why?

"Her story is the same as mine," explained one purple-haired young lady.

"She understands me, where I come from," said a feisty young man. "She gets what my life is like." So there was the rose, hidden in the thorny brambles. My heart rejoiced. It was apparent that she had much to offer her students, if she could just get control of her emotions.

I dug into the stories of the kids who were willing to share.

The Screamer had experienced a hard childhood, like many of those students. She loved school because it was her escape from home and the ugly relationships there. She found a new world in the pages of a book. She could use that world to build her own, after she got away from home and started her own life. She only screamed, the kids explained, because some knuckleheads didn't appreciate the opportunity that school and learning gave them. She got frustrated because they wasted their time and their opportunities. They didn't see that education was their way out. She wanted them to get it and she thought by making herself louder, they would hear her.

She had really taught these students something. They had learned important lessons about life and human nature and many kids had already applied those teachings to their own lives. They were grateful that a teacher had gone through such similar experiences to theirs and had been willing to share them. They felt a connection and were able to create beautiful relationships with her.

I awarded her Most Impactful Teacher of the Year.

As I handed her that award, I saw behind her mask of self-protection a recognition that I had seen her through a different lens. It flashed in the briefest micro-moment of light in her eyes, an imperceptible softening of the corners of her mouth, so subtle I'm not even sure she was aware of it.

So many of these ancient emotional reactions happen below the level of our conscious awareness. But I saw the micro-flash of light, and I held onto it. It helped me see her as a unique individual, not just one more person in an overcrowded school building. Seeing her inner light for even a fraction of a second was the saving grace of that whole year's worth of struggle.

Amber might not have been consciously aware of her Why. Had I known more at that time, I might have been able to help her explore the deeper reasons she had become a teacher and her true goal behind educating students. If we don't go deep enough in the discovery process, there is the possibility of getting trapped in a superficial or negative Why. Amber needed to be the Authority Figure, to always be right. It is quite possible that her Inner Critic, driven by fear of being discovered as inadequate, had supplied her with a Why that did not serve her.

Learning from Matt

Let's contrast the story of Amber with the story of Matt. He was in the last portion of his university's teacher education program, the final requirement to earn his license: the six-week student teaching practicum.

A desperate call came in one afternoon from the Office of Teacher Licensure. I'd previously had three practicum students assigned to me and was always thrilled to turn my classroom over to a budding educator, and to help create the space and environment for soon-to-be teachers to get a taste of the reality of being in charge of a classroom full of hormonal adolescents.

Anne oversaw finding placements for the student-teachers, and we had developed a great relationship. She urgently needed to get Matt out of the current practice classroom, where he was suffering greatly. Could I help?

"Send him my way," I said. "I'll do what I can to restore his confidence and love of education."

Matt called me about an hour later, tearful and incoherent. I did my best to ease his agony, and asked him to come in before school the next day so we could meet face to face. His crying had me wondering if I might have made a mistake by saying yes. Did he possess the emotional resilience and maturity needed to manage a classroom?

He showed up the next morning looking very professional, with a bow tie and rosy cheeks. His glasses were shined to a sparkle, matching the light in his eyes. It was hard to believe this was the same young man I had spoken to yesterday.

I walked to the door. "Matt?" I asked.

"Yes! Thank you, Ms. Dahl!" Bypassing my outstretched hand, he practically leaped onto me with a grateful hug. He looked barely old enough to be out of high school, and could easily have been one of my students the previous year.

"Now, now. You're welcome," I said, patting him gingerly. I was a little uncomfortable at his unfiltered display of emotion, but also laughing inwardly at his child-like enthusiasm. I wished my students greeted me this way every day.

We sat together at two student desks at the front of the room. He shared the nightmare of his two-week experience at the school across town, how the lead teacher, known by students as Old Yeller, had continually belittled and berated him. She did not and would not support him in his efforts to manage and teach her students. She yelled at him in front of the students. And she screamed at them, too—all day long.

Matt lamented the unruliness and meanness of the students and started to cry again when he told me how often they had cursed at him, and even thrown books at him! It happened on a daily basis. He could not gain control of the classroom, let alone teach them anything.

No support came from anyone, not Old Yeller, not the school principal, not the school counselor—not even the Dean of Student Life, who was charged with instilling kindness and compassion within the walls and halls of the school building.

Matt confessed that he cried every day on his way to and from school. He had spent a fortune on his teacher education program, but wasn't sure he even *liked* kids anymore, referring to them as "the little bastards!"

At that point, I knew it was time to cut him off. I shared with him that I myself had spent a hellish year at that very school about five years before, in the classroom right next door to Old Yeller. I was astonished that she was still there. We commiserated as we connected on a very visceral level. I shared that those little renegades had managed to get under my skin, too.

I assured him that not every classroom had to be that way. He could create his own unique learning environment, a place where he and his students loved to be every day. I would welcome him into my classroom, and eventually turn it over to him so he could practice and develop his teaching skills with my students.

He spent that day and the next observing my class. He returned the third day with his teaching outline complete, everything he hoped to teach my students in the next four weeks clearly and explicitly planned with the utmost care and detail. He seemed the picture of resilience, determined to achieve his goal of becoming a teacher and instructing his students to Spanish language fluency they would be proud of. I did not doubt he would accomplish all he set out to do.

We chatted every day after school that first week in the sweaty, teenage-stinky heat of my classroom. That Friday afternoon, we decided to have our feedback session outside. Walking around the sidewalks of the campus, he thanked me profusely.

"Ms. Dahl, you have no idea how you've rescued me! I was about ready to quit, to walk away from it all, to go work in a coffee shop. It would have been a waste of a $140,000 education, not to mention four years of my life," he told me. "You've given me your trust from the get-go and I've been able to bounce back. Now I'm super-excited again to be a teacher. I really do love kids. It's so awesome to share the Spanish language with them, to hear them speaking it, to watch their learning process. They learn so fast!"

Matt had come a long way in that week, regaining his confidence and his love for students. My week-long observations revealed that he had exceptional teaching skills and that he knew the Spanish language inside and out. He knew more street lingo than I did and made quick relationships with the native speakers. He was so close in age to my students that he was a non-threat, even a friend from whom they could learn. He was fun and funny. I was ready to fully hand over the reins of my classroom.

The following Monday morning, he stepped into the role of teacher—not student-teacher, not practicum-teacher, but full-on teacher. I spent the first ten minutes of each different class explaining that Mr. Brown would now be the teacher and that I would not be in the classroom except for an occasional drop-in where I would be an invisible observer. They should ignore me and see Mr. Brown as the teacher.

I dropped in two or three or four times during the course of each day that week. Things seemed to be going pretty well.

Thursday afternoon in our feedback session, Matt was troubled.

"Ms. Dahl, the students are different when you're not in the room," he confided. "They're disrespectful. They don't listen. They won't stay on task, and they won't speak Spanish."

I was astonished!

"What?! My little honeys are misbehaving on you?" An incredulous furrow creased my brow. "Well, this looks like your chance to exercise all your skills and step right into the full mess and magic of the life of a teacher."

He bit his lip and nodded. "Yes. I guess so."

"What's your plan?"

"I'll let you know tomorrow."

He had a sly edge to his smile the next morning, but when I inquired about his plan of attack, he only winked at me. I found this a tiny bit disturbing, but it also piqued my curiosity.

I hung around the closed classroom door all day, anxious to sneak a peek inside if ever any student should leave. Or, as Spanish class ended and students left for another class, to ask what was happening with Mr. Brown. I waited to hear a raised voice or some sort of ruckus or commotion.

But no. Nothing. All day long, not a peep was heard from inside classroom 217. And it was equally silent out there in that lonely hallway. Not one student left class during instructional time.

At the end of the day my nails had been chewed to the quick. As the school building emptied, I found Matt relaxed back in my desk chair, hands crossed behind his head.

"So....?" I prompted, my eyes wide with expectation and pleading.

Leaning toward me, he re-crossed his hands on the desk, shook his head, and beamed me his smile of success. "All good."

"And....?"

"I love teaching. I love these kids. *Soy profesor.*"

Matt never did let me know. My students were like clams, I couldn't pry it out of them. But something had changed. They had gotten the message, however it had been delivered, that as students, part of the expectations for them was to respect their teachers and to engage fully in the process of learning and speaking Spanish.

When Mr. Brown's four weeks drew to an end, we had a little ceremony for him in each class. The students loved and respected him. They wanted him to stay.

"Ms. Dahl, we don't want him to leave! Mr. Brown, don't go! Can you both teach us?"

We all learned a lot from Mr. Brown that year. And I think it would be fair to say that he learned a lot from us, and from himself.

So what had happened, exactly?

First, Matt was confident in his abilities, his knowledge, his goals, and life dream to become a great educator. He had a clear vision of what he wanted, and had made a serious commitment.

Next, he was willing to receive feedback, to spend time observing and adjusting his plans and perspectives according to the realities presented to him in two different high schools. And even when it was hard, because of his commitment, he was not willing to give up on his goals. His commitment enabled him to ask for help. And then, ever-so-importantly, to be receptive to the help and support that was offered, allowing him to make the necessary changes that created of his classroom an engaging dynamic learning environment.

And so Matt became Mr. Brown. He overcame his challenges. He created relationships of trust with the students and they were able to learn and flourish under his care.

You Teach Who You Are

We can take a couple of great lessons from the world of being a teacher in the educational system. "You teach who you are" is a common saying among educators. "What you model is what you get," is another. The good teachers know that if they don't model resilience, emotional self-management, kindness, and compassion, their students never will either.

Our teachers are some of the first leaders that we encounter in our young lives and can make an indelible impression on us. But "you teach who you are" is equally true for everyone who supervises, manages, leads, and parents.

If we shirk responsibility and instead offer excuses and justifications, we will find these same behaviors, not only in our subordinates, students, or kids, but in our colleagues as well. If we are fault-finders and negative-Nellies so too will be the people who surround us. People who object to these behaviors will move on, but the ones who remain will self-reinforce the dysfunction.

Modeling emotional resilience is one of the greatest gifts we can give the people in our lives that we lead and influence. By using the power of his deeply held intentions to persevere, Matt was able to give this gift to his students and his coworkers. He was able to achieve his goals and spiral up to the next level of educational expertise that he could then use to expand his positive influence.

When your intention becomes the guiding force of your life you will, like Matt, be able to pause, regroup, consider your options, and move forward in a new or different direction that will ultimately take you to your goal. Even if you don't know exactly how you will get there, when you know where you're going and why you're headed there, the power of your intention infuses you with a perseverant willingness to move forward with integrity and confidence, in a way that honors the voice of your Inner Wisdom and solidifies your sense of self-worth.

Solidify Your Intention with a Mantra

Mantra is a Sanskrit word that means "mind protection." When your mind is about to go berserk—when your Inner Critic starts in on you or events around you seem to be spinning out of control—a mantra is a like quick blast of fresh air for your mind that will bring you back to current time, back to your center, back to your values, and back to your discipline. It can protect you in times of dire upset. At the cliff-edge of an unfortunate emotional incident, your mantra can literally protect you by protecting your mind.

Your personal mantra can be as short as one word, or a phrase of a couple words. As you think to yourself what your mind might need protection from, you will have a good idea of what your mantra will be.

A mantra is sort of like an intention, but just for a micro-moment of time. Your intention is over-arching and colors the whole of your life's canvas. The mantra might be compared to the tiny hint of color that covers a wee mistake or draws the eye to something beautiful. Maybe we can think of the mantra as emotional first aid—immediate help, right now, so we don't melt down in an emotional heap. In Matt's case, his intention was to be an influential educator. In times of struggle, when he couldn't get students to engage in their learning, he may have used as his mantra, "I am calm," or "I am in control of my emotions," as a way to come back to center and avoid an unfortunate emotional episode with his students.

Some examples of mantras that can help protect your emotional resilience:

- I am cool, calm, and collected.
- I manage my strong emotions.
- Breathe. Breathe.
- Be still. And listen.
- Beauty in, beauty out.
- Kindness in, kindness out.
- Goodness in, goodness out.
- Purity in, purity out.

Positivity is the protective factor of a mantra. And the shorter the better. You want to be able to remember it quickly so it can come to your rescue and protect your mind in the blink of an eye. Create one for yourself now and write it here:

_____

If you need to change your mantra later, that's OK. You are free to change it when you need to, and as often as you need to. But eventually, create a single, reliable, and powerful mind-protecting phrase that will work for you in every difficult situation. And then use the heck out of it.

Use it at every turn. And observe what happens. As your mantra succeeds in protecting your mind from being sucked under by a strong negative emotion and you experience the benefits of this simple but potent emotional resilience practice, it will steadily become more effective.

Protecting your mind is an enjoyable and enlightening experience.

You Can't Do It Wrong

In addition to formulating your own mantra, there are other practices that will guide you toward a state of emotional resilience.

Let's take a brief look at the core ideas that are presented in much greater detail in later chapters, and how you will be able to apply them in your life for the most delicious results.

While the whole process of becoming the artist of your emotional resilience is a step-by-step undertaking, sometimes the steps will end up out of order. You might find yourself on the same step for several weeks or months. That's OK.

At one point in my own journey, a teacher shared a useful and very profound phrase:

You can't do it wrong.

Yes, ironically, the Inner Critic may show up to judge your progress toward emotional resilience. This is a wonderful phrase to dismiss this Inner Critic, to give yourself the breathing room to try on all the principles and practices, and see what works for you.

As you connect with your voice of Inner Wisdom and apply the science and the art of emotional resilience, your process will become uniquely yours. It's *your* process, *your* life—thus, you can't do it wrong. Your life is not the *shoulds* and *should nots* of others. It is yours. You have the power to choose how you want to do it—to do your own life. The only way you might throw a little wrench into the whole process is by *not* listening on the inside.

Let's also be clear that just because you can't do it wrong is in no way license to do whatever you want. It most certainly does not mean that anything goes. Understanding that you can't do it wrong requires a very deep sense of personal ownership and responsibility, and a deep understanding of who you are and your own personal Why. Living by the phrase "I can't do it wrong" means that you trust yourself, deeply, and that you have a sense of meaning and purpose to your life that guides your thoughts, your actions, and your decisions. It means that when you are authentically living your own unique genius, you will have the presence of mind and the strength of heart to know that how you show up is beautifully aligned with your inner values and strengths.

The Emotional Resilience Artist's Palette

To create your masterwork of emotional resilience, you'll need to use a "palette" of practices and approaches. In Chapter 1, we covered Current Time and Breathing. In later chapters, we'll be discussing and experiencing the following techniques and strategies:

- Taking Perspective
- Setting Your Intention
- Loving Yourself
- Being Self-Responsible
- Being Patient

These and other useful and potentially life-changing practices are the tools for your artistic expression.

Like any artist, you may find that you have favorite colors—in this case, practices—on your palette. You may discover that certain mixtures of these practices really work for you. Emotional resilience requires different practices and approaches of each of us. For example, maybe you're a natural at taking perspective, but you have not formulated a clear intention, or Why for your life. You'll need to practice harder at setting and using intention. Maybe you have a brilliantly clear intention, but could benefit by cultivating deeper patience and perseverance in order to fully live it.

Say for example that you are clear on your Why: "To provide a good and happy life for my family," but you are short on patience. Eager to shower your family with the spoils of the good life, you may end up going into debt to buy a big fancy toy (a boat, an exotic trip to the islands, or a vacation home) before you're financially prepared. The burden of the debt will increase your level of anxiety and stress, which can easily overflow into relationship stress. Your lack of financial patience rolls over into emotional and behavioral impatience. It shows up in your shortness with your children, the lack of time for your spouse, and the strain of owing more money than you're comfortable with. It colors your mood and attitude on a daily basis.

Being self-aware, knowing how you operate, and being able to gauge the appropriate level of stress for yourself are essentials on your palette of emotional resilience skills. Take a little time and make these practices and approaches your own: make them fit your life and your schedule and your personal preferences. My teacher once referred to this as "morph and core." You will keep the *core* of the science, the core of the practice or technique, but you will *morph* it to fit you. As you do, you will develop and deepen a habit of knowing both yourself and what works best for you in any given situation.

There is just one more tiny possibility that might bring this whole thing to a stop: not doing it at all. But in these words we can find comfort and hope that we cannot do it wrong. The *do* in the sentence is the critical component.

As you set out on your journey to master the art of emotional resilience, you must make this promise to yourself: *I can't do it wrong*. How will you be able to do that with any sense of authenticity, not seeing it as just some superficial phrase—*you can't do it wrong*—that might sucker you into this whole thing?

As much as you must learn to trust yourself and to live your unique genius, you will have to learn to trust in a great organizing principle of life, knowledge, and process.

Oranges to Oranges

Grandpa Dahl managed a 220,000-acre ranching and farming organization in central Florida for many years. The ranch included 1,600 acres of citrus groves.

Grandpa once explained to me that an orange is not an orange by chance. Every orange that has ever grown to full fruit is the same. It has a protective outer peel, the rind, that is orange in color and contains citric oils that repel bugs. Inside that peel is white membrane, the pith, surrounding the globe of fruit. Inside that pulpy inner membrane, each orange grows in segments, separated again by a membrane, or a wall, this one transparent and not pulpy. The inside of each segment of every orange in the entire existence of oranges is filled with tiny teardrop-shaped sacs, again each surrounded by a thin membrane. Each more inward membrane is finer and more delicate. Inside the very innermost membrane is the sweet juice of the orange. If we take away all the membranes, an orange is just juice, just liquid sunshine transformed by the magical yet methodical and repeated processes of photosynthesis, pollination, fertilization, setting fruit, and then ripening to maturity.

This happens for lemons and limes and for grapefruits too. The process is the same for any fruit that comes from a blossom. We can look at vegetables that come from seeds, that turn into sprouts, that send their roots down to become carrots or radishes, turnips or beets.

Trees and bushes and shrubs all follow their process of becoming. All the natural world does. All animal life does too. And as part of the animal life on the planet, we do too. We have a process of becoming that almost always works in the same manner for each human being. As physical beings, except for a rare few, we will all develop the same body. The great organizing principle of life ensures that each fetus will become a baby and then grow into an adult human being, with one torso, two legs and two arms, one head, with a face with two eyes, one nose, and one mouth.

We can trust that same great organizing principle when it comes to the personal cultivation of our consciousness. It is that consciousness that makes each one of us individual and unique, but at the same time, allows each one of us to understand the deeply interwoven connection we all share as human beings. As we learn to trust this great organizing principle, we come to understand that it is this very principle that gives us the capacity to think and reason, to make connections, and to create our own unique stories.

You have the opportunity to surrender the need to know it all and/or to always be right, to this great organizing principle that never makes an orange peel purple or a carrot blue. You can come to know that this principle is the organizing principle of anything that ever was, is, or will be, and that it doesn't get things wrong. As you tune into and create a relationship with the principle by learning to trust it, you learn to trust yourself. You learn, steadily over time, that you are an integral part of the process of life and that as such, a necessary part to the proper functioning of it all.

When you can see yourself in connection with this great organizing principle, when you learn to trust this, you will be able to say with perfect understanding, "I cannot do it wrong."

Preparing for the Journey

The work of becoming the artist of your emotional resilience must be undertaken with a mindset of "continuously, over time, without ceasing."[5] What does that mean for you, the emotional adventurer? It's like climbing a mountain. When you get tired, you don't go back to the bottom of the mountain to rest. You sit down where you are, find your breath, have a sip of water, a snack, and gather your strength, *right where you are*. And this is what you will do emotionally, on any given day, at any given moment— right where you are.

And sometimes, climbing the mountain alone is just not fun. Sometimes, we need a companion. Is there someone who can be your cheerleader, your supporter, and maybe your objective, third-party reality check? If you work better with an accountability buddy, get one! Perhaps it's someone who'd like to take this journey themselves, too.

It might not be the best idea to have your accountability partner be your husband or wife, or girlfriend or boyfriend, or even a sibling. Personal transformation can involve some social risk, and those closest to you may actually trigger rather than help you. For example, if your journey to emotional resilience involves re-assessing big life decisions, a family member or partner might inject their own fear of change into the process. Choose someone a bit more removed, and someone you trust. It could be a whole lot easier for everyone that way.

Should you choose to undertake this journey on your own, welcome aboard! But if this is your chosen style—flying solo with no accountability partner—will you please be kind and gentle with yourself as you stand in the role of your own accountability buddy? If you find it hard or impossible to demonstrate self-compassion and to allow yourself to be fully human, you might not find the success you hope for.

Let's recognize, and then make real and true in our awareness, that we are human. That means we do, and we will, make mistakes. As much as we try, as much effort as we put forth to move ourselves on the scale from reactive outburst to calm response, as many tools and practices and strategies as we know and try, we will fail on some days. And that can really be disappointing and make us want to call it quits.

Yet it does not mean that we're doing it wrong. Our failures can show us many things. They can be our best teachers. They are essential to building resilience and perseverance. As you make mistakes, rejoice! Oddly enough, that rejoicing can help you see your defeats as friendly allies on your journey.

At the beginning of the process, we will probably fail a lot. And that's OK! It has to be OK. It's through failure, when we are aware of it and see it as a learning opportunity, that we can grow. That we *do* grow!

Please repeat these words to yourself often. Copy them down and put them on your mirror:

Consistently. Over time. Without ceasing.

This is a gentle reminder that what you are undertaking will not happen overnight, and that steady effort is required to create your masterwork. No one is waving a magic wand. Your life is not a TV reality show that skips all the actual work and only shows the marvelous results.

Another useful phrase worth keeping close at hand:

I give myself permission to be fully human.

This can provide mind protection from the Inner Critic.

And most importantly:

I love myself.

Loving It All

Our time together on these pages is meant to help deepen your own sense of truth and OK-ness of living in the phrase, "It's like this now." Sometimes yes, we do love it here in the fullness of this moment of Now. And sometimes we don't.

How do we manage the sometimes-not moments with grace and dignity? How can we find emotional strength and stability when things are falling to pieces around us? How can we gracefully manage ourselves when things don't go our way? And you know they won't, because they don't and that's just how life is.

Some of us have already experienced losses, setbacks, disappointments, and regrets—experiences that have helped us become an emotionally resilient superstar. Some of us have yet to go through the depths of such events. We all fall somewhere along that continuum.

How much do we need to consider or worry about emotional resilience when things are going our way? Not too much, really. When things are going well and according to our plan, then we just live life, and we enjoy it.

It's when life reveals its true nature—ever-changing, impermanent, and often painful, that we need some emotional backbone. We need emotional resilience when our plan doesn't come to fruition, our goals cannot be reached, or we find that our hopes and dreams will forever be just hopes and dreams.

Dr. Wayne Dyer offered an intriguing perspective when he said, "Nothing in my life ever goes wrong."

I remember the very pinpoint-moment when I first heard this life-changing phrase. I was listening to one of his podcasts[6] as I was making panzanella salad on a perfect summer evening, the tomatoes and basil fresh from my garden. My life was shining and my joy at its zenith. The summer had been magical in every way; clear blue skies with never a cloud, delightful temperatures in the mid-80s, a cooling breeze every afternoon, blazing sunsets of red, mauve, and violet. Every day I asked myself "How can it possibly be any better than this?"

And there I was, mincing garlic and chopping tomatoes, whisking olive oil and thick, sticky, purple-black balsamic, listening to Dr. Wayne. Those profound words sliced into my awareness, sank deep into my heart, like the blade of a very sharp knife, piercing right to the core. I stopped. I pressed pause and then hit the ten-second rewind. *What?*!

Yes, sure enough, those were his words: *Nothing in my life ever goes wrong.*

I pondered this for days, rolling it around not only in my mind, but also in my Sacred Heart, in dialogue with Ms. Inner Wisdom. I wondered how such a thing could be true. And then an old saying of my teacher's came ringing into my ears: "It's all perspectival," he used to tell us.

Yes, sure enough, it *is* all perspective. I wanted to make those words as true for myself as they were for Dr. Wayne. And so I did.

I had to take perspective. Often. Sometimes several times an hour! But eventually, and through much practice, I learned to see everything as either an opportunity for learning and growth or a blessing—often deep, deep in disguise.

On that panzanella-making summer night, it was so easy. Everything was just exactly like I wanted it to be. My life was the sum total of almost all the dreams I had ever dreamed of as a young girl: married to the most amazing man on the planet, who happens to be my best friend; making dinner from the bounty of my own garden; all the windows and doors open to the perfect summer weather; birds chirping outside the kitchen windows; enjoying wonderful health, with everyone in my family healthy. A true portrait of the perfect life.

And then the sun went down and the next day dawned with its trials and inconveniences. As it does, life kept me on my toes. I continued to practice this theory for myself and then began to share this idea with others.

I decided to take this principle to my high school students to see if they could make heads or tails of it. At first, they puzzled. They didn't quite get it. So we dialogued and wondered together, and came up with scenarios and situations, toying with possibilities and perspectives. Eventually, we all came to agree that each person *could* actually say this about his or her life, but it would take a seriously open mind, and according to several students, a good measure of faith that things would work out in the end.

Consider now for yourself: can you fully and truly get behind this phrase, even in the really difficult situations? What would it be like for you, for your life and your relationships, if you could see every event and situation, every trial and tribulation, every loss and even every gain, as just exactly the way things are supposed to be? What would that be like?

Would you need emotional resilience in order to get to that point? Probably so. And probably a lot of it.

And since *no one is coming,* this is where you get down to the nitty gritty—understanding that life's vicissitudes will continue, things will not go your way, and you will have to somehow deal with and manage them, hopefully with an ample measure of grace.

Suffering and stress, sorrow and worry, uncertainty and trouble are certainly not new conditions for us as members of the human race. They are indeed a prevalent, elemental feature of the human condition. If we get mired down by thinking things will always go our way, and that somehow we'll be exempt from these trials, we are certainly going to need a lot of emotional resilience to get ourselves unstuck.

Emotional resilience is a practice. And just like so many other things in life, we will often need to try, try again. During some of our emotional episodes, we will remember lightning-quick to get a hold of ourselves and manage our reaction. Other times, we might let fly a string of word-knives designed to slash our opponent to ribbons. Or unleash that savage attack on ourselves, berating ourselves for our stupidity or our incompetence. Ouch.

Wherever we are on the path of emotional resilience, we can all either learn a bit more for ourselves or support someone else on their path. We have either been there, will be there, or will watch someone else land flat on their face.

We are all in this together. We all suffer. Whether it's a hangnail or a dying spouse or anything in between, it's all suffering, to one degree or another. And all of it is real; all of it is valid. But we move through these struggles; eventually, we can make it to the light on the other side of the tunnel. And mostly, we do it alone. Emotional resilience is an inside practice. We must have an inner reckoning with ourselves, we must see clearly on the inside that we do have strength to press on.

But as much as it is an inside job, we need each other. We need the support and love of those people we love most. We need words of wisdom and stories from those who have had similar challenges and have made it. If we're on the couch for the seventh day in a row, in complete despair, with unwashed hair, we most likely need someone to come and physically help us up, brush those greasy locks from our forehead, and say, "I love you. You can do this. I will support you. Now go get in the shower."

You were born with the seeds of emotional resilience in the space of your Inner Knowing. They are there, lying in wait for just the right moment to germinate and send forth their tender shoots, from which will eventually blossom the fully ripened fruit of your efforts.

There is so much good in you, around you, and for you. You have much wisdom and strength to offer the world, no matter the world situation. No matter your situation. Be your strong, resilient self. You can. You must. You will.

Press on.

Art Class: Nuance

"When you are inspired by some great purpose, some extraordinary project, all your thoughts break their bonds: Your mind transcends limitations, your consciousness expands in every direction, and you find yourself in a new, great and wonderful world." ~ Patanjali

Let's summarize here with a review of your intention, your Why, and your mantra.

Your intention and your Why might be very intricately linked, even spilling into each other and swirling together. Your intention might be considered the voice of your Inner Wisdom encouraging you toward your life's meaning and purpose, the *what* of your life. It can be a truth or perspective that you hope to live by, something you are willing to give your time and energy, your devotions and commitment to. Maybe it can be considered your personal North Star.

It can be overarching for your entire life, or situational for one of the many hats you wear. Before each teaching, workshop, or presentation I share, I center myself by coming into current time, taking three deep breaths, and asking myself "What am I doing?" In this way, I get a feel for the people I'm spending time with and a sense of how I can best serve them. Most often, the answer that surfaces becomes my intention of connecting with people at a level of joy, positivity, and the potential for beneficial change.

My overall intention for this stage of my life is to live my unique genius as much as I can, sharing my skills and talents with others to create more love and positivity on the planet. When I need to tap into my intentions quickly and get right to my center, I use the short version, "I intend to share goodness and love."

Looking at it from the perspective of something to *connect with* rather than something to *do*, my intention connects me to one of my deepest core values and strengths: love.

Does it feel like the right time to connect with your own intention? Let's explore.

Whatever words you use to capture your intention, your Why, and your mantra, they need to have deep personal meaning. Use vocabulary that resonates with how you want to live and with the presence you want to be. If you are a funny person, include humor in your phrases. If you are flamboyant, use extravagant and flashy words. If you're calm and steady, allow your phrases to mirror your character. As you find your authentic phrases, they will dovetail with your personality and spirit in an expression of your unique genius.

Your Intention:

- Please come into current time with yourself. Find your breath. Give yourself the space of time to enjoy several deep breaths, expanding and contracting the belly with each one.
- Connect to the space of your Sacred Heart. If you're not comfortable there yet, please simply find a place of inner peace and quiet and connect with the stillness.

Now consider: What is the most important thing I can do with my life (or a specific arena of my life)?

_____

You might also consider some supporting questions: What do I value? Where do I spend my time? What excites and motivates me?

_____

Listen on the inside. Soften around the eyes and let go of tension in the jaw. Breathe into the stillness. Connect with your deepest sense of Self. Set your intention for your life (or a specific arena of your life), positive and powerful, the image to capture those thousand words.

_____

Your Why:

Now comes your Why. Why are you doing what you're doing? Why are you here?

As I start each presentation or workshop with my intention of what I'm doing firmly in my awareness, I ask the participants to ask themselves, "Why am I here?"

I learned the nuances of setting an intention in my yoga teacher training courses. The instruction I received from my dedicated teachers was to know clearly, at the beginning of each class I would eventually teach, that I was connecting with beautiful yogis. I must learn to see them as beautiful in order to guide them toward fluidity of movement, openness in their joints, length in their muscles and their spines, and steadiness of balance. If I wasn't seated in my own Why, my instructions wouldn't resonate from my own deepest truths, from my own intention. If students weren't aware of their own Why, yoga class would be just another way to spend time.

I learned to ask myself before every class, "Why I am teaching yoga?" Over time, the answer became, "To share possibility with others so they might find and experience freedom."

As you delve into your Why, again come into current time and find your smooth, even breath.

Identify an area of your life you'd like to focus on, or expand into your whole life.

Now ask yourself, "Why am I here?" Add any specifics you might need, such as "Why am I here, leading this team?"

Your Why can be as short or as detailed as you prefer. Make sure it resonates with your deepest sense of Self.

Your Mantra:

And now for your mantra, the emotional first aid that protects your mind. You will want your mantra to be short and concise, easy to call to mind when you're about to step over the ledge into an unfortunate emotional chasm.

I didn't know it at the time, but back in my tear-stained-face days, I would eventually come up for a breath of air and say to myself, "It will be OK." I believed that. And eventually, it *was* all OK. Some days, I still use that little mind-protection phrase.

Please think of one that will work for you, in a quick hurry when you find yourself in need of protection.

Dog-ear this page. List here for easy reference for the future, until you have them committed to memory:

- Your Intention:

- Your Why:

- Your Mantra:

> Your authentic expression makes your unique genius most known to the world.

CHAPTER 3

Emotions:
An Owner's Manual

Emotional resilience is built on a foundation of emotional ownership. But before we continue this exploration, we need to establish a common understanding of what emotions actually are.

Human emotions are a neurobiological phenomenon that serve as a survival mechanism, an efficient, automatic, inner appraisal of threat or no-threat. Emotions happen in a split second in order to keep us alive. The occurrence of emotions as a neurochemical response to the possibility of threat is short, from a half-second to five seconds.[7] In that short time your body sends out neurotransmitters that move you to fight or flight in order to give you the best odds for survival.

> We *need* all of our emotions.
> They are paramount to our full
> development as human beings.

What we must understand is that our behavior is *not* our emotions. These are two separate and distinct things. We'll explore this in more depth later in this chapter, but it's important for this discussion that we do not mistake them for each other.

Your Brain on Emotions

We're all aware of the complexity of the human brain. Advances in modern technology have taken us deep into the brain, and we are able now to see more through fMRI (functional magnetic resonance imaging) than ever imagined. The field of neuroscience has exploded into many branches: neurobiology, neuroanatomy, neuropsychology, and neurophysiology, among others. What we now know about the brain can shed light on important ways the brain relates with itself, with the body, and with other bodies.[8]

Broadening our understanding of the basics of brain structure and function, as well as neuroplasticity (the amazing capability the brain has to restore, reorganize, and regenerate itself), can help us better understand and ultimately manage strong emotions.

In the education world, thanks in great part to the amazing work of Dr. Daniel Siegel[9], acclaimed psychiatrist and professor at UCLA, and Dr. Tina Payne Bryson[10], renowned author, educator, and researcher, the terms *upstairs brain* and *downstairs brain* are becoming more and more common, and increasingly impactful. These phrases make it easy for children and teens to understand their brains and which parts are associated to what outcomes (behaviors, physical movement, and automatic internal process such as digestion and respiration). They also make it easy for the adults in the room to understand, too!

The downstairs brain includes the lower, or more primitive regions, of the brain. It is also referred to as the *reptilian brain* (labeled by Dr. Paul McLean in 1990[11]) because it resembles the brain of reptiles. It is one of the oldest regions of the human brain and is incapable, and absent of, thought process. It is our instinctual brain that maintains the fundamental functions that keep us alive. It also makes possible our memory, our basic drives, and our emotions. It includes the limbic system, (*aka* the emotional brain), and the brainstem, which is responsible for the functions of heartbeat, breathing, and physical movement.[12]

The limbic system has many component structures, but the ones most commonly known are the amygdala and the hippocampus. According to Dr. Richard Davidson, author and professor of psychology and psychiatry at Wisconsin-Madison, the amygdala is associated with and plays a complex role in "certain kinds of negative emotions, particularly fear"[13] and anger. The hippocampus is associated with "formation and recall of long-term memories and information consolidation"[14], especially the processing of general knowledge and facts, as well as personally experienced events.[15]

Its role in the dynamics of emotion is critical, as it is associated with recognition of the *context* of the events.[16] The limbic system is also labeled our survival brain because it acts impulsively and automatically to assess and then to remove us from a potential threat or danger that could result in serious harm or death. It's responsible for the flight/fight/freeze response to an automatic, internal appraisal of danger.

The upstairs brain links many different networks and is associated with higher-level thinking and mental processing. It is composed of the higher cortices, those regions directly correlated to complex and increased capacities for learning, thinking, and processing information. The upstairs brain is what makes us human—enabling fine motor and precise motor skills; language, both spoken and written; comprehension, evaluation, analysis, and correct application of detailed and abstract information; and empathy and compassion.

The higher brain can learn; it can be trained and shaped by the experiences it goes through. It has the capacity to interpret and take perspective. It creates the stories around emotional episodes, recognizing both the destructive and the positive ones. It is in these higher regions of the brain that we can develop and cultivate our emotional resilience. Here is where we bring our thinking brain back online and override the automated reactions of the lower brain. Our capacity for change and transformation lies in our ability to exploit the power of the upstairs brain.

Emotions are our biological, internal, automatic assessment of a situation and the possibility of threat in that situation. This assessment happens in the downstairs, the reptilian brain, and is surprisingly short, from a half-second to five seconds. It immediately forces our survival mechanism to kick in so we can cope with the circumstances of the event. In response to that automatic assessment, our biology sends out a chemical cascade of hormones and neurotransmitters signaled by the amygdala and the hippocampus. Sometimes our biology moves us to fight, sometimes to flight, and other times, we simply freeze.

Emotions as Messengers and Teachers

Emotions are also an internal barometer, clueing us in to our inner state of affairs. They have messages for us that often reveal our wants, needs, unmet needs, and our deep desires and goals. (Unmet needs are a psychological phenomenon, as of yet unfulfilled, that will provide a feeling of well-being or contentment when satisfied.) Emotions can provide warnings and protection. As we heed these messages, we can identify what adjustments need to be made so we feel safe, both physically and psychologically.

In our quest for emotional resilience, we can ask ourselves what an emotion has to teach us. Or if necessary, we can ask for clarification, gaining a deeper understanding of our own psyche. As we learn to befriend our emotions, they can show us many things, including profound truths as well as changes that are due to be made. Emotions can help us identify old, worn-out patterns that, with a tiny push, will forever vanish from what Dr. Paul Ekman calls the "emotional alert database,"[17] the storage unit in the brain packed with all your previous emotional experiences and events.

Our emotions can also reveal to us our greatest sources of joy, love, and hope. They are the medium we use to create a masterpiece of our lives.

Emotions 101

According to Dr. Paul Ekman,[18] we all experience "the big five" emotions. Dr. Ekman's research on the universality of human emotions took place in the mid- and late-1960s in Papua, New Guinea, with a group of several hundred people in a place that was virtually uninfluenced by any outside forces or factors. His study group was naturally isolated from the progressive, technological, and business world of both Eastern and Western cultures, and therefore, the perfect group to observe and study.

His many years and careful experiments led him to a conclusion that supported much earlier findings by Charles Darwin—that facial expressions are innate and therefore universal. Dr. Ekman concluded that we all experience these five emotions, and display universal facial expressions of them—regardless of geography, race, culture, societal norms, religion, or ethnicity:

- Anger
- Fear
- Sadness
- Disgust
- Joy

In addition to these universal big five, others, such as pride or shame, are experienced in a cultural context.

Dr. Ekman further identifies and explains these five as "emotion families", which include a wide range of intensities as well as states. The anger family, for instance, includes mild irritation, frustration, annoyance, bitterness, and a complex mixture of what I call *frustranger*. This is not your common, garden-variety frustration, but a thorny, barbed mutation that digs its way in like a cocklebur and cannot be easily plucked out.

In the joy family, we find the immense collection of all positive emotions: sensory pleasure, happiness, relief, contentment, pride, amusement, wonder, bliss, and gratitude, among others.

Becoming emotionally resilient requires the study of human emotions—if not direct scientific or academic study, at the very least an examination of your own life. Since most of us come equipped with the full array of emotions, we take for granted that we know what they are. After all, how can we not be an expert on our own feelings? But when we actually begin to examine emotions in earnest, we see that they have tremendous depth and complexity.

Our study of the art of emotional resilience should begin, just as the study of fine art does, with a thoughtful exploration of our materials and methods. Unless you've carefully observed and studied human emotions, you would probably be hard-pressed to define them, or to differentiate them from feelings. The materials that we will work with in our study will be the emotions themselves, the context in which they occur, and the resultant words, actions, and behaviors. The methods will be personal observation and tracking of those observations.

The methods to change the behaviors that you observe and don't find useful or beneficial will be provided throughout the book. You've already experienced a couple of them in Chapter 1, and will experiment with several more in Chapter 8.

As you progress through your study of emotions, you will expand your awareness and understanding of the depth and intricacy of the emotional process. Hopefully, you will also widen your appreciation for the emotional events of your own life, how they teach you who you are, and your pattern of reaction/response to the happenings of your life. Through this examination, your sense of self-awareness will grow and you may see things about yourself that you've never seen before. Stay open to the process and available to the revelations!

To simplify this process, I've created a table that summarizes years of my own study and careful reflection on action research carried out in the laboratory of my own life (which I strongly encourage you to do also). I have distilled the teachings and observations into what I hope will be an easy-to-read overview that includes each of the big five emotions. It also includes, in summary form, some of the work of Dr. Barbara Fredrickson, *Love 2.0* and *Positivity*; Dr. Daniel Goleman, *Emotional Intelligence* and *Destructive Emotions*; and a collaboration between Dr. Daniel Goleman and Dr. Richard Davidson, *Altered Traits*.

The chart is meant to clarify the survival purpose of emotions, the ways they manifest physically and psychologically, and how each is expressed through demonstrated behavior. As you spend time observing your life—your emotions, the gap between the emotion and your reactions or responses, as well as your reactions and behaviors—you can use this chart as a way to track your experiences.

Please include your own observations in the empty cell, which provides some space for your fieldnotes. You might be surprised, or even pleased, at what you observe. Pay attention to your emotional response as you pay attention to your emotional events! The information you gather may come in handy in Chapter 6, where you will be encouraged to take a deep, honest look at your quality of mind and how it affects your experiences.

THE FIELD GUIDE TO HUMAN EMOTIONS

EMOTION	SURVIVAL PURPOSE	FACE	BODY	BEHAVIOR	Other Noteworthy Observations
Anger The anger family includes: *Annoyance *Frustration *Rage *Frustranger*	To remove an obstacle on your path to a goal, to right an injustice	Eyes glaring and beady in order to narrow their focus; brows lowered, giving a mean or sinister look; tight, narrow lips; clenched/tight jaw; in rage—the mouth becomes square	Big and aggressive to scare the obstacle off of the path toward the goal; hands clench into fists; leaning toward the object of anger during yelling; tightness around the heart	Voice can become a roar, or have a sharp edge; advancing toward the object of anger; pointing and stabbing at the air; if not controlled— moved to fight	Feeling powerful and righteous, justified and infallible. Sometimes tears and crying if you cannot prove yourself right or make your point. Sometimes stonewalling as a defense, making your argument impenetrable to your foe

Fieldnotes: Your observations

EMOTION	SURVIVAL PURPOSE	FACE	BODY	BEHAVIOR	Other Noteworthy Observations
Fear The fear family includes: *Anxiety *Panic *Terror	To remove yourself from a harmful or threatening situation, either physical or psychological. "Help me!" is the message conveyed through fear	Eyes open very wide with upper eyelids lifted; eyebrows lifted and drawn in toward each other; lips stretched wide horizontally	Muscles of neck tense; body moves away from object of fear	Freezing or fleeing; screaming; shallow, rapid breathing; jumping or backing away from the frightening object	Feeling extra strength in the legs as you prepare to flee or to right your physical balance. Sometimes, in extreme fear, the legs will give way, resulting in collapse

Fieldnotes: Your observations

EMOTION	SURVIVAL PURPOSE	FACE	BODY	BEHAVIOR	Other Noteworthy Observations
Sadness The sadness family includes: *Disappointment *Hopelessness *Sorrow *Feeling dejected	To elicit support from others in times of difficulty; to draw the tribe together; shared support in the face of loss or grief	Frown, corners of lips pulled down; inner eyebrows lifted and brought together; outer corners of eyes pull down; loss of focus in eyes	Slumped; heart drawn in, back, and down for protection; heaviness in posture	Sobs, tears, quavering voice; withdraw from life; remote, distant or self-isolated; dragging the feet; slouching through life	With self-isolation, the desire can be to draw others to you so you don't have to ask for help (sometimes the vulnerability required to ask for help adds a level of fear to an already burdened system that cannot be dealt with, let alone managed.)

Fieldnotes: Your observations

EMOTION	SURVIVAL PURPOSE	FACE	BODY	BEHAVIOR	Other Noteworthy Observations
Disgust: 1) Physical	To remove a toxic, poisonous, or potentially threatening substance from yourself	Nose wrinkling up, nostrils lift and widen; upper lip lifted yet relaxed; with social disgust, the corners of the mouth may turn down	Leaning back away from toxic substance or person; head turned to side, hands up to repel object or person	Spit to remove disgusting substance from the mouth; possible vomiting; hands up to block or move the disgusting object or person; head moves back to increase distance from the repulsive object or person	In social disgust, some might respond by wanting to know more about the offending person(s) and their behavior, sometimes without being able to explain the interest. Others might start or take up an ongoing crusade against the offender(s)
2) Social	To remove a harmful, dangerous, or threatening person, or faction, from the tribe				
The disgust Family includes: *Dislike *Revolution *Loathing *Despising					

Fieldnotes: Your observations

EMOTION	SURVIVAL PURPOSE	FACE	BODY	BEHAVIOR	Other Noteworthy Observations
Joy—the big umbrella of all the positives The joy family includes: *Amusement *Contentment *Awe *Excitement *Happiness	Procreation; to create prosocial behaviors that bond the tribe; create connection and cooperation; progress and growth of the human race	"Duchenne smile"— lower eyelids tighten to create wrinkling at outer corners of eyes; lifting corners of the mouth; sometimes lips open to reveal teeth, sometimes not	Lifted, open and bright through face and across heart; easy and comfortable; shoulders relaxed; laid-back posture	Smiling, laughing, engaging, loving, loving-touch, playfulness, teasing, humor, kindness, tenderness, compassion, flow states, connection, reciprocal positive actions	Most who enjoy the positive emotions are open and available to others; they demonstrate empathy and compassion, they are other-aware and not overly concerned with self. Some will authentically demonstrate a live-and-let-live attitude where others will make efforts to improve the world around them and the lives of others

Fieldnotes: Your observations

The Two-Year Old Self

Even though the initial time frame of the emotion may be a fleeting ½ second to five seconds, the time frame of the response can be extended and last much, much longer than mere seconds. How so? Well, we "import a script," based on our "emotional alert database."[19] Every experience that we ever have is stored within the folds and contours of our memory. Included in the memory are the emotional neurobiology and the sensory details—the song playing in the background, the look on the other person's/people's face(s), the tone of voice of those involved, the scents in the air, the temperature, and the lighting.

Also included is the *outcome* of that emotion and the behavioral reaction: did you get your way? Getting your way equals survival. Not getting your way is the equivalent of extinction—at the survival level, when the amygdala in the downstairs brain is running the show. When we have a powerful emotional experience, whether positive or negative, at a young age, we lay down a strong and powerful neural network for that emotion.

Take for example a child who throws a major fit in the middle of the grocery store aisle. He wants the candy bar he was told he couldn't have. His yells and screams pierce the air, snot and spittle fly from his red, enraged, and contorted face, tiny fists pound the air and the handle of the shopping cart. His poor, embarrassed mother trying to soothe and calm him only seems to exacerbate the situation. Hopeless, she gives in and hands him the candy bar.

He is immediately soothed. And happy. He got his way. Pitching a fit worked! And you can guess what happens next time momma says no.

Because he was rewarded, that behavior will most likely happen again.

The world of behavioral psychology describes it like this: All *untrained* human behavior is to seek rewards and to avoid punishment.[20] We either move toward what we like and want, or away from what we don't like and don't want. It's very rare that we can suspend judgement and find ourselves comfortably in neutral, without grasping to a reward or pushing away a punishment.

An educational attorney I know describes the phenomenon this way: "Behavior that is ignored tends to diminish. Behavior that is rewarded tends to increase." The rewards we desire can be both external as well as internal. The outer rewards probably come easily to mind—money, material things, praise, recognition, attention, and fame. Stuff. We love stuff, like shoes, and cars, and cigars, and clothes, and summer homes. The inner rewards we strive for also fulfill powerful ambitions and aspirations, but can be more abstract or transcendental—a sense of meaning and purpose, self-mastery, altruistic aims, or self-fulfillment on a spiritual or relationship level.

And the same can be said for the punishments we hope to avoid: both outer and inner exist. No one wants to be broke, no one wants to be ignored or exiled from the tribe, and no one wants to be embarrassed in front of their peers or colleagues. And we certainly don't want to feel yucky on the inside. We don't want to be depressed or anxious; we don't want to wander aimlessly through life; and most of us don't want to be alone, always going home to an empty house.

Often, unknowingly, we behave in ways that we think will get us what we want—like our tiny, fit-throwing friend who felt so cheated by being told "no" at his request for a candy bar. He acted out in ways that would get him what he wanted. He turned his request into an aggressive, hostile, manipulative demand. For whatever reason, momma then said "yes," and a pattern was born in his fertile mind.

He now "knows" that when momma says "no," all he has to do is rage and yell and he'll get his way. This boy is of course too young to actually know, through cognition and recognition of cause and effect, that his negative behavior actually produced the result he wanted. This is all happening in a part of his brain far, far away from the executive functioning and logical thinking/reasoning region, the pre-frontal cortex. At his age, the pre-frontal cortex is a long way from maturity.

That's part of the reason the habits and patterns of mind that are laid down in early childhood are so potent. They are happening in the survival part of the brain, without the cautionary intelligence and rational guidance of the executive functioning and reasoning part of the brain that has yet to develop.

When we win, or get our way, we survive. And when we conquer and overcome a foe (i.e. being told "no" when we want something) or we remove an obstacle from our path toward a goal, we get a big rush of dopamine, the pleasure and reward hormone. This hit of dopamine feels so good that we repeat the behavior that produced it so we can get it again. This is also how addiction develops.

In a very simplified version of explanation of the above scenario, we lay down a memory in the hippocampus that is linked with the reaction of the amygdala in these steps:

1. We're denied something we want, or feel we won't reach our goal.
2. The amygdala sends out the anger message, and we throw a fit.
3. We get the candy bar. Dopamine is released. Hurray! We win! Goal achieved.
4. The hippocampus lays down the memory of getting our way, the equivalent of surviving.
5. When we are in a "threat" situation next time, the amygdala and hippocampus swing into action for us, working in tandem to recreate the grocery store scene from above.
6. Our display of anger is impressive, scaring those around us into submitting to our demands.
7. We win again! We lay down yet another layer to that memory network. The negative behavior has been rewarded and reinforced, so it will continue, if not increase.
8. It all repeats the next time we don't get our way.

Fast forward to this boy's life as a fifty-five-year old man. Probably, like many who comprise the adult population, he has not had the opportunity to do much internal reflection and work, and so demonstrates little to no control over his angry outbursts. His spouse and children suffer, his colleagues suffer, the people who drive in traffic with him suffer. And probably, because he's now become such a master of manipulating others with his anger, he gets his way most of the time. In his mind and brain, this is reality. This is the way things work to keep him alive. And in his world, being alive means being the conqueror!

Remember, in the survival part of the brain, being right equals staying alive. And yes, in the John Travolta way too. We feel good—sexy and powerful—when we come away as the conqueror.

Also worthy of mention here is that when we are in the throes of a powerful negative emotion, and we import this script, we lose touch with reality. We think that the whole situation is true. It is certainly *real*. However, just because it's real doesn't mean it's true.

Back to our grocery-store-toddler-turned-adult who has not yet explored the depths of his lack of emotional maturity. Perhaps he finds this book and is willing to give it a try. He may discover that this emotional self-regulation stuff is a lot of work! Unless he has a strong incentive to change (maybe his wife is ready to leave), he may give up, and return to his comfort zone, where he feels powerful.

It can be scary, even downright terrifying, to look at the reality of cultivating emotional resilience. As we undertake the adventure, we can be thoroughly miserable—drawing our awareness to our emotional chaos can make it feel like it will certainly get worse before it gets better, which just might be the case. There is nothing easy or pleasant about owning our behavioral ugliness. Our "aha" moments might be followed, in rapid succession, by "oh, hell!" moments.

Yet, we have to try. If we ever hope to master the Art of Emotional Resilience, we have to start at the very, very beginning. We have to own what is ours: all the fits we've thrown in the style of our two-year old self. All the variations of unfortunate emotional incidents: the ranting and raving, the tears, the self-pity, the withdrawal, the stonewalling, the sullen silences, the disappearing.

What is your go-to method for escaping strong emotions or manipulating a situation to get your way? This must be looked at and owned before you can clear it out and move on to a level of emotional resilience that you will be proud of. It's like clearing the weeds from a patch of ground you'd like to turn into a beautiful garden. Consider this emotional inventory the weed-pulling stage. (Maybe you'll need a Bush Hog.)

You can do this. If it is your heart-felt desire and your intention to gain emotional and behavioral control of yourself so you can be the leader you want, the partner you want, the parent you want, the (fill in the blank for yourself), you can do this.

Learning from Jack

Jack, a colleague in the leadership training field, shared a story with me one afternoon.

A couple of nights ago there had been some tension at home. Big differences of opinion about navigating the blending of two families finally came to a head. No one, neither parents nor children, was communicating clearly. Tension was increasing, voices were rising. Jack was about to put his foot down and become the dictator to make sure he got his way.

As he became self-aware in a moment of thinking and emotional lucidity, he knew that were he to say what he felt must be said, he might do irreparable damage to a fragile relationship he was cultivating with one his "bonus" children. He took a deep breath, and in his lucid mental state, excused himself from the room.

He went out to the back yard and took several deep, cleansing breaths. He looked up at the twilight sky. He surveyed the yard and noticed that someone had not done their chore of cleaning up the dog poop, for several days, from the family's three dogs. He went and got the shovel and the bucket and began the pooper-scooper task.

He told me how much he hated the poop pick-up chore. I agreed that it could be pretty disgusting. Jack continued, "Molly, what do you think might have happened if I had decided to stay inside, carrying on with my side of the argument, not really communicating, just trying to prove myself right? Do you think I would have been able to take perspective? Do you think I would have been creating a poo-poo situation in my relationships?"

He was able to use his backyard clean-up experience as a way of avoiding the big emotional mess that was inevitable were he to have stayed inside and continued to press his argument. The real poop was outside and could easily be cleaned up. The potential poop that he might have created would not be so easy to straighten out.

He shared his experience with his kids the next morning at breakfast. They loved how Jack could talk about poop as a real thing in life and how they could easily create poopy situations if they were not careful. They also appreciated how he could be mindful and imagine that each pile he picked up with the shovel and dumped in the bucket represented a potential unfortunate emotional incident that was being avoided.

The oldest kid summed it up perfectly, in an oh-so-obvious and quintessentially teenage way: "I don't want my life to be one big pile of shit!"

Emotions vs. Behaviors

We need all emotions. They are essential components of our make up as human beings. Emotions, in and of themselves, are neither good nor bad, right nor wrong. They are outside of the moral domain—they are amoral.

However, we *cannot* allow ourselves all behaviors. We must draw the line at behaviors, which include actions as well as words, that are harmful. We can clarify "harmful" by defining it as *harmful to self and others*, including all living beings, and even to the property of others. If we think we can destroy the property of others, no matter what the object might be, we would be well served by thinking again. It might fall under the same ideological definition of stealing—taking something that isn't freely given. Call upon your ethical understanding of life and property and how you expect others to treat you and yours, and this concept is clear.

Let's summarize:

- We need all emotions.
- Not all behavior is OK.
- Behavior that is harmful to self or others is not acceptable. Ever.
- Behavior that damages the property of self or others is not OK. Ever.

Now, if you like things spelled out a little more clearly so there can be no mistaking, we can add the clause "willfully or intentionally" harmful. Because of course, there are accidents. So be nice. To yourself. To others. To birds and dogs and lizards. To the trees and the rivers. To the Earth, as our home.

We must allow all of our emotions. We must feel them and experience them. Know that they are an integral part of you, and that it's OK to have and to feel each and every one of them. Learn how to identify and name them, and then appropriately respond to them, especially the negative emotions that will surely arise within. Know how and when to manage them so that you *can* be nice.

Let's look a little deeper into the significant difference between emotions and behaviors. At first glance, and certainly in the moment of a heated emotional episode, it might be impossible to separate them. We typically think, "I'm yelling because I'm upset." But when we really stop to examine them, we can tease them apart.

When we dial in our self-awareness microscope and go in between the threads that weave an emotion into a behavioral outburst, we see that an emotion is a process that *results* in the behavior—either patterned, reactive, and destructive, or intentional, chosen, and constructive. We see tiny spaces, little gaps, where the trigger stops and the emotion arises, and then where the emotion stops and the behavior arises. You'll really have to pay attention in the lab of your own life to see these small gaps, but the more you focus your attention, the less elusive they will be.

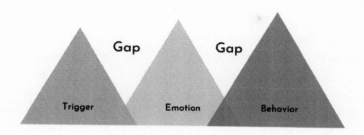

The trigger is a result of a combination of factors:

- The stimulus from the environment, both outer and inner
- Your personal history
- Your hard-wired responses (shared universally by all humans—such as flinching from an incoming object)
- Your current state just prior to the trigger being activated

The stimulus from the outer environment might be a threatening person, occurrence, or object (even an animal). In the inner environment the stimulus might be a memory; an imagined, future scenario; or the replay of the last negative event you were involved in. For example, you see in your rearview mirror that the person behind you in traffic is speeding toward you way, way too fast and there's nowhere for you to move out of the way. Certain collision is an instant away.

Your personal history includes the previous events and relationships of your life, your beliefs, your thoughts, your patterns of behavior, and your perceptions. You may have been in a traffic accident when you were young and the damage was horrific and irreparable, making you extremely cautious, or even afraid, when you're behind the wheel. This vehicle speeding toward you makes that memory come back to life, lightning-fast and intensely powerful!

The hard-wired responses are built-in safety features that follow an outline of instructions to protect us. All us have them as protective mechanisms to keep us alive in a split second of impending danger. They are not learned, but rather they come pre-installed in all human beings. Dr. Ekman found that we have an innate fear of falling and of rapidly incoming objects (the car you see in the rearview mirror barreling uncontrollably toward you). We also have an innate anger response to being physically restrained, and an in-born reaction of sadness at the loss of something important. (Here we find yet more support for the idea that we cannot do it wrong. These emotions and certain reactions are hard-wired into us.)

Your current state—your mood, even your attitude—is multi-faceted. It includes your physical, psychological, and emotional status in current time. Maybe you've had a very long and stressful week, with too many people hurling tasks and projects your way, and you just don't have band-width for one more stressful, incoming thing.

All of these factors contribute to the experience of the emotional process—certainly fear in this case, and perhaps anger as well. If you cannot remove yourself from the path of the oncoming car, your fear can easily and quickly turn into anger, the response of not being able to get to your goal. Your goal, in many cases, and especially this one, is safety. Maybe it's a complex combination of both fear and anger that you experience.

The actual *process* of the emotion, which occurs as a result of the multiple components of and around the trigger, is automatic. It has to be. If you are to survive a potential threat—and your biology really, *really* wants to survive threats—the emotion must happen without the interference of the thinking mind. Having to process the threat through the rational, cause-and-effect thinking centers would drastically slow down and hinder the immediate and necessary response to remove yourself from threat, or to remove the threat or obstacle from you.

That microscopic gap between the trigger and the emotion, as well as the gap between the emotion and the behavior are mostly indistinguishable *during* the emotional event. But they do exist! The practice of the art of emotional resilience is learning to *see* the gaps, to create space around them (it will eventually feel like these gaps expand), and then to utilize them as perfect opportunities to get a hold of ourselves, come into current time, breathe, and shift our neurochemistry away from survival mode. As we calm down and our rational mind becomes available, we can make a conscious decision to respond constructively.

And all this can happen in the space of those tiny gaps! But only if you're willing to spend the time on developing the skills of observation and deep inner reflection.

Emotions in Action

Let's walk through an example of how quickly and powerfully an emotional response can hijack a situation.

Wendy is helping her husband, Ben, put the star on top of the Christmas tree. Creating the holiday magic is something she looks forward to every year and she is as excited as ever to beautify the tree and their home. It's decided that she'll be on the ladder and Ben will be on the ground, steadying both ladder and tree.

Now this is no Christmas sapling. This beauty is over eight feet tall and massive around the middle. As Wendy sets up the ladder next to it, she grows concerned that the top of the tree is farther away than anticipated. Seeing her hesitation, Ben pokes fun at her: "C'mon Wendy! Don't be a wimp!"

As Wendy makes it to the top step of the ladder with nothing left to hang onto but the branches, Ben jiggles the ladder. She shrieks, "Stop it!" as she regains her balance. Reaching out toward the top of the tree, she realizes it's too far away for her to reach.

"Ben, can you bend the tree at all? I need it to be closer."

"Bend the tree? Are you crazy?" he replies. "Trees don't bend in the middle."

The emotional episode begins.

"OK, *fine.*" responds Wendy through clenched teeth. "Please hold my ankles. I really have to reach."

Before Ben can get hold around her ankles, Wendy reaches out and a blinding fear grabs her. Her heart goes icy in her chest. Her face turns white. Her eyes widen. She yells, "No-no-no!" She is too far off balance. She is going over, with nothing to hold onto, and will certainly smash into the tree and crash to the floor.

Ben grabs her hard around the lower legs. He leans back and braces himself with his feet wide and firmly planted. Wendy's biology sends a rush of blood and energy to her legs. Her innate sense of righting a wobbly balance kicks into high gear, contracting her stomach and leg muscles, strengthening her core, allowing her to find stability. She is upright. And safe.

This all happens in the space of about eight seconds.

In a fear response, our body naturally moves itself away from the object of fear—typically, we flee. In this case, the object of Wendy's fear is a forward free-fall into a giant Christmas tree. Her body's innate wisdom, all in the space of a microsecond, assesses the threat, goes into its automatic, instinctual reaction and sends blood to her legs, which strengthen to move her backward away from the threat of a forward fall into danger. And she regains her balance.

As she descends the ladder, she breaks out in a cold sweat and her knees buckle. Ben reaches out to catch her before she hits the floor, and at the moment of physical contact, she comes back into current time in herself. The fear over, her emotions switch in a split second to anger at Ben. Why would he make such a stupid move as shaking the ladder and jolting her? Did he push her? Why wasn't he more careful? Wendy raises her voice, "You could have killed me!" She strikes with her hand toward Ben, but he reacts quickly and catches her fist in mid-air.

Her anger is also a microsecond's worth of her existence, designed to keep her alive and functioning, allowing her to remove the obstacle to her goal.

Her goal was to safely place the star on the tree. Ben was an obstacle to her safety and thus the object of her anger. She needs to, even after the actual event, make sure he knows how badly he could have hurt her, which is certainly antithetical to her safety.

The entire emotional episode took less than three minutes. Yet it felt to Wendy as if time were moving in slow-motion. She was hyper-aware of the distance between herself and the top of the tree, the height of the ladder, the length of the fall that could have happened. She was aware of Ben moving to the back of the ladder to grab her legs, but his movement seemed lethargic and at a snail's pace. She was acutely aware of the physical sensations of fear, being out on the edge with no support, and nothing to grab onto.

Yet if you asked Wendy if she could distinguish the micro-moment when the outer situation turned to inner fear, or the emotion of anger turned into behavior—yelling and striking with her fist—she most likely wouldn't be able to. Often, and especially as we begin the practice of paying attention to our emotional events, we cannot distinguish the timeline of the emotional process until reflecting on the event at a later time.

Mind the Gap

Remembering that the actual time span of the emotional reaction is short, we can marvel at how well the nervous system functions to keep us alive in a fraction of a second! As we make the split-second, automatic assessment of threat or no threat, our biology can determine whether or not we need to remove ourselves from danger or fight to protect ourselves from it. This internal processing must happen fast. Or we stand the very real chance of dying. The rushing of the chemicals through the body triggers the innate fight or flight response.

As we automatically react to the threat, we are doing what has proved successful for thousands of years. Thanks to our emotions and their survival intelligence, we are all still here. And now, because we've made it this far as the human race, because we have evolved and developed in myriad ways, it's high time to refine the destructive, reactive patterns that lead to trouble.

Almost always, the *behavior*, not the emotion, is what gives birth to the unfortunate emotional incident; the unfortunate part is the destructive outburst and behaviors.

For example, how do we know that someone is angry? We intrinsically recognize the facial signature and the body postures that are precipitated by the emotion of anger. Those might include things like a scowl with narrowed brows, tight lips that draw the mouth into a straight line, a red face, hands becoming fists, or the angry person moving in toward the object of anger. The behaviors we associate with anger can include a raised voice, harsh words, and in Wendy's story, a physical lashing out.

These anger signals on the face of the upset person create a scary or frightening mask to announce the threat of danger to the recipient of that anger. If we happen to be on the receiving end, the facial expression and body posture seem threatening to us, which triggers a fear response that passes through our biology, preparing us to flee from the angry person in front of us.

When one person displays anger and the other person reacts in fear, both have a better chance of survival. The angry person's facial and postural display is scary enough to create fear in the other person, who flees the scene. The fight is avoided and both survive. Both get what they want. The angry person wants the obstacle out of the way on the path toward the goal. The frightened person wants to get away from the threat to physical and/or psychological safety and to avoid the conflict.

Even though both get what they want in this scenario, because the anger display was radical enough that the frightened person had to flee, we consider it an unfortunate emotional incident.

The good news of becoming aware of what occurs during the emotional process is that we can learn to see the gap between emotion and behavior and begin to work there, to short-circuit the behaviors before they erupt.

It isn't easy. The gap is tiny, full of the fantastic and dynamic power of the survival mechanisms of brain and body. But with consistent practice of being and staying aware, over time, the gap can seem to widen as you become more and more tuned in to the geography of your personal emotional and behavioral map. In the wideness of the second gap— the one between the emotion and the behavior—you will eventually be able to short-circuit the habituated, learned behaviors supported by your survival instincts. You will have a chance to consider and carry out a meaningful behavioral response, making it more likely that you can respond constructively rather than destructively. But until you become aware of and mind these gaps, you will most likely continue in your same old patterns of learned behavior, many of which aren't so useful.

An Interlude:

Human Emotion, Illustrated

As you read the following story, see if you can identify the big five emotions, paying close attention to the facial signature, the body postures, and the physical displays of behavior. Underline or star them if it helps you keep track. Think about which of these emotions are on display, and what might have triggered them.

One bitterly cold winter in the early 1990s, I found myself on a mission trip at the bottom of the world in Punta Arenas, Chile, accompanied by my friend Karen. The cold was bone-biting and mind-numbing, far beyond anything I'd experienced during winters growing up in Northern Nevada. I was young but had the good sense not to complain out loud—we were surrounded by people who were suffering much more than we were, both from the cold winter weather and grinding poverty.

Karen and I were called to the home of a young mother, Anita. Coming home from the hospital after delivering her 3rd baby girl, she had slipped on the ice and broken her ankle. With two other little ones at home, and a fisherman husband out to sea, she was in urgent need of some outside help.

On the bus the next day, as Karen and I bounced our way through the potholed, frozen dirt streets of Anita's ramshackle neighborhood, we saw a part of the city that was new to us. We soon realized that this might not be the typical help-mom-take-care-of-new-baby experience we had expected.

From the bus stop, we picked our way through those antarctic streets, punished and whipped by the stinging polar wind from the South, stepping over muddied trash, carcasses of dead, frozen dogs, and piles of waste. We finally found Anita's house in the labyrinth of littered streets. Like its neighbors, it was a pitiful shelter made of tin, both walls and roof, and had a sickly chimney barely peeking through the top. We stepped around a frozen puddle of water and stood before the fatigued, paintless front door. Karen and I exchanged a long glance, each gathering strength from the other, and braced ourselves for what we would find.

At the sound of our knock, the door boomeranged open on squeaky hinges and slammed into the jamb, revealing a beautiful chestnut-brown face, shining black eyes, and smile of tiny white teeth. It was as if that small, jubilant six-year old, heart outstretched in welcome, lithe body leaping and exuberant, was just daring us to flinch at the poverty that surrounded her.

"¡Hoooooooooooooo-LAAAAAAAaaaaaaaaaaaaaa!" she sang at the top her lungs, offering her greeting of *bienvenidos* to us. Then she announced with the grandest authority, "¡*Mamá, están aquí! ¡Las misioneras!*" Momma, they're here! The missionaries!—as if we were the finest people ever to have visited their simple home. Humbled, I experienced a deep moment of gratefulness that I had managed to keep my complaints about the miserable weather and squalid streets to myself.

We hurried inside to prevent the frigid outside air from stealing the precious warmth of that meager yet cozy home. As Karen and I stood shoulder to shoulder in the tin shack, our spirited little door-opener danced in circles around us, singing and pulling at our sleeves and hems, so excited to have visitors.

Up against the wall, under a window papered over with old newsprint and a layer of tattered, yellowed plastic, was a double bed that also served as a couch. There sat Mamá, leaning up against the wall, new baby at her breast, broken ankle stuck out straight on the bed, her plaster cast three times as thick as it needed to be. She patiently soothed an older daughter, who stationed herself on the edge of the bed, skinny arms folded tight against her chest, a mean scowl of distrust and fear making her face a dark and impenetrable mask. Her shiny black hair was a wild, uncombed mess.

Karen and I took in this whole scene in the blink of an eye. We also took in the walls and ceiling of the living room/kitchen/dining room. They were black and greasy, covered with year-after-year of smoke from the coal-burning stove that was the source for both heat and cooking. Smoke seeped out from the chimney, filtering through the space around us, clinging to our hair and coats. It had also adhered to the spiderwebs and dust on the walls, designing a "wallpaper" that was grease-slick yet coal-dusty at the same time. What we imagined to be a kitchen sink was piled high with dirty dishes, old food, and trash. There was no kitchen table, but three rickety wooden chairs lined the edge of the back wall.

I pulled up two of the chairs to the edge of the bed, while Karen piled our bags in the corner near the door. I kept a respectable distance from the fierce little beauty guarding mother and brand new sister, perched like a sentinel at watch over her beloveds. I could now see that her hair was filled with an incalculable number of lice eggs. Knowing that lice could hop, I scooted back so that none of them could make me their new home.

During our conversation with Anita, we decided that our first task would be to bathe the older girls and see if we could rid the oldest of lice. Somehow, the little sister was miraculously lice-free. We were not allowed to cut the child's hair—not even a trim. The kids at school were merciless and Anita didn't want her daughter to suffer further embarrassment and harassment. We also were instructed to gather enough clothes to last a week, and take them with us to a laundry facility. There was no point in having clean children in dirty clothes.

Karen gave me the task of going to the back rooms to gather up the clothes. The little one was eager to help. She clasped my hand and pulled me toward their "closet." She opened a flimsy door to the back rooms and I was accosted by a stench so pungent and repulsive that I immediately grabbed the door knob and yanked it closed. My eyes watered, my nose and throat stung, I could hardly breathe. My mind reeled at what could have possibly created such a stink. Then my thinking mind said, "Molly, you don't want to know." And I didn't. But I needed to get some clothes for those girls, so I girded my loins, gathered all my courage, took the deepest breath I had ever taken in my whole life, and holding it for all I was worth, opened that door and followed my new friend into her closet.

I hurried to pull some clothes from the heap on the bed, but the little girl wanted to make sure she had both her and her sister's favorite clothes. In an epic display of patience and good humor, I let her pick through the pile and find a couple of sweaters and pants. But it wasn't long before my good humor dissolved. I desperately grabbed an armful of sticky, dirty clothes and fled the hideous room.

Meanwhile, Karen had been learning all about the difficult situation of Anita and her family. I was not very happy that she got to sit in that nice, rickety chair in that smoke-filled room, eyes watering and struggling to breathe while she enjoyed a conversation and pleasantries, all while I was gagging my way through many years' worth of piled up, dirty laundry.

Is your nose wrinkling in disgust yet? I knew my face couldn't hide the discomfort I felt. Not wanting to be rude, I forced as smile as we bid Anita and her children goodbye.

On our way home, with a plastic grocery bag full of dirty laundry, we stopped at the *farmacia* to pick up a lice kit, which contained shampoo, a teeny-tiny narrow-toothed comb, and a pair of tweezers.

Arriving back home at our warm and comfortable residence, Karen and I felt an extreme sense of gratitude, compassion, and sadness. We were overwhelmed with feelings. We told our *mamita* about the experience. She was not surprised in the least. Over a warming cup of tea, she shared a little history of that neighborhood to help us understand. We were better prepared the next day when we went to collect the girls.

When the four of us got off the city bus near our house, the girls were fascinated. They'd never been to this part of town. "Wow!" they exclaimed, the houses were so big and so pretty! They loved the bright colors of paint. They loved the fence around each yard.

Into the house they trooped, these darling, dirty children, one just overjoyed and dancing into this new adventurous outing, the other cautious and guarded, her striking, cagey eyes taking in every detail. On their heels we came, our courage at the ready for the task at hand. We got the girls into the bathroom and ran lukewarm water into the tub. It was just a shallow bath—hot water was expensive. We got the girls stripped down and told them what was happening. They were both curious about the bathtub, and why were we putting so much water in it.

In a simultaneous flash of insight, clarity, and shock, Karen and I both realized they had *never* taken a bath. The older sister was eight years old. The little one was six. And neither had ever taken a bath—a fact we later confirmed with Anita.

Karen lifted the little sister and settled her in the water. Her face lit up in a bright radiance of wonder and joy! Her perfect white six-year-old teeth flashed a wide smile. It was like magic for her. So warm. So wet. So *splashy*!

I took hold around the bony ribcage of the older girl. Her hands cuffed tightly around my wrists as I lifted her over the edge of the tub. She dipped one dirty foot in that water and let out a howl that instantly sent icy terror coursing through my veins. She gripped my arms hard and those scrawny little legs flew up and clamped around my waist in a split second. She clung to me and screamed holy terror, as if she was about to be sliced to bits.

Sharp little fingernails scissored through my blouse, and then into my skin. It felt like I was trapped in a human straitjacket, the little girl was wrapped around my body so tightly. My eyes went wild with fear and shock at this sudden onslaught of screaming and clinging, gnashing and wailing, clawing and crying. As Karen reached out to pull her off of me, the girl's fear intensified, and so did her clawing and clinging.

She was determined to get as far away from that water as possible and started climbing me like a frightened bear cub climbs a tree. She clawed her way up my chest and used my shoulders and hips as steps to summit my head, pressing her belly to the side of my face, her hands clinging tightly to fistfuls of my hair.

Karen took one look at this spectacle and started laughing. My fear burst into fiery anger. This was not funny! Not in any way. There was a naked, shrieking child on my head!

Karen collapsed in a fit of laughter, doubled over in tears. The little one in the tub had no idea what was going on, but Karen's laughter felt good to her, so she started to laugh too, splashing away obliviously.

So there we were, this tangle of four girls, the two tiny ones naked and howling—one with fear, one with laughter—and the big ones completely at a loss of what to do next.

After much coercing and soothing we finally lifted big sister from my head and set her on the floor. We got her a drink of water. We had her talk to little sis, who encouraged her, "Yes, come in. It's so warm. It's fun!" We got her calmed down. We asked her if she was ready to try again. She managed a tiny, brave nod and a whispered "*sí*," so we tried again.

Nope. She was not having it.

Karen and I were ready this time and didn't let her latch on to either of us. We faced her toward the tub, away from us, and again I lifted her up and over the edge. Again, that toe into the water and she came unhinged. She couldn't grab onto me, so instead she latched on to the opposite edge of the tub, a free-standing model about a foot away from the wall. Her hands curled into a death grip, and her feet actually grasped the near edge, too. Her voice erupted in wild terror. Naked little bottom right up in the air, her arms and legs were stiff, made strong by the intensity of her fear. She was not going in that water!

I have never experienced such human strength. And this from a scrawny, wiry eight-year-old girl whose amygdala was on highest alert, savagely and viciously protecting her from danger. She was not going in that water. She would not let go of that tub. We could not get her arms or legs to bend. We could not pry or peel her hands or feet from the lip of that bathtub.

There was no way we could get around or through that fear. It was a fear whose purpose was to keep that child alive at all costs. Throughout her ordeal, she howled and cried, sparks of fear-turned-anger flying from her enraged face. And the little one, right below, sat playing and having the time of her life.

Karen and I were thrashed. We didn't know what to do, so we just let her howl, triangled up there on the edge of the tub. And finally, as most children do, she exhausted herself. We were able to peel her from the bathtub. She trembled and whimpered, shivering and snotty.

We gave her a sponge bath and brought her a cup of hot chocolate, wrapped her up in a warm towel and eventually got her to settle down enough so that we also began to relax.

We couldn't coax the little one out of the water! So we let her stay in, adding a little warm water to keep it comfortable, while Karen and I got ready to work on the hair and the lice. Karen perched on the toilet and I positioned myself on the edge of the tub, clasping the big sister tightly between our knees. We knew we were in for a serious event with the lice removal. We wanted to have every chance of success.

We obviously didn't use the shampoo. Could you imagine trying to get her head wet to wash her hair? What otherwise might have been a little easier of a chore became an exercise in patience and nerves, as well as a stomach of steel. (Did you know that lice burrow? They burrow.)

Karen took the tweezers and I took the comb, and we set to work.

Whew. Let's pause for a rest here.

What emotions were happening during that experience?

The strongest was fear, with disgust and enjoyment running a tie for second.

In the experience of fear, the common reaction is flight. We have to get out of the danger, to physically remove ourselves from the threat, real or perceived. This little one was not going in that water. Her whole system was on high alert and doing everything in its power to keep her alive. Even seeing her little sister right there in front of her, splashing and playing in the water, happy and enjoying herself, she was not able to experience this event as something safe. Her perception was so much stronger than the reality of the situation, so strong in fact that it became not only her reality but her *truth* that she was in life-threatening danger.

What was she afraid of? The unknown, mostly. She had never in all her eight years of life been in a bathtub filled with water. How was she to know that it would be safe? Or maybe there was a water or bathtub-related trauma in her personal history of events. We'll never know for sure, but what we do know is that *now* there is a bathtub-related trauma in her emotional alert database.

How many times in our lives do we fear the unknown? Our reaction probably isn't as outwardly impressive as hers. But what is it like on the inside, when you are in big moments of fearing the unknown, afraid of what comes next, what your next move must be? Afraid to make a mistake? Afraid to make things worse?

Karen and I experienced a fair share of disgust. The survival purpose of disgust is to remove a toxic or harmful substance or object from us. Our nose wrinkles up, with nostrils widening as we detect the stench of rot, decay, or spoilage, or even the feeling of creeping things on our skin. Our hands move up to push away the offending object, substance or creature. *Get it away now!* Don't let it get on you. Don't let it get *near* you. Creepy crawlies provoke disgust in many of us. Filth and squalor and extreme poverty do too.

Disgust is interesting and unique in that it also includes social disgust. With social disgust, we experience those who would harm or poison the tribe, those who do unspeakable things to children, or those who perpetrate horrors like Jack the Ripper, as toxic. We must remove them from the tribe in order to protect it, to keep it safe from threat and possible death. We must protect the weak and vulnerable from the predator.

Humor and enjoyment, oddly enough, were also present. The tiny sister was as happy as a lark, minding her own beeswax, splishing and splashing like it was a Saturday night. Karen was doubled over with the giggles at my mix of disgust, fear, exasperation, and frustranger, which flashed momentarily into anger.

The purpose of joy, which is the colossal umbrella for all the positives, is to help us make it through the hard times. It creates social bonding and encourages us to work and play together as we have fun with each other. Its main purpose is procreation. Additionally, joy facilitates the progress and advancement of the human race.

There was also anger—my lightning-quick experience of terror triggered Karen's laughter, which then ignited a spark of anger in me. It was quick and died easily, but I didn't think the whole crazy episode was one bit funny! Anger is designed to remove an obstacle on our path toward a goal. My goal? To get free of this clawing girl who had me in a strangle-hold, a death grip on my whole body.

And finally, there was sadness. Perhaps not during our hour-and-a-half adventure in that bathroom together. But surely there was sadness in our recognition of the desperate circumstances that Anita's family faced. What was to become of that brand-new baby? How did she stand a chance at having a good and happy life, let alone a bath on a regular basis? What about the fisherman father, who didn't know his girls and couldn't spend time with his wife?

Sadness is an emotion that brings us together so we can help each other through the tough times, revealing our compassion and tenderness toward others. It creates social cohesion and forms bonds of support that unite the tribe. We instantly recognize the facial signature and body posture of sadness and often feel our hearts open as we approach the person and inquire after their well-being, "Are you OK?"

We need all of these emotions. They keep us alive and progressing as individuals and societies. But, as mentioned earlier, we must be sure to distinguish between emotions and behaviors. As much as we need and must experience all emotions, we have an unmistakable line we must not cross when it comes to behaviors.

We must refrain from those that are harmful or destructive to self and others. They are not acceptable.

We must practice more often those behaviors that are helpful to self and others, often enough that they become our habits (frequent and repeated). And often enough that the gradually erase the harmful habits, which will eventually dissolve from our internal library of reactive patterned behaviors.

Emotional Re-Runs

Let's explore another scenario that can help us make the connection between childhood experience and our patterned reactions as adults.

Let's say you're continually upset with your boss, whenever he behaves like a boss toward you and corrects some minor error or outlines a new project for you. Yet you go out for dinner every now and again, you enjoy lunch together, you have even spent family time together, all the kids and dogs piled into the truck for an occasional weekend nature hike.

You cannot figure out what it is that creates the friction of the work relationship. You like him as a person. He seems to like you. You share some of the same understandings and philosophies of life. You just don't get it.

In your quest to understand and to improve the working relationship, you have begun to look deeper at the dynamic—beyond the workplace, beyond your roles as subordinate and boss. You spend time talking with a trusted friend to get perspective. You even take the time to journal about it.

The last big upset you had was not that long ago, and it kept you awake several nights in a row. The tension at the office felt thick and unfriendly. Exasperated after months of not understanding and the situation not getting any better, you finally decide to just let it go. You need some peace of mind. After you make this decision, you take yourself for a congratulatory bike ride on the outskirts of town, on a forest trail.

Pedaling for all you're worth up a long, steep trail, you exhaust yourself. As you crest the peak, you pull to the overlook and gaze out at the sea of trees. As you suck in air, regaining your breath, you realize how mentally and emotionally exhausted you are. The struggle with your boss has really taken its toll. You exhale and let your head drop forward.

In a flash of understanding, you hear your boss criticize your work in the same harsh and unwelcome tone your father used when you were a small child.

As a child, nothing you did was ever good enough. Constantly berated and belittled, you learned to fear the knife-edge of your father's voice and to bristle in self-protection.

This is the script you have been importing, triggered by the surprisingly similar sharp edge you hear in your boss's voice. As this revelation sinks deep into your understanding, you are able to see that your boss is not your father. And like a film reel, your entire experience at work shows you exactly how you have unknowingly been recreating a false present-time reality of a very real, hurtful childhood memory.

Your situation with your boss is real, and painful. But it is *not* true that he is critical and judgmental. It *is* true that he has the same tone as your father, but his intent is not to criticize and demean your work, making you feel like an incompetent child who isn't good enough. He is only doing his job, trying to get the best outcome for the company, and letting you know when your performance isn't meeting his expectations.

This understanding is enough to enable you to see him for the man and the boss that he truly is—supportive and encouraging, even with his sharp tone of voice. But he is not your father. As you adopt this new perspective, the tension in the working relationship gradually resolves itself. In a couple months' time (during which you often remind yourself that he is your boss, not your father) you notice that it has significantly dissolved and your relationship is better than ever.

Heading in to the Way-Back

Learning to observe and label emotions can be a really fun practice. At the very least, it will be interesting. You may notice things about yourself that you've never seen before. The tenor of your expanding self-awareness may be delightfully surprising to you. Or, you may feel a bit dismayed if the observations are not as flattering as you might have expected or hoped.

An interesting phenomenon that often occurs is the emotions we have around our emotions. When I see clearly that I have a tendency to express my fear as anger, I get angry that I get angry! A recent social media post sums it up very accurately: "The fact that it bothers me bothers me too."

Don't let the process of emotional discovery bother you too much. It's normal to find less-than-pleasant things in your mind. Like turning on the lights in a dark storage unit, until you do, you have no idea what's in there. When the lights illuminate the space, you can see the stuff. Then you can make a decision as to whether the whole mess should be loaded up and taken to the dump, or if it's worth sorting through the contents to find the valuable items.

The mind, like that storage space, can be full of all kinds of stuff. Your observations allow you to see, a bit more clearly, what you'd like to throw out and what is useful to keep.

Below you will find an activity to help "turn on lights." Begin in a place of non-judgment. Who knows, you may possibly be headed into a wormhole. Prepare yourself the best you can by keeping an attitude of adventure and light-hearted inquiry. And then pick up your sword. There may be some big uglies hiding in the dark, in the way-back, behind the light and fluffy, easy-to-manage stuff. You don't want to be caught unaware by these monsters.

But once you turn the light on them, they will dissolve faster than a shadow when the sun appears directly overhead.

Art Class: Field Observations

> *"I am still unable, as the Delphic inscription orders, to know myself; and it really seems to me ridiculous to look into other things before I have understood that."* ~ Socrates

You'll be keeping track of your emotional world for a week or so. Map out ten days on your calendar. To keep it manageable, you'll track yourself for most days, at least six of those ten.

You might like to record your notes in your phone or on your computer. Or even just a small notepad on your nightstand. If you find yourself in a pinch, a cocktail napkin will work just as well! Be creative. This is a fun undertaking and the more positivity you bring to it, the more fun you will have. The brighter your attitude, the more likely the big uglies will run from your mind, tail between their legs. And the less chance you'll get wound up around some not-so-pretty things you might find.

For your ten days of field observations, you will tally how many times per day you experience the big five emotions. Be sure to jot down any pertinent observations around the emotional occurrence.

Information that will be useful later:

- Your attitude just *prior* to the strong emotion

- Your physical status (tired, hungry, totally concentrated on another task, etc.) before the emotion
- The underlying mood for the last twenty-four hours, or so
- Your intention as you entered into the conversation or interaction with another
- Who was involved in the interaction
- Whatever else you feel is important

Big Five	Day 1	2	3	4	5	6	7	8	9	10
Anger	|||			|||\	Not Today	||	(And	so	on	...	...)
Fear			||||	||								
Sadness	-	||	-	|||\ ||						
Disgust			-	|||\ ||||	||						
Joy	|||	||	-		||						

NOTES:

Day 1—Overall, a pretty balanced day. Got angry with my cat for throwing litter all over the bathroom. Damn cat! And at the drivers in traffic today. They were so, so slow. And . . . I did leave about ten minutes late. I own my part there. My kids are so amazing! They make me laugh. Ah. ☺

Day 2—Just a so-so day. Felt kind of emotionally removed from it all. I am tired. And just need a break. I'm Zoomed out. If I have one more Zoom meeting, I think I'll tear my hair out. Fear is high because I'm afraid I will say something inappropriate on a Zoom call. I'm close to that edge.

Day 3—Spent too much time on Facebook, got really trigged over the stupidity of people! My faith in humanity is dwindling. My social disgust is off the charts! Why? Too many people out there using their words to hurt and incite fear and division. My perspective gets narrow when I'm so angered by *their* narrow-mindedness. And it exhausts me. I have little patience, so I find myself flopping over from disgust to anger so easily. And then I get angry that I'm wasting my time on these ignoramuses. And now I'm name calling. Very mature! I need a break to keep my sanity. Maybe tomorrow will be a social media-free day.

Day 4—Oh, I did it! I went Facebook-free all day! And didn't bother to keep track because it felt so freeing not to worry about too much. I might have to do that again!

Day 5—Oh gawd, my poor cat died. And I had just cussed at her for being a pig in the litter box. I'm a horrible person. Not really, but it feels like it right now. My kids were so supportive. What's gotten into them? Better not question, just enjoy it. They're good and getting better all the time. Hey! I just non-criticized myself. I know I'm not a horrible person, but I do have a habit of thinking so when things go "wrong." This must be progress.

This is just a snapshot example.

At the end of your ten days, check in with how you feel about how you feel. Does any of this data provide useful working material? Do you notice any patterns? Do you observe that anything in your current reality is reminiscent of your childhood? Patterns of behavior, contributing factors, similar characters?

Please go through the following questions with an attitude of lightness toward your process. Jot down your thoughts in the space provided.

As you look back over your ten days' worth of observations, what is one thing worth rejoicing about?

What is one thing, based on the data provided by your field notes, that would be useful for you to spend some time investigating or changing?

How ready do you feel to take action toward this change? Rate yourself below:

Not at all!   Totally ready!

If you're ready to begin, what action will you take as a first step toward improving that situation? (If you need some ideas of practices that can support your change efforts, jump ahead to Chapter 8 for a full range of exercises.)

If you're not ready yet, what might give you a gentle push in that direction?

If you're ready, but not feeling confident, what potential barriers can you identify? What are some strategies for addressing them?

What results do you most hope to see as you put into practice your action plan?

And finally, how committed are you to that practice?

I'm not.   100%

How much time will you set aside on a weekly basis, to cultivate a positive emotional/behavioral habit? (Hint: don't set yourself up for failure by over-committing time here; be realistic but keep your promise to yourself.)

If you've jotted down any notes here, please congratulate yourself. You have just taken a powerful step toward emotional resilience. And, this moment of congratulations can also serve as a self-administered dopamine hit, laying down a strong foundation of positive, self-supportive behavior.

CHAPTER 4

The Power of
Positive Emotions

Back at the end of the twentieth century, I began my official teaching career in a prestigious, private Catholic academy near Washington DC. It was an exclusive, sophisticated school and several levels up for a country girl raised in the dirt and the sticks. Luckily, I had an aunt who schooled me in the proper etiquette and manners of "society," which she had mastered while serving as the Social Secretary in the White House for three different administrations.

We had Mass every week in the school gym. Our athletic director (we'll call him AD for this story) said the Our Father at each sporting event and teams prayed in the locker room before taking the field or court. Many students prayed over their lunch in the cafeteria, and many teachers prayed at the beginning of class, too. I attended my first Stations of the Cross at this school, and later helped direct the production for a couple of years.

You get the picture. Even if we weren't, we were practicing Catholics while at school.

During my wonderful years there, I also coached several sports teams, and so worked fairly closely with AD, a very religious man who took his faith quite seriously. Now, I'm not Catholic, but I did grow up in a strong Christian household, going to church every Sunday. I knew how to pray the Our Father, but most of the Catholic practices were new to me. I was on the steep up-sweep of the learning curve and highly aware of not disrespecting the Faith. I did not want to end up in teaching purgatory, so I minded my manners and even learned the Hail Mary.

Did I mention it was Catholic?

Early in my first year, at the end of a hectic teaching day, I sat finishing up some grading at my computer before volleyball practice. I had kicked off my shoes and was carelessly slouched behind my desktop, typing in grades and comments, when AD walked through my classroom door. He stood there, just inside the threshold.

"Good afternoon, Ms. Dahl."

I glanced up and smiled, then seeing it was AD, quickly sat up straight and moved my hands from the keyboard, assuming a formal and respectful posture.

"I know you have practice in a few minutes, but do you have a quick sec?" he asked.

"Sure, I have lots of secs!" I responded with a big smile.

My eyes widened in horror! My mouth fell open in an *Oh my gosh! I am such an idiot!* expression. My face turned fourteen shades of red. I wanted to crawl under my desk and die of embarrassment.

Not something you say to a single, very Catholic guy.

He cleared his throat and his lips tightened. A very stern, weighty expression crowded his facial features into a mask of disapproval, displeasure, and distress. His eyes narrowed as he instructed me on the details of the plan for my volleyball practice. Clearly vexed, he turned on his heel and marched off down the hall.

Our relationship never did grow into one where we could fully appreciate the spontaneous arisal of joy and laughter that this moment *could* have provided. Rather, it forever hung between us as an unpardonable slip of the tongue.

How unfortunate. Something *really* funny had happened! If it weren't for such strict codes of word and deed, we could have whooped it up together. I did, with many other of my teaching friends. We laughed until we almost wet ourselves over that story and AD's stiff refusal to even crack a smile.

Humor is a vital and necessary emotion. We know this, and we love the fun and funny moments of life. What is it that makes things like this moment so funny? The unexpected. The coming together of two disparate ideas, the clash of wit and incongruity that catches us by surprise. Humor helps us negotiate difficult moments. It enables us to access our delightful dopamine, refreshing and re-energizing our brains. It relieves tension.

Best of all, humor opens us to connection. It makes us want to engage, to join in, and to play. What if every classroom, every boardroom, every meeting, and every HR training session began with a little light humor? The genuine humor that we share with our closest friends. Wouldn't we all be in a better mood and feeling a little more connection with our students or colleagues, our bosses or our clients?

Humor invites us in. Laughter is to the soul what water is to the body.

Think of the last time you enjoyed a good belly laugh. What was the situation? Who were you busting up with? How long did the mutual crackup last? Did you snort?

Simply remembering this situation probably made the corners of your mouth go up a tiny bit. You may feel a bit more expansive and spacious in your mind. You've just released into your biology some of the same chemicals and hormones that you did during the actual fit of laughter. Just by *remembering*.

Your brain and nervous system are extraordinarily skilled at their job. They keep you functioning on all levels with precision and perfect timing. Yet there is an interesting phenomenon about your experiences—not only actual events, but remembered past events, or even anticipated future events. Your brain and nervous system can't entirely distinguish between real and imagined. This is both good and bad news.

The power of your thinking, your remembering, or your imagining can trigger the release of the same neurochemicals that flood your body during the actual event. This helps us understand why we become re-upset when we recall the last negative conversation we had. We can drop right back into that emotional-upset groove as our system releases the chemical cascade of stress hormones, including cortisol and adrenaline. And there we go, off to the races, re-running the entire negative situation not only in our thinking mind, but in our biology and physiology as well. This is part of the reason it's so easy to confuse the real from the true in these unfortunate events. That's the bad news.

The good news? A similar thing happens when we remember or imagine something positive, or when we recreate the experience of laughter by remembering a funny story or occurrence. The difference being a flood of happy hormones and neurotransmitters is released. We can take advantage of this process to ensure that we experience more positive emotions than negative on any given day. And it serves us well to remember that these positive experiences work their best magic when they are heart-felt and genuine.

We all know the phrase *guilty by association*. Another useful phrase is *positive by association*. When we move into the habit of showing up in a positive frame of mind, happy, or optimistic, those good vibes radiate from us. They can be felt and picked up by others during our interactions. We can spread goodness by association.

It could be argued that this is really how we create a good world; we "infect" each other with goodness, with joy, with love, and with hope.

In our world right now, it might be useful to experiment with this. After all, we have seen the damage and destruction recently caused by spreading fear and hate and violence. Most of us know Gandhi's powerful phrase, "Be the change you want to see in the world."

If we would like to see a world where people respect each other, where listening to understand is a regular and genuine occurrence, where we take care of each other, then we—each of us individually—must first do exactly those things. There is no great mystery in Gandhi's statement. We simply have to make some inner adjustments to affect the outer world. And as we know, all change is self-change.

If you struggle with the concept of you being the epicenter of change, go to the pages of your journal. Explore why this doesn't sit right with you. Ask a lot of questions of yourself. Be willing to listen on the inside. And then, as always, hold yourself in the gentlest of hands as you come to understand your own story and your own perspective. Your story has value. All of it has something rich and useful to teach you. You are not bad or wrong. You are simply where you are, coming to new and different perspectives and understandings as you learn and grow.

Allow yourself to change. Let knowledge change you. Let a new perspective change you. Allow life to change you. As a result, you can then change the world, just by simply being the new version of yourself, maybe new and improved. But maybe just the simplicity of new.

Imagine with Me . . .

In your role as leader (or coworker, or parent, or teacher), pause for a moment to imagine the beauty of harmonious social bonds among your people.

Can you see in your mind's eye the happiness, the engagement, the desire to play and be a part of things? How would your world change if you, as the "adult in the room," could bring a sense of lightheartedness and emotional buoyancy to your undertakings, especially the challenging and troublesome ones; to the people you work and associate with; to the people who live under the same roof as you?

Could be fun. Might be funny.

The goal isn't to be rolling in the aisles every moment. But offering some kind and appropriate humor, just a bit, each time we gather for a meeting, shifts the energy toward the positive side of the mood-meter. Each time we need to have a face-to-face with our child or children, with our beloved, our boss, our team, or our employees, we can choose to boost the positive energy by consciously choosing a positive mindset and *emotionset*—the timbre of the emotions we bring with us to any given situation.

At the last school where I taught, posted on the door of a classroom just down the hall from mine, was a placard with a powerful message:

You are responsible for the energy you bring into this room.

What positive emotions can you bring to the table to create more harmonious and enjoyable situations, whether at work or home?

Heart-Felt Positivity

In the work of Dr. Barbara Fredrickson,[21] we learn about the *positivity ratio*, the term she coined to summarize why positive emotions matter so much and how they can help cultivate the character traits shared by successful individuals and organizations.

Through her research, she has found that in order to thrive and flourish, we need, on a regular basis, to have more heart-felt positive emotions than negative ones. In fact, she identified a ratio: 3 to 1. Three positive emotions for every one negative emotion and you're on the fast track to well-being. Positive emotions boost our emotional immune system, acting as a buffer against stress, anxiety, and overwhelm. They create emotional resilience. And we like them a whole lot more than the negative ones.

The experience of positive emotions, especially when we are aware of and can notice them, builds within us a reservoir of durable resources. Joy, from the big five, is a powerful emotion family with many relatives, including awe, wonder, pride, contentment, and excitement. Any of these relatives can create within us the desire to persevere when things are hard. They can offer us hope that things will be better. They fill our self-motivation tank and can push us toward personal excellence.

When studied in the realm of education, we see that children and teens who have a high positivity ratio can more fluidly overcome the struggles of academic challenges. They set goals, and more often than not achieve them.[22] These young people move easily between their inner and outer worlds, noticing how they affect others and are also affected *by* others. They demonstrate more compassion and empathy. They go on to achieve more than their peers who don't enjoy frequent and repeated positive experiences.

As we bring these positive inner resources into the world of adult leadership, we see the same. When adults in a work situation are given choice, when they are recognized for their efforts and their contributions, and when they can work from their strengths and their talents, they flourish. Subsequently, they are more willing to contribute, more willing to up their level of dedication, and more willing to be a team player. Experiences of positivity in work life are critical to cultivating emotional resilience against the inevitable struggles that are part of being a working adult.

If we are continually beaten down and feel like nothing ever goes our way, or we are never recognized for the good that we are and the good that we do, we languish. We succumb to learned helplessness, thinking, *Nothing I ever do is right or good, so why bother? Why try?*

This is a scary and potentially dangerous place for anyone to be. If we end up in Why Bother Land, we will need to really dig deep to notice goodness around us, to experience gratitude, or to feel a sense of hope. It will be an uphill struggle to move beyond the resignation, but heart-felt positive experiences will be key to your progress and eventual success.

As a leader in your field, or an aspiring leader, it is critical that you recognize and appreciate those with whom you work and associate. Be specific in your praise and spread it around generously, like sunshine or confetti. Make sure it is authentic and appropriate to the actual behavior you are recognizing. All of us can smell false praise a mile away. Keep the respect of your people by being genuine. The recognition and positive acknowledgment that you share will contribute to a dynamic environment where learned resilience can be the norm.

Some days, it will be extremely tricky to maintain an optimal positivity ratio. Other days, it can feel like we're completely manipulating every aspect of life, so much so that we feel sticky and sycophantic. There will be days, no matter what we do—what we think, how much we mindfully breathe, how much we use our mantra/mind protection—we simply cannot avoid overwhelm and negativity.

And sometimes, sadly, we move from overwhelm to megawhelm. If you are there, or live there frequently, keep reading! Later chapters offer several practices and strategies to steadily eliminate the megawhelm from your life. Through the genuine, felt experiences of positive emotions, we develop the durable inner resources of resilience, perspective-taking skills, and self-motivation that help see us through the rough-and-tumbly times of life. The resources help us move up through the megawhelm, out past the overwhelm, into the clear, uncluttered brightness of Just Enough.

Now let's be clear. This is not some "pie-in-the-sky" idea. You know for yourself that when you experience positive emotions, you want more of them. It feels really good when you have experienced the reversal of a negative mood through shared laughter with a friend or pure appreciation from your faithful four-legged friend. What are some of the other results of feeling more positive emotions than negative on any given day?

Go inside: think to yourself. How do you act toward others when you feel content or engaged or humbly proud of your accomplishments?

When our life is on the positive end of the happiness gauge, we are less worried about ourselves and have more time, energy, and attention for others. We have more time to do the things we enjoy because we spend less of our time in emotional upset, and less time afterward cleaning up the resultant fallout and emotional shrapnel.

Happy people, who possess the qualities shared by Seneca in the epigraph of this book, those who experience the deep, inner contentment that comes from living in alignment with their core values, are nice. Happy people become available to others. They move beyond the self and into a place where they are other-focused.

And did I mention that they are friendlier? When we're happy, we create friends, and build strong friendships. And here's the juicy nugget of that— we aren't mean or inconsiderate to our friends. If we do say something that hurts their feelings, we quickly say, "Oh no. I'm so sorry. That wasn't what I meant at all." We take ownership of our words and actions, and we apologize.

Imagine, just for a moment, if you were actually in the space of mind that you could consider every person on Earth as your friend. That might be a little overwhelming—but how many people would have your back? How much more harmonious would our world be? How much more would we allow for, respect, and honor differences and diversity?

We need positivity. Not just for our thinking mind, but for our heart, which we might consider "the seat of life"[23] and our Sacred Heart. When we live under the darkness of negativity, our Sacred Heart withers. It recedes from our priorities. We forget that our Sacred Heart is even there. We move through the world from our conceptual mind, continually weaving a story devoid of the strength and goodness of the heart.

It can be easy for the mind to create a story about reality that isn't actually real. In fact, many of us live in that false reality most of the time. We judge without knowing the perspective of others. We jump to conclusions. We prognosticate. We re-write history to our own liking. And so we create mental constructs that support our perspective, beliefs, and viewpoints. It can be a really good story! But it is ours alone, and might not necessarily be accurate or true.

Do positive emotional experiences help to dispel that false perspective? Maybe. This is one of those situations that is best summed up by the words of Brazilian author Paulo Coelho, "People never learn anything by being told, they have to find out for themselves." I like to say, "You don't get it until you get it." But when you *do* get it, when you realize you have been living in a false reality, and then use your emotional resilience as a skill and as a tool to move beyond it, you can change in a split second!

It might be useful to integrate into your understanding that heart-felt positive experiences encourage us to move away from a state of constantly narrating our life, to a place where we can just live it. We can dismiss the inner Howard Cosell and his play-by-play commentary and simply live from the heart, without getting wound up in the false world of appearances.

Positive emotions can help us be in the heart-felt moment of now on a more regular basis—a reality unmediated by the narrating mind, but lived from the heart. And it is in current time where we experience emotional resiliency, maturity, and freedom from the burden of emotional enslavement and chaos.

Accentuate the Positive

Armand worked with a lady he just couldn't stand. Try as he might, he could not be understanding, patient, or friendly to her.

Early one morning on his way to work, the words of his grandmother came to mind, offering long-forgotten advice. "The world needs kindness. Be kind, Armand, especially when you don't want to. Know that at the very least, kindness won't ever hurt the situation."

We can adopt that attitude here. *At least it won't hurt.* We know that the heartfelt experience of positive emotions won't hurt us! Perhaps the more often we are bathed in the neurochemistry of positivity, of love, of joy, of deep compassion for and connection with our fellow humans, the easier it becomes to stop living in our own mental construct of what we think the world should be or has to be. Maybe that will enable us to become open and available to unmediated reality in current time. And as we let go of the rigid belief that our perspective is the right one, perhaps we can see others as they are: just like us, trying their best to do their best, trying to live a good life, trying to be happy. What are the possibilities?

How can we use our heart-felt moments of positivity to help us navigate and manage the powerful blasts of negative emotions that force us to react from the amygdala rather than respond from a clear, reasonable, thinking mind, or better still, from the space of our Sacred Heart?

Each time you become aware of the inner workings of your nervous system experiencing the good and the positive, begin to cognitively recognize that for yourself. You can start to lay down a neural pathway of positivity by giving yourself a little extra dopamine hit when you realize that you're awash in a yummy endorphin rush. Congratulate yourself and say, "Yes, *this*! This feels good. I would like this again!"

We love dopamine. When our brain and body receive those hits, it makes us want it again, and more. The natural effect of a positive emotional experience is that dopamine hit. And when we use the thinking mind to recognize, "Hey, this is that heart-felt positivity thing I'm working on. Nice job, self!" you can actually create a stronger habit of positivity.

A habit becomes a habit by frequent and repeated occurrences. So the more frequently you experience the positive, and then intentionally recognize it for yourself, the better chance you have of repeating it down the road.

What if your whole life were one big positivity habit?

Look for the Good

Another lovely practice that cultivates positivity is to look for the good that is all around you already, right now. Be on the lookout every day for beauty. Listen for the sounds of laughter. Watch for the smiles, for the physical posture of joy or humble pride or amusement. You find what you look for.

As you start a practice of being aware of the goodness that already exists, you'll notice more of it. You'll start to see it everywhere. The sky will be a deeper, more radiant blue. You'll see so many smiles around you. You will hear the laughter that accompanies the spontaneous arisal of joy. And then you will laugh too. We all know, but it is so easy to forget, that happiness is contagious.

How enjoyable is it for you to be with someone who knows just the right thing to say at just the right moment? How do people do that? They pay attention. They are outside of themselves and are able to see you. They see the facial signature of the emotion moving through you, they see your posture. They open to their innate desire to tend and love you. They just pay attention. They have this wonderful capacity to see you because they are living in positivity and they are other-aware. They do not live in fear; they have lost the habit of critical judgment.

Wouldn't it be fun if you were the one to infect others with the lightness of joy, the big-heartedness of love, the breathlessness of awe and wonder? Wouldn't it be fun if you were the leader who could inspire these in others? Wouldn't it be amazing if you had a leader like this?

You can be that someone, if you choose.

Decide now.

Is that what I want to be?

Can I be that for myself?

Is that what I'd like to be for others?

Can I be that for them?

Is it necessary for all of us to be the inspirational spreader of positivity and goodness? Maybe. Maybe not. It's up to you how deep you go into the positive and into a place of being aware of and available to others. It's your choice how much of yourself you are willing to give to and share with others. You decide how willing you are to let go of a victim mindset or limiting beliefs. And you get to choose how much you let the positive change you.

Let Life Change You

One of the potent results of living more and more in the positive, is that you will move into a place where you can appreciate, with the depth of your soul, this idea: *Let life change you.*

My husband and I have an acquaintance who used to work in the casinos here in Nevada. As a young man, and for many years, he was a concierge for the high rollers and made buckets of money. He has no education beyond high school, but banked over $100,000 a year. He drove the fanciest of cars, wore the finest of suits, and the top of the line thin-soled Italian shoes. He was living the high life of a well-to-do bachelor, at a very young age.

Then he got married. His wife is a prominent doctor. They quickly had twin daughters. He is now a stay-at-home dad to two very smart, fun, and lively girls.

One night over his home-cooked, restaurant-quality supper, we spoke with him about this big shift in his life. In his very mild and peaceful manner, eyes radiating genuine contentment, he said he was as happy as he's ever been. We inquired as to how he could so easily slide into this new and oh-so-different role. He set down his fork, and said simply and gently, "You have to let life change you."

When we consider this word, *change*, we all have our own ideas and experiences around it, yet we all have a common understanding as well. One dictionary definition of the word really moves me. It clarifies that change is the process of making something "different from what it is or from what it would be *if left alone*."[24] [italics added for emphasis]

If left alone. How do you feel about that? How willing are we, in general, to leave things alone and let them run their course? Mostly, not very willing. Some would argue that if we could just let things be, we would reduce much of our suffering. My teacher used to say, "Don't pick the scabs." (We get a vivid image.) Can we leave the "scabs" alone, let things be just as they are, and find a sense of contentment in that space? Is it always a good idea to leave things alone? When might it not be?

Change brings up many, many questions, for many, many people. Much recent literature from many sources and sides of the topic confirm for us that all change is self-change. You can't change the outer until you change the inner. As you make your inner changes, you are enabled and empowered to move into places you were not previously willing to go, places that seemed scary or dangerous. You can look deeply enough and find inner answers to a powerful question that moves you forward on your path of emotional resilience: *What is the point at which I have to do something?*

As you gain strength to explore the depth of your inner self, you can come to know that you can indeed affect outer change, in a positive and powerful way.

As we seek to change old, habituated reactions and behaviors, intentional positive emotional experiences can build an inner reservoir of skills that will ultimately help us better manage and direct those changes. A positive and grateful heart opens up the thinking centers of the mind. It brings our prefrontal cortex into a fully functioning state where we can carefully consider cause and effect relationships, set and achieve goals, and plan for a better future. It allows understanding and compassion to color our relationships with others as well as the decisions we make.

As a positive emotional experience, gratitude powerfully and directly affects our neurobiological functioning. It can move us out of fear of or anger toward beneficial changes. It opens us to a new perspective, to possibility, and to potential. Even the words we use to describe our physical feelings during gratitude point the way to a lighter and brighter way of being.

I feel so lighthearted.

I feel so uplifted.

These are expressions we use often as we experience moments of gratitude. As we come up out the stress, out of the despair, out of the agony by finding something to be grateful for, we experience heart-felt gratitude and then are inclined to express that gratitude. According to positive psychologist, author, and professor Dr. Tal Ben-Shahar, in his book *Even Happier*, we learn that expressing our gratitude to others lives right at the top of the chart of most effective ways to increase overall well-being—not only our own, but that of others as well.

Positive emotions steer us toward optimism, which increases creative thinking, which in turn moves us toward an expansive awareness of the goodness that already exists in our lives. Positive emotions soften us, enabling us to receive and appreciate that goodness. It is so easy to get stuck in thinking that life isn't good, that it is all hardship and misery. It's easy to get suckered into thinking that because it's so hard, we cannot make the changes we desire to make.

How We Change for the Better

Let's take a quick look at the stages of change according to James Prochaska, et al., in the book *Changing for Good*. In their model, they outline and describe six stages of change that happen—first in sequence, and then as a cycle.

A lot must happen before the "action stage" of actual change, the authors explain. In the "preparation stage," you come to a point where you must decide if you really want to change or not. Unless you decide that you *want* to change, that the time, effort, and sacrifice necessary to see your changes realized will be worth it, you will not change. You will stay stuck in the "contemplation" or even the "pre-contemplation" stage and never get yourself off the ground.

Knowing that your negative behaviors are harmful to self and others is not powerful enough to counteract the strong and long-lived patterns of your reactive behaviors.

To change your emotional reactivity and your emotionally destructive patterns, you must decide whether you *actually* want to change or not. Without that firm decision and your commitment to it, your pre-conscious patterns will win the day.

Where do positive emotional experiences come into this picture? How do they support you in your change efforts?

Let's look at gratitude. Recent scientific studies conclude that gratitude activates regions in the brain that are heavily connected to areas of the brain that "control basic emotion regulation" on the physiological level: heart rate and arousal level.[25,26]

As we feel gratitude, we can override the fight-or-flight responses of racing heart; the short, rapid breathing; and the shunting of blood away from the core of the body out to the limbs. As we settle the sympathetic nervous system by coming into the felt-experience of gratitude (real, remembered, or imagined) we decrease both the respiratory and heart rate. We move from the very narrow and focused brain and mind of fear or anger (or other negative emotions) into the more expansive state of a calm and settled nervous system.

When we are calm and settled, the thinking brain—the upstairs brain—comes back into the equation. We come back to ourselves and remember who we are. We can tap into our intentions, recall our goals, and remind ourselves of our commitment to change. We are then able to move forward with authentic action to self-regulate a potentially damaging emotional incident.

Positive emotions also "broaden and build" our cognitive capacity, allowing an expansive perspective-taking ability and the development of durable inner resources. They also "engender flexible and creative behavioral choices rather than rigidly pursued behavioral addictions."[27]

Expressed feelings of heart-felt positivity have a sizeable list of benefits:

- Improved sleep, which increases your patience, your decision-making skills, and your ability for self-restraint and self-management
- Improved immune system functioning, which protects your health and allows you to recover more quickly from illness
- Increased motivation on many fronts—for physical activity and exercise, polite and considerate behavior, positive involvement in relationships, and productivity at work or in career
- Increased levels of overall health and well-being[28]

As we are able to experience more and more positive emotions, we strengthen our inner resources and motivation that support us on our path of change. We can feel more confidence that we have what it takes to be emotionally resilient and to actually demonstrate that resilience. In short, as we align our inner desires and our outer behaviors, our sense of self lands in the sweet lap of coherence and harmony.

Getting Up Close and Personal with Change

There are times when we all want things to change. We're not comfortable with how things are. We might feel angry, or sad, feeling that "Life isn't going my way," or "Things didn't turn out how I thought they would," or worse yet, "how *they* said they would." We may be grieving the loss of what we had been planning for our whole lives, but that have never materialized.

So we want things to be different. We can't leave things alone. We pick the scabs. We plead and pray for change. We do everything we've ever heard of that will help us get the life we want; we meditate, we visualize, we do The Secret, we set positive intentions, we send out positive intentions to the Universe, we do affirmations, we pray, we beg, we "do unto others that which we would have done unto us," we make bargains with God, and some of us might even make them with the Devil. But mostly, we resist what is, trying to force the hand of fate, unable to leave things alone.

Let's call this *forcing* change.

Then there are the times when we don't want things to change. We want things to stay just as they are. We have finally achieved the good life. We are making our home-grown panzanella in the perfect setting for our perfect family. Our prayers have been answered! The Universe granted our wish. The affirmations have worked. The Secret is true. Karma is true. Life is perfect and we want it to stay like this forever.

"Don't ever let it change," we say to ourselves. And again, we resist what is.

Let's call this *resisting* change.

Then change happens, as it will. And we toggle from forcing change, to resisting change. When we want change to happen and it does, we like it. In fact, we love it. We feel like someone Big and Mighty is on our side. We feel like we have finally tapped the secrets of the Cosmos. We feel powerful and in charge. We feel good, really good.

When we're living in the place of not wanting things to change, that we are living life exactly like we want to, and things do unexpectedly change, oh how easily we fall apart. We did not invite this change and we want it to turn on its heel and go back where it came from. Right now.

It is not a welcome visitor. It is ruining things. In a big way. And we are certainly not interested in letting it stick around long enough to see if it just might be a blessing in disguise. "Oh no thank you! Beat it, will ya?" we might say to this change.

Our love-hate relationship with change swings back and forth like a pendulum. Either we want it and try to force it, or we don't want it and try to barricade ourselves against it. We are not willing to make friends with it. We are not willing to simply let it be, as one of the irrefutable facts of life. We are not willing to let life change us.

Why this love-hate dichotomy? Why the resistance to just letting things be? Why so uncomfortable with change on one hand, yet so hungry for it on the other?

Maybe we don't know how to manage it.

Maybe we're afraid we don't have, or won't have, the inner strength and resources to deal with changes that happen when we don't want them to—the resisted changes. And conversely, when we are living a horrendous life that we never planned for ourselves, we're afraid that we don't have the strength to do this for just one more day, so we try to force change.

It's tricky. And to make it even a little more thorny, let's add one more area of change: *change that needs to happen.*

At one point along the way, Andrew's life was almost too painful to tolerate. He often spoke with his close friend Sam about a disrespectful situation at work, a situation that desperately needed to change. Sam listened for hours at a time as Andrew recycled past events, inciting himself to reexperience these past situations in current time—his blood pressure off the charts, his breathing ragged, and his face red with the heat of unresolved injustice. Andrew pounded his fists on the table, solidifying his commitment to say something and to make serious changes.

After several months of conversational self-torture, Andrew said to Sam, "Something's gotta give, Sam. I just cannot allow myself to be in this situation for one more day."

That very night, Andrew found himself re-reading some notes in his calendar from years prior. He had written to himself, "Something has to give. And I guess it's going to have to be me." The scrawled note was a powerful memory of a situation in which Andrew was determined to keep the heat of his anger alive. He was struggling with profound perceived injustice, hurt, insult, and injury done to him by an old flame. He'd been done wrong and he was not about to let her forget it. He wouldn't let himself forget it. Things had not gone his way, and he was pouting like a five-year-old.

Through the wonderful synchronicities of life, a mentor from days gone by had reentered Andrew's world at that very time. She explained, ever-so-patiently, that by clinging to anger, the only one Andrew was hurting was himself. He couldn't hurt his ex by being so mad. She had most likely moved on, as was her habit. This mentor led Andrew to see, and then to understand in his bones, that by staying angry and not forgiving, the only one suffering was him.

He pondered how he could apply the wisdom from that past event to the situation at hand. Andrew decided that he was the one who was going to have to give, that he would have to rise above the situation and take the high road. He realized that if he didn't, he was simply deepening and prolonging his own suffering. He would have to accept and allow that not every problem had a solution; not everything would go his way. He would have to find his own voice, never yelling and vehement, but firm, powerful, and authoritative. He would speak his peace and truth and then let it go.

When Andrew found his footing, when he surrendered, he actually found his strength. He made the necessary changes. Consequently, he was no longer held hostage by the behaviors of another. He was no longer the victim.

And where did those changes happen? On the inside. Andrew had to find his courage, his strength, his voice. And he had to use them to face an ugly situation. And he did.

Did things change from the outward perspective? No, not in an apparent way. But what did change was that Andrew no longer allowed an abusive person to have power over him. He stopped feeding into the drama. He stopped reacting to caustic remarks and hurtful gossip. He stopped giving his time, energy, and attention to the perpetrator, and when she felt his disengagement, she finally stopped. And the situation eventually dissolved.

The best part about it? Andrew had masterfully worked on his inner world. He came away from that months-long situation as the victor, not because he had beaten his opponent, but because he had taken ownership of himself. And in so doing, he took control of the situation, his response to it, and his management of it.

The Inner Resources Needed for Change

So, what is the root of all change?

Let's look at change from the perspective of our inner resources.

What is it that helps us navigate the bumpy ride of unwelcome, forced change? What is it that allows us to really savor the good life when we're right in the glorious middle of it, while knowing that one day it will inevitably change? And what is it that will empower us with the wisdom and courage to make the changes we know must happen?

Self-knowledge. Self-value. Self-confidence. These allow us to appreciate and live from our own power, from our own truth. They dispel the paralyzing fears in the mind. They buttress our inner strength and enable us to build our inner resources. They give us courage to accept that no one is coming and to understand that we can't do it wrong. They enable us to trust the encouraging voice of our Inner Wisdom.

What is it that prevents us from allowing and living the truth of the ancient wisdom, *It's like this now,* able to simply accept and leave things alone?

Fear, probably. Or other members of the fear family: doubt or self-doubt, anxiety, or dread.

But it might be something else. And that is for you to discover for yourself. Go inside. Look around. Ask yourself what it is that keeps you from living fully in current time, whatever the state of affairs of your life, or the world. What is it that keeps you pressing for change when things aren't going your way? What is it that prohibits you from living fully in the deliciousness of your life when things are going according to plan? Are you too afraid to enjoy things *because* you know they will change?

Our inner resources of perseverance, resilience, fortitude, strength, hope and faith, optimism, humble pride, and self-motivation are what get us through the passages of change. Without these, we flounder. We languish. We fall short.

We need these inner resources. They are paramount to our happiness, to our thriving and our flourishing.

How do we get them? Some are born lucky and come with a generous portion of positivity. These folks show up on the scene fully stocked with protection against the adversities of life, able to smile no matter what. (I really do know people like this. Several of them, the lucky ducks.)

But most of us have to work really hard to develop these—and then to maintain them once we've got them. On days when we find ourselves asking, "Will today ever end?" we must constantly remind ourselves, "I can do this." Or "It's all OK." Or even, "It will all be OK."

Positive psychology shares some insider's secrets with us on how we can cultivate more of these durable inner resources[29,30,31,32] for and in ourselves. And like all things that must be cultivated, we have to practice, we have to *do* certain things. And in the doing, patience is an absolute necessity, for the results of our practice will take the time they take.

What are those things?

Art Class: Practicing Positivity

> *"Though we travel the world over to find the beautiful, we must carry it with us or we find it not."* ~ Ralph Waldo Emerson

Please remember that having a positive outlook, seeing the good, and maintaining a good mood in no way discounts your struggles and challenges. They are real. They are sometimes arduous. They sometimes hurt—a lot. Being positive does not mean that you will always have a blissful smile plastered on your face. It does not mean that you will laugh and dance your way through every hardship you face.

Not at all. It means you know that life is sometimes rough and difficult and tiring. And even in acknowledging those realities, you know that you have the durable inner resources to make it through. You know that there *is* good in your life and in your heart and that you can access that goodness and use it as a tool to support your growth process.

The more positive emotional experiences you enjoy on a regular basis, the better your odds at finding success. And the better your chances of developing and nourishing those inner resources that will move you beyond the realm of unfortunate emotional events and into a life rich with joy and well-being.

We must practice positivity. We must have more and more experiences of heartfelt positivity each day. We would probably do well to play and have fun every day. And to laugh. We know that laughter is the best medicine. It makes the blues slink from the room on tiptoes, back into the shadows. It wipes away the facial signature of sadness, replacing it with a slight, genuine smile, the corners of the eyes crinkling. Laughter helps us see a little light in the darkness, helps create social bonds with others, and helps us get involved and engaged in life.

Let's practice a little bit of positivity right now, shall we?

Strength-Based Living

At the top of the list of positivity practices is knowing, appreciating, and working from one's strengths.

When we can shift our life from weakness-based to strength-based, we carry with us a sense of self that reminds us that we are enough. We can then move through life certain of our capabilities and skills, our talents and our gifts. And we use these as our primary tools to accomplish our goals, our work, and our play. We use our strengths to develop and cultivate relationships of trust with others.

Do you remember the last time someone asked you, with genuine interest, what you were good at, or what you really liked to do, or asked you about your art? How satisfying did it feel to inventory the positive about yourself?

And now the converse. How did it feel when someone asked you about your biggest weakness? (It's a very popular question in employment interviews.) Unfortunately, it's not always a useful question. It can easily send you into a downward spiral of not enough, of lack, of deficit. And it's especially disempowering if you're tired, stressed out, or running low on mojo.

We know we cannot perform to our fullest capacity when we are weak or sick. We just don't have the physical strength. It works the same way for our mind, our psyche. When we dwell on our weaknesses, we become weak. When we focus on our strengths, we become strong. It is from strength that we accomplish, that we set and achieve goals, that we create the good life.

If you have to pull a stuck car out of the mud, are you going to use a flimsy little chain that you'd find on a table lamp, or one that has visible wear and tear? No. Of course not. You're going to get either a really strong chain or rope that has no weak links, no fraying, no tears.

When you're cultivating your emotional resilience and working your way to the good life, please use your areas of strength to help pull yourself out of the emotional mud, should you ever end up there. Remember, you're only as strong as you make up your mind to be.

Let's explore. Please consider:

What are you really good at?

At what tasks, chores, jobs, or activities do you feel joyous?

What do you love to share with others?

What do others *say are your strengths?* (Sometimes an outside perspective can provide us with valuable insights.)

These answers can move you from self-awareness to self-knowledge. And when you know yourself, you move one step closer to living from your strengths-based approach to your unique genius.

Remember to give yourself a little dopamine hit by patting yourself on the back if you actually took time to respond to these questions!

Positivity Boosters: Creating a Life Where Nothing Ever Goes Wrong

In the catalogue of positive psychology research, teaching, and practices, we find a very useful yet simple way of increasing our positivity ratio. As often as we need to, we can give ourselves a little "positivity booster." It's just as straightforward as it sounds.

What in your life always makes you smile? Maybe your spouse, or your children? Your pet? Your sailboat? A favorite song? The thought of such personally meaningful, smile-producing things is a very handy positivity booster.

Let's say it's the memories of wonderful times you've spent on the water, out in your sailboat. When you picture your boat in your mind's eye, you summon vivid memories of being out on the water with friends, the wind in your hair, the warm scent of sunshine and salt, and the freedom of being on the open water. As your mind becomes immersed in those sensory memories, the chemical cascade of joy floods your brain and nervous system, changing your neurobiology. Simply by remembering and smiling, you can begin to dissolve some of the neurotransmitters of unhappiness, discontentment, or frustration, and release those of pleasure, joy, and contentment.

Our inner and our outer selves work in tandem. The designs of nature are so amazing! If we change our physiology, softening the jaw, lifting the corners of our mouth, taking a deep and pleasurable breath, we can change our mood, our attitude, and our emotions. We can either work from the inside, by imagining a favorite memory or scene, or we can work from the outside, by changing our posture and our facial expression. Both approaches can profoundly influence our emotional state. Much to his surprise, Dr. Ekman found that his research[33] confirms that when we voluntarily make the facial signature of an emotion, we produce the physiology of that emotion.

Create a little collection of positive boosters that you can reach for immediately when you feel the first pangs of loneliness, frustration, guilt, or unhappiness—or whatever negative emotion drags you down.

I actually had, for a very long time, a list of boosters that I wrote during my positive psychology studies. I even carried it, most days, in my back pocket. It finally went through the wash and dissolved into tiny filaments of lint that stuck to all the black sweaters in the laundry that day.

On that list was my favorite song, at the time, Accentuate the Positive[34] which encouraged me to *eliminate the negative*. I certainly did not want to *mess with Mr. In-between.*

Other boosters on my list included:

- Be grateful.
- See beauty everywhere.
- Laugh! A lot.
- Take a deep breath. Exhale. And breathe again.
- Love your students.
- Listen to the birds sing.
- Feel the wind against your skin.
- Call your mom.

Reminding myself of this list now makes me smile. I feel a deep sense of contentment and peace. I have hope that the future will be good, even though there is a whole lot of uncertainty in the world right now. (Isn't there always?) But my positivity boosters are a quick and easy way to help me take perspective, and that in turn enables me to live in current time as I focus on what is real and tangible and good in my world. These simple prompts can help me avoid getting mired down in the big What Ifs of life and remind me that I can choose, that I do have options. And my first choice has, over time, become a positive outlook. A *habit* of positivity.

What might win a place on your own list of positivity boosters? What are some things that almost always lift your spirits? What makes you feel good, deep down inside where it really counts?

Build your own inventory of positivity boosters by writing your list here:

Positivity Is in Our Nature

A powerful positivity booster is connecting with nature. Many of us know this through our own experiences. As we sit in a moment of awe and wonder at the ineffable beauty of a violet-fading-to-lavender-melting-into-peach-dissolving-into-pink ombre of the twilight horizon, we are developing the inner resources to see things with fresh and appreciative eyes. We are better able to take perspective and also to move into a sense of gratitude. When we experience feelings of awe and wonder at the natural beauty that surrounds us, the extraordinary uniqueness of each member of the plant or animal kingdoms, or the astonishing feats of our fellow-human achievers, it helps create in us deep appreciation and allows us to cultivate hope and even new worldviews.[35]

It doesn't matter where you happen to live on this amazing planet; these experiences are available to you everywhere. All you have to do is gaze up or gaze out with open eyes and a desire to *see*. Autumn leaves blaze away along city streets, falcons soar between skyscrapers, red squirrels spiral around tree trunks in a park, and the moon waxes and wanes in the night sky. Stunning cloudscapes appear over the freeway during the commute. Flowers blossom from the cracks in the sidewalk.

Look and you will see.

Awe Inspiring

Take a moment here to reflect, to let yourself slip into a moment of awe and wonder.

1. Scroll through the camera roll on your smartphone, or look at your social media feed. What were the last three pictures you took, or shared, of nature's beauty?
2. Why did these inspire you to capture them?
3. What feelings do they evoke in you? Can you identify specific emotions that you experience when contemplating these images?

Or . . .

1. If you have a favorite view of nature—from close to home, or from a vacation, what is it? Why that view?
2. What feelings does this view evoke in you?

And now, capture your thoughts about the following: One thing about nature that really inspires me is . . .

As we feel inspired—by observing and rejoicing in nature, in our fellow humans, even in ourselves—we feel that something in the world *is* good, that there *is* beauty, that the cycles and rhythms of life continue and endure. We can use this inner celebration to gather strength and hope that will motivate us to press on and move through and beyond our struggles, and to make the changes that need to be made. As we overcome our challenges and work on our change process, we feel a sense of pride in our accomplishments: *I did it!* We thought we would never make it through, but we *did*. We came out on the other side, victorious. And now we can take pride in ourselves, in our resilience, in our inner strength, in our determination. And oh, we feel good!

This sense of pride allows us to envision a bigger future for ourselves, for our community, even for our world. We know that we can accomplish whatever it is we set our mind to, because we have just watched ourselves achieve something, great or small. Every achievement counts. Every victory strengthens us. This further motivates us to press on through difficulties. It makes us brave to cheer on others we know who are struggling. It gives us courage and self-assurance to stand up and let our voice be heard. And as we, from the deepest heart of love, share our optimism and encouragement with others, we nurture them with hope and valor.

When we are living from a place of self-assurance and confidence, we relax into a sense of contentment, of deep soul-happiness. We feel fulfilled and can savor the present, the goodness of what we have achieved, and the goodness we see in others. One powerful phenomenon that can happen when we are living from a contented heart is that we easily and joyfully rejoice in the goodness of others. Where once we may have felt jealousy, envy, or frustration at the success of another, we now genuinely smile and celebrate when others succeed.

This joy we feel for self and others makes us want to get involved, to play, and to join the fun. We develop a *can-I-try?* attitude. As we connect with others on the level of fun and humor, we deepen our relationships, and what were once just casual friendships can become profound relationships of trust.

As we play and engage in life, we grow more willing to try new things. We are open to learning and we gain skills that we otherwise wouldn't have because we are participating in activities, not just watching on a screen or from the sidelines. Maybe we decide to play frisbee golf with some colleagues that have been asking us for a while to join them. So we say yes, and we get out into the fresh air and sunshine. We hone our frisbee throwing skills, our attention skills, and our teamwork skills. And, we're getting some good exercise, all while having fun.

We love having fun. Most teenagers live for it. For little kids, it is their way of life.

What happens to us as we move into adult territory? Do we get too busy? Do we take ourselves and life too seriously?

Recently, in the high school classroom, I had a student ask me, "Ms. Dahl, do you think adults take themselves too seriously?" I burst out laughing. Of course we do. And isn't it a shame?

Let's lighten up. Let's look for moments to play, to be playful, and to get involved with our friends and colleagues in a fun way. There are tons of fun things we can do every single day: put a miniature race car in your spouse's lunch box, purse, or briefcase one morning; put a small, blown up balloon in your kid's lunch box or backpack; place smiley face sticky notes on the bathroom mirror; bring lunch to a coworker, with no silverware—or better yet, if it's a salad, bring a spoon or for a bowl of soup, bring a fork! In line at the grocery store checkout counter, have a five dollar bill in your hand, bend over, and as you stand up, hand it to the person in front of you and say, "I think you dropped this." Watch their face. If they say "No, wasn't me," then you respond, "It must be your lucky day!" and make sure they take the bill.

Get creative! Life is fun. Sometimes we have to create our own fun. Sometimes, it's just there for the enjoying.

Learned Skills

We know from the studies of positive psychology[36,37] that those who thrive and flourish despite unfavorable circumstances have several defining characteristics:

- They are future-oriented, focusing on meaningful goals that provide direction and a sense of purpose
- They focus on their unique and individual strengths, yet do not ignore their areas of potential growth
- They have a grounded sense of optimism, knowing that life will certainly have its challenges, but that these can be overcome with effort; dedication; and primarily, working from a strength-based focus

All of these are learned skills. They are developed and cultivated over time and supported by the use of several easy protocols.

Practicing positivity boosters, simple prompts that can help you achieve and ultimately maintain a high positivity ratio, is one protocol that allows you to thrive and flourish rather than languish in self-doubt, uncertainty, or fear.

Your list of positivity boosters may include a person you can call for support. Please remember to call them when things are good, too! Yes, they may be happy to support you and be a listening ear in times of upset. That's why they made your list in the first place. And they deserve to hear from you when you have good things to share, too. Don't wear out your welcome on their supportive shoulder.

According to the Christian teachings we find in the Bible, as well as in the Indo-Tibetan lineages of Buddhism, we will get back what we give out to the world, or "reap what we sow." You've probably heard of the word *karma*. *Karma* means "action," and according to some, it means "reciprocal action."[38] If you hope to have someone there for you in the trying times, you would be well advised by the ancient teachers to be that someone for others. If you know of a friend or colleague, or even a mere acquaintance, who is in the midst of hardship or conflict, how willing are you to lend your support? To listen to their frustration, their sadness, their struggle?

It can be hard to make ourselves available to others in that way. The encouragement here is for you to try it out for yourself. The beauty of these teachings is that you can try them out with a personal experiment before deciding if you want to accept them as your truth. So put your emotional resilience skills to the test and offer support to another. See if "support others in their challenges" makes your list of positivity boosters.

And if you're just not ready to take it that far yet, that's OK. Good for you for knowing yourself well enough to understand where you are and what you're currently capable of. As you learn to listen on the inside with mindful awareness, you are building your positivity reservoir. As you honor your own boundaries, needs, and availability, you are adding to your emotional resilience palette.

We know that listening is a learned skill. How much greater is the learning process of listening on the inside, listening to your own truth shared by your Inner Wisdom? It requires a high level of self-awareness and non-judgment toward the self, too. Please honor where you are at each moment on your path of becoming the artist of your emotional resilience. Please know that if you have nothing left to give, you will simply wear out on many levels: physically, emotionally, and psychologically. You're not much good to yourself when you're worn out. And you're certainly not ready to step in and help others when you're exhausted.

Listen. Consider. Take the time to reflect and make the best choice for yourself so that you can make the best choice in your efforts to support others.

CHAPTER 5

Gratitude: The Heart of Emotional Resilience

"I was just sitting at my usual cafe table, watching the comings and goings of the patrons, the bustling liveliness of the baristas, when a sense of 'really living' came over me," my good friend wrote to me, describing a visit to his favorite coffeehouse that triggered a surprising epiphany about the potential of gratitude.

"I'd seen the same young man in the apron on so many mornings, and briefly exchanged pleasantries with him, but today, when he came out from behind the counter and set down my morning coffee and blueberry scone, I felt a sense of gratitude that I had not experienced before. I could barely say 'thank you,' I was that choked up.

"In a dawning moment of deep connection, I saw this young man beyond his apron and his coffee-making skills. In my heart, he flowered as a young college student who was working to pay his own way through university so as not to burden his mother with something she could not afford. His time and effort on my behalf took on a new dimension, a cinematic quality that gave me an insider's peek behind the scenes of his coffee shop life. I saw his efforts as part of my *own* time and effort spent on happiness. He was spending his morning to make my life pleasant and enjoyable.

"I then looked at each of the cafe's baristas and recognized that they were there for my well-being—the happiness that I found on so many mornings at the bottom of a cup of coffee.

"And then my awareness expanded—moving beyond the walls of the cafe, to the people who planted and picked the coffee in some far-off place on the globe. I imagined them, bent over the coffee bushes, again spending their time and effort for me.

"I saw the people who roasted the beans, those who packed them into burlap bags and loaded them onto trucks bound for the shipping docks. The whole story unrolled in my mind . . . the people who made the tires for the trucks, the truck drivers, the gasoline industry people. I took a bite of my scone and saw the bakers, the farmers who grew the wheat and the blueberries. The scone-delivery people.

"As I swallowed my last swig of coffee with my last crumb of scone, I leaned back in that comfy cafe chair and thought of the furniture designers and builders. The architects of the building, the builders, the plumbers, and the electricians.

"As I came to rest in this complete sense of gratitude, I had to ask myself, 'Why in the world do I ever complain? Even in the slightest, tiniest way?' And I made a vow with myself then and there to be grateful on a daily basis for everyone who crossed my path."

The Gratitude Web

Like my friend who was moved by his morning joe and scone to an awareness of the interdependence of all things, we too can know that gratitude binds us together as human beings, as friends. We are all, in one way or another—depending on the type of work we do—taking care of each other.

Gratitude moves us to a sense of creative reciprocity. As we receive the goodness of others, we also want to *give* goodness. It opens in us a deep and far-reaching generosity: of material resources and time, of spirit, and of human connection. Gratitude truly is the mother of all virtues.

Gratitude can stem from awe and wonder. We can expand our entire sense of being as we witness grandeur and majesty. We can be steeped, saturated even, in appreciation that we are a part of it all, no matter how small we are or how vast the world seems. We are part of the magic.

Gratitude can also come from receiving an unexpected gift or good fortune. Think of the last time someone did something really nice for you that you weren't expecting. Feelings of deep appreciation can well up in the heart. A sense of wanting to give back, to reciprocate, can emerge from a heart full of gratitude. We develop the skills of showing care and concern for others, and of creativity as we think of how we can repay this kindness.[39]

A deep sense of appreciation can engender in us a recognition of something greater than the self—a benevolent force that knows us and cares for us. We may also begin to appreciate others for who they are and what they do, and taking it a step further, we might just acknowledge that goodness. We may even be moved to very prosocial behaviors, spreading our positive vibes to the tribe. We may vocalize our sentiments of appreciation and recognition for others, making "Thank you" one of our most-used phrases in our vocabulary.

We then spread positivity by association rather than negatively infecting other people with a contagion of habitual skepticism, bitterness, or meanness.

Gratitude can be one of the most powerful and potent experiences for helping us move away from a mindset, and an emotionset, of slumped cynicism and defeatism into emotional resilience.

Saying Thank You

In his important research on gratitude, Dr. Robert Emmons at UC Davis, shares a long list of the benefits of grateful living and grateful thinking.[40] He usefully divides these benefits into three categories: psychological, physical, and social. Through these myriad benefits, Dr. Emmons concludes that gratitude is a relationship-strengthening emotion that increases our overall satisfaction with life.

Having one positive, supportive relationship is the number one *indicator* and *predictor* of overall well-being.[41] If we live a life of heart-felt, authentic gratitude, we will improve the quality of our relationships. If we enjoy supportive relationships, we will enjoy a greater degree of well-being and contentment. Take a moment to contemplate the extraordinary potential of positive relationships.

While I was in the classroom, I conducted my own action research with my students around gratitude. I wanted to see if the recommended gratitude practices would have any effect on attitude toward school, engagement in learning, and overall academic grade.

I asked each of my students to write, *en Español*, a letter of gratitude to a close friend or relative. They then had to either read or send this letter to their person.

We had a couple of objectives: to express their feelings and explain why these feelings occurred, and to pay attention to the inner experience of expressed gratitude.

Over the two weeks of the assignment, I watched my students become happier and more engaged in their studies, not only during our in-class time, but also the time they spent practicing their Spanish outside of the classroom. They attempted to speak more Spanish, they helped each other more, and they laughed a lot more.

In a class discussion, they expressed feelings of connection. They felt closer to the people with whom they had shared their gratitude, prompting feelings of being known, cared for, and loved. They felt lighter and less stressed out, so it was easier to pay attention in class. Their minds were more focused, so they learned more. Communicating more in Spanish in the classroom, writing their letters, and for some, reading them aloud, increased the students' language fluency. The academic result was high test scores for that unit.

Of course, as any teacher would be, I was pleased that they had found a school assignment so beneficial. They wondered aloud why they didn't have more projects like this, ones that connected school to real life. I wondered the same. So we decided that we would incorporate more positive psychology practices into our Spanish language lessons.

Gratitude was our jumping-off point. And indeed, we did see the promised results. From there, it was a smooth transition to interweave practices from positive psychology into each new lesson. We worked on self-concordant goals, taking perspective (super interesting and fun when considering other cultures and societies in the Spanish-speaking world), positive self-talk, making positive changes, and using skillful communication in our closest relationships.

We can easily see how gratitude is a primary player among the character strengths of positive psychology. It not only creates a sense of being known and valued, but it also creates a sense of wanting to be involved and engaged, or wanting to share goodness with others. It truly can transform even the most challenging of social institutions.

Let's look at the benefits of expressing heart-felt gratitude:[42]

Psychological and Mental

- Increased positive emotions
- Increased alertness, aliveness, and awakeness
- Increased pleasure
- More enthused about life
- Increased resilience to trauma
- Decreased depression

Physical

- Increased exercise and physical activity
- Better sleep, waking more refreshed and revitalized
- Increased immune system function
- Increased heart health
- Decreased blood pressure
- Decreased symptoms of poor health

Social and Relational

- Increased prosocial behavior
- Increased generosity
- Increased compassion
- Decreased isolation and loneliness
- Decreased hostility
- Decreased destructive behaviors

We would be wise to also consider several factors of success that impact business environments. A lack of gratitude on the part of supervisors, managers, and leaders is a common complaint among employees across all industries. How many workers, regardless of their job description, truly feel seen, heard, and valued by their bosses?

Feelings of not being appreciated, or being overlooked and undervalued, lead to poor morale. This loss of engagement results in a loss of productivity. Finger-pointing, scapegoating, blaming, and complaining further erode morale. Most of us know this from our own experiences in the workplace.

When these things occur in the work environment, poor customer satisfaction is sure to follow, which then cycles back around, with a negative impact on employee engagement.

When leaders come to a personal understanding of the power of gratitude, then easily and authentically say "thank you" to employees, team members, and colleagues, these leaders will see increased creativity and innovation. If you're a leader, expressing appreciation supports your people in achieving success, and motivates them toward achievement of both personal and company goals.

From the work of research psychologists,[43,44,45] we learn that gratitude builds the self-regulation circuitry in the brain, which guides a person's prosocial behavioral capacity. (Prosocial behavior refers to "voluntary actions that are intended to help or benefit another individual or group of individuals."[46]) Self-regulation, and certainly emotional self-regulation, leads to increases in teamwork, organizational awareness, increased motivation and productivity, increased efficiency and increased cognitive resources. Gratitude also produces beneficial decreases in harmful behavior, hostility, aggression, and anger. In short, those who both express and receive authentic gratitude are happier, are using more of their strengths and talents, and are more willing to work toward shared goals.[47]

Our work experience is so much better when we say thank you to each other. But these expressions of gratitude are effective only when they are authentic and specific. Rather than offering a general "Thanks for showing up today," find a specific reason that you're glad your people showed up: "I know it's a holiday weekend and many of you had plans with your family today. The situation we face is critical and our customers are depending on us. We need to deal with it today. Thank you for giving up time with your family. I appreciate your dedication and commitment." Specific and personally significant. Genuine. Heart-felt. This is the gratitude that supports you, those you work with, and those you work for, in your efforts to be emotionally resilient.

Cultivating Self-Gratitude

Just as it's important to express thankfulness to others, you will benefit from having a self-gratitude practice as well.

Goethe eloquently described the way we create a worldview when he wrote, "A man sees in the world what he carries in his heart."

Having a grateful heart can give us hope for a world that often seems so hopeless. It can also help us see the good in others and to give them the benefit of the doubt. And oh-so-importantly, it can help us remember, that given the chance, most people will do their best.

Sometimes, that is not an easy idea to wrap your mind around. Sometimes, it's virtually impossible to hold the perspective that others are doing their best. But we can. And we must. Otherwise, we will be fraught with agitation and judgment, criticism and fault-finding, and end up in a black pit of despair.

At the end of every yoga class I teach, I offer the participants a little phrase of hope: "The world is a good place, full of good people, all of us trying to do our best."

For several weeks, I had been listening to the news, trying to get a sense of what was happening in the world, trying to find balance in the topsy-turvy upheavals of our current society and culture.

One night I had a little *crisis de fe*, a crisis of faith around the goodness of humanity. I asked my husband how I could go on saying that the world is a good place, that people are good. I implored him to provide some sort of answer, some sort of hope.

All he said was, "It is. They are. Your world comes from you, not at you. If you are good, if your heart is good, then you will live in a good world, full of good people."

I pondered long and hard. I turned off the news and started paying attention to my world, to the reality of where I spent my days—the people who drive on the same streets as I, the people in the grocery store, at the gas station, in line at the post office. The people I work with and for. I said "Hi," as a personal experiment to see if others would say "Hi" back.

And they did. They smiled and they waved in return to my friendly gestures. They held doors open and talked with me about the weather while we waited in line together. They said "please" and "thank you" to the postman, to the check-out girl, to the office clerk. And to me.

A couple of weeks later, back in my yoga class, I shared my concerns about teaching that the world is a good place, and my action research around that concern. My inner gratitude practice had blossomed. As I was able to appreciate my ability to question and ponder, to observe without judgment, I opened to possibility and to potential. These all became salient points of my self-gratitude that I was able to share compassionately and kindly with my yogis.

"I know we worry about the state of the world. I know that there are a lot of weird and crazy things happening right now. I know we worry about the future, which is very uncertain. But we never really know what tomorrow will bring. We know about today. Actually, we know about right now. We know that we live in a place where people are good and kind. We know that we are good and kind. Or, at least, we can lean on the idea that most of us will do our best whenever we can."

I looked around at my yogis, my dear friends who I have come to love, and my heart opened wide. Here was my world, full of good people, doing their best to be good and kind and share their goodness with others. In a moment of fluttering and light, I knew that what my husband shared was true. My world *does* come from me.

As I was able to eliminate negative input that created fear and doubt, and focused on seeing and experiencing the good that is all around me, and in me, the anxiety and worry dissolved. My hope blossomed. My faith in humanity as good was restored. And then with certainty born of the felt experience, I was able to authentically and confidently share my experience and my knowledge.

What does it take to know in your bones that the world is a good place? How do we do this without negating the awareness that some things are not beneficial and useful? I think the secret is being able to find gratitude for the self, for all your goodness, your perseverance, your talents, and your gifts. When you can practice self-gratitude, you create a heart that is available to gratitude. And just as Goethe observed, you will then see a world full of grateful people.

So please be grateful for you who are, for all the experiences that have gotten you here, to this very moment of time. Be grateful for your inner strength and sense of determined commitment. Find a deep sense of appreciation for all you have struggled through and overcome. Your character is a result of your life's experiences. Don't let any of those experiences be in vain. Honor who you are and where you've come from. Honor your own goodness.

You are good. And you are good enough.

Our work here is never meant to encourage or cultivate arrogance or hubris. Self-gratitude is actually the opposite of self-aggrandizement. Instead, it enables us to build a confident sense of self, each one of us honoring our own unique genius, helping us to develop a *good heart*. It is only with a good heart that we become available to others and can share our goodness as a way to make the world a better place.

Gratitude as Choice

Thankfulness and appreciation can glide smoothly and effortlessly into a sense of hope. With hope, we may be anxious that the worst could happen, but we still have faith the something better will happen in the end—or at least the long run. As my grandma used to say, "If it hasn't worked out for the better, it isn't the end yet."

Hope can inspire us. When we see the strength and resilience of the human spirit and the way it enables us to overcome adversity and struggles, we are encouraged. We all have our challenges, but we can seek inspiration by observing the successes of others where we feel we are failing, or flailing.

One afternoon when I was in my early twenties, I was out for a drive to cool off from a heated argument with my mom. My old pickup truck rattled down the rough county roads of northern Nevada, out past the canal, and over to the other side of the valley.

As I slowed to manage an especially wash-boardy section of road, movement out the open passenger window caught my attention.

A young mother, barefoot, in a tattered and thread-bare dress, hair in a tangled jumble on top of her head, was hanging clothes on the line in a dirt yard. The yard, barren except for a few scattered twigs, puncture vines, dried weeds, and dandelions, was an expanse of dust surrounded by a worn out, sagging, missing-picket fence. That fence was, once upon a time, the crowning glory of someone's dream come true. Now, it was only a reminder that all things change and that life is uncertain.

Sitting in and covered with dirt, waving a small branch in some internal victory salute, a tiny girl, naked save for a diaper, amused herself in the sun. Playing in front of a dilapidated house that resembled the old picket fence, she laughed and smiled, unaware that she was living in poverty, filthy and unclothed. Her happy face turned up to the sky, searching for the bird she had heard chirping overhead. As she saw the bird, she pointed her stick at it and let out a scream of delight.

The mother turned to watch her daughter, perhaps unfazed by the poverty in which she was living and raising a child. As she watched her little girl, so spellbound by the bird in the heavens, a beaming smile broke out across Mom's face, highlighting the beauty of her lips, revealing the brightness of her eyes and the creases of true joy in the smile lines gracing the corners of her eyes.

Anyone who observed the scene would have been moved deeply, understanding that despite their circumstances, love, and joy—yes, even hope—were present within that young mother and her child. The observer might well conclude that happiness is where you find it.

Contentment does not come from outside factors, but arises from an inner wellspring of goodness. It is the reward we reap from being kind. It can be found in abundance in the meagerest of external situations. Maybe that is how our Chilean mother Anita felt about her life and circumstances: that it was OK to have three children to raise by herself, and that it could even be joyous.

If this mother and her child could be happy there, in the dirt and dead weeds, without the conveniences of modern life, then how many of us can be happy and content with all we have and all that is available to us?

Recognizing in the depth of our knowing hearts where contentment comes from, we can understand that it is up to each of us, individually, to create the life we desire by creating an inner well that is the source of our peace of mind, thriving, and flourishing. We will come to know, as we continually take perspective, stay self-aware, cultivate self-knowledge, and skillfully self-manage, that profound joy is available as our own reality.

What are some simple ways you can boost your experiences of joy, fun, and light-heartedness during the day? Let's return to positivity boosters. A few suggestions:

- Listen to uplifting music, a humorous podcast, or watch funny videos (but not fun had at the expense of others)
- Get a joke book for late-elementary aged children (all the jokes are clean, and totally corny!)
- Reminisce and laugh with good friends about a funny situation you shared
- Take a few minutes to play with your dog or your cat
- Call a friend you haven't spoken to in a while and tell them something you appreciate about them
- Pay for the coffee order of the car behind you in the drive-through
- Rather than offer a reflexive "thank you" to someone who helps you in a store or restaurant, tell them something specific that you appreciated about their service

These inner resources that we cultivate are interwoven into each other and are cumulative. They're kind of like rabbits. Rabbits breed and suddenly we have exponential rabbit population growth. The gestation period for rabbits is only about thirty-one days, just about the same time it takes to dissolve an old habit and establish a new one.

As we begin to enjoy just a couple of truly heartfelt positive experiences each day, our feelings of positivity and optimism can multiply exponentially.

Maybe not as fast as rabbits. But we can certainly observe the benefits of enjoying ourselves more. The more we enjoy ourselves, the more inner motivation we have to persist in our efforts to practice positivity. The more we enjoy ourselves and our lives, the more others notice this, and in noticing, can't help but be a tiny bit affected by us and our happiness.

Virtue—the Guarantee to the Good Life

Let's summarize the inner qualities that can help you magnify your efforts toward thriving and flourishing. We can call these inner qualities *virtues*. I read once that "virtue is a phenomenon that necessarily results in goodness."[48] Dig in there just a bit and you will find the answer of how to create a good life. And don't we all want a good life? I think it's fair to say that we can define a good life as one in which things are mostly going our way, perhaps with just a few hiccups here and there.

We can also expand into a more altruistic perspective and understand the good life as the experience where we all mostly have what we need, where we all see and appreciate each other, where we all have capacity to give each other the benefit of the doubt and the time of day. (Not an easy perspective, but achievable.)

This definition of *virtue* is just about the closest we're going to come to finding a guarantee to the good life, although it may take a while for the fruits of our virtuous living to grow to full ripeness.

What is the near-guarantee? *Necessarily results in goodness.* Which means that there is *no other option.* It's like making a free throw in basketball. A free throw is only ever worth one point. No one will ever earn partial points for style and form. No one will ever lose points for missing. A successful attempt at a free throw *necessarily* results in only one point on the scoreboard. There is simply no other possibility.

And so with virtue resulting in goodness. Goodness must be the result of our patience, our resilience, our hope and faith, our appreciation of beauty, our optimism, our generosity, our attentional awareness focused where we want it, our compassion, our empathy, our perspective taking, our kindness, our honesty, our dedication and devotion, our generosity of spirit, and our love of life and fellow man and woman. (Among others. What else would you add to this list?)

> Virtue is a phenomenon that
> necessarily results in goodness.

As we are living these virtues, it's easier for us to keep our attentional awareness focused on the present moment. A positive mental state necessarily expands our awareness and experience, which becomes wider than "me and my needs right now." Attention broadens to include an awareness of others, and their needs and wants. As we cultivate a positive outlook and worldview, we nourish our own capacity to practice virtue. How? Positivity is like sunlight, generating energy and life force, reviving the world after a long, dark winter. It allows your gifts and talents to flower and expand, letting you be a light for others who need one.

The more you practice living a virtuous life, the more other-oriented and available you will become. And let's be clear that this does not mean "virtue signaling" (making public statements or performing symbolic acts intended to demonstrate moral virtues that you may not actually practice). A virtuous life is lived authentically from a heart that understands that kindness begets kindness, you get what you give, and that what comes around goes around.

We are not in this for ourselves. Science shows us repeatedly that depression is partly caused by loneliness and isolation. We move into a state of constantly thinking and worrying about me, me, me. *Why can't I be happy? Why is my life so hard? Why is this happening to me?*

When we move beyond the binds and limitations of *me and mine*, beyond our small, self-focused world and reach out to others, we begin to change our neurochemistry and our biology. By connecting with and serving others, we experience biological renewal. Our systems are invigorated with light and compassion, joy and love, hope and resilience.

This goodness and optimism can help us remain grounded in reality if we balk at the idealistic nature of this new take on virtue. It can be a slippery perspective to hold, or even to grasp. Yet practicing virtue as a way life has merit. It has survived the trial-and-error method of figuring out if something works, or is useful. As you expand your capacity for virtuous living you will move from comprehension to knowledge, born of the felt-experience, that goodness is indeed the result. As you apply virtue across the "curriculum" of your life, you will gain applicational mastery, able to add your own finesse and flair.

And then you will begin to see results. You will see your life get better; people will become nicer and you will find yourself showing up more and more as your best self. As you have personal experience with both the elements and the results of living a virtuous life, you will be able to move away from any obsession with things, prestige, or power and start re-valuing your relationships and the development of your inner life.

Demonstrating virtue as a regular habit means that you are living from your true center, aligned with your values, strengths, and goals. You might experience deep and meaningful connection to others. You might create friends of mere acquaintances or colleagues. Your problem-solving ability will gradually take on a more creative flair, generating more internal motivation for you to be involved and engaged. Rather than awaiting the promise of the future, you will be content in current time, enjoying what life delivers to your doorstep today.

Practice virtue. And then, necessarily, goodness will be yours.

Of course, if we're in the throes of sadness and gloom, the last thing we want to do is think of performing a virtuous action. We have little desire to get up and go help someone else. It can be a very real and heart-felt struggle. So, turn on your favorite upbeat song, open the drapes and let in some light, wash your face, get dressed, and at the very least, go outside into the fresh air, into the sunshine. Let the sun shine right on your heart, warming it and nourishing it. Sunlight creates energy. Soak in this energy. Let this light get inside you, on a very real and visceral level, and it will begin to dispel the inner darkness.

Turn your face to the sun and lift the corners of your mouth into a teeny smile. Be confident in the idea of faking it until you make it. It works! Just lifting the corners of your mouth can stimulate the release of the happy hormones and neurotransmitters, including dopamine, serotonin, and oxytocin—another effective yet almost effortless positivity booster.

Program Yourself for Positivity

We need heartfelt positive experiences on a very regular basis, and especially during times of stress and high anxiety. You are in charge of the type of experiences you allow yourself. To stop feeding the stress and anxiety, you can choose to turn off the TV, turn off the news. You can choose to distance yourself from toxic social media and negative, emotionally charged posts and pages.

"Curating" these inputs is an empowering practice. You can also replace them with inputs that feed your positivity, such as reading or listening to uplifting stories, inspiring biographies, or, when you need a brain-break, things that just make you laugh. You might even enjoy doing nothing for a little while, allowing your whole self to rest with nothing to think about and nothing do. Doing nothing is a lost art. Maybe it's time to bring it back.

You can also use the time previously spent consuming content produced by others in creating your *own* content. Journaling, sketching, and photography are all easy ways to tell your own stories, make your own observations, find new meaning, and enhance your awareness of current time. Explore something new, maybe even something out of your comfort zone, or something that seems just beyond the reach of your skill level. You just might discover a whole new artistic layer of yourself.

Detox Time

If we are full to the brim with negativity, comparison mindset, fear, or anxiety, how are we going to add happiness or contentment to that cup? We must first empty the cup by steadily pouring off the negative, and replacing it with positive inputs. Try this for a couple of days.

- **Do a digital detox.** It doesn't have to be long; even one day can have powerful benefits.
    o Unplug, disconnect, and clear negativity out of your mental and spiritual space.
    o Consider changing the way you use technology to communicate. Do you commiserate with friends or family via text? Do others expect you to listen or respond when they vent their frustrations?
    o If you plan to continue using social media, you can curate the algorithm of your social media accounts for greater positivity by deleting negative posts from your feed and commenting on the positive ones. You can fine-tune your feeds once a week for a month. As the algorithm searches for new, similar posts it thinks you'll like, it will choose steadily more-positive ones.
    o Go through your social media apps and delete followers or connections who you don't personally know, who you haven't had direct contact with, and those who really get you emotionally fired up.
    o Turn off all alerts and notifications on all your devices to avoid interruption when you're in the flow.
    o Make a conscious choice not to let your social media own you.

- **Review your list of positivity boosters.** Choose prompts and simple activities you can easily and quickly reach for when you need some levity and joy. This practice is so powerful that it's worth the time to revisit it here. In Chapter 4, you found space to write your own list. Below, you'll find a list of possibilities to help you revise your previous list, or create one if you haven't yet. Please put a check mark next to the three that feel good and right to you. Then in the space provided, formulate one, just one positivity booster, that is perfect for yourself.

- o   Listen to a favorite song
- o   Read a beloved poem
- o   Re-read a cherished card or letter from a friend or family member
- o   Visualize a vivid happy place (maybe it's your favorite vacation spot, or somewhere you dream of visiting) and go there as you close your eyes for a few moments
- o   Go on a quick walk around the block
- o   Spend some time with your pet in the park
- o   Feed the ducks in the pond
- o   Sit in the sunshine
- o   If you're a yogi, do three sun salutations
- o   Keep a supply of cards, and write a short note expressing your appreciation to someone
- o   Sketch or doodle for a few minutes. For an extra burst of creativity, use your non-dominant hand!

You have the power and self-control to change your mood by changing where you place your attentional awareness. You don't have to be a victim of the whims of your mind, your mood, or your attitude. You can choose to be in control of yourself, your mindset, and your emotional responses. You can choose to be happy and content.

Art Class: Gratitude Practice

"If you see no reason for giving thanks, the fault lies only in yourself."
~ Tecumseh

Let's conclude this chapter with a simple gratitude practice that you can do anywhere, without having to write anything down. As you do this practice, please set aside mental distractions.

1. Come into current time. Be fully present with yourself.
2. Close your eyes. Take a deep breath, a really deep one, expanding the belly.
3. As you exhale, become aware of your lungs and the amazing and miraculous way they function to bring fresh oxygen and life into your body and to dispel carbon dioxide and waste.
4. Breathe again and become aware of your vascular system, your veins and arteries. Find a sense of awe and wonder as you consider the intricate detail of their architecture and design, able to carry nutrients to the exact point where needed and to remove waste by moving it to the lungs to be exhaled.
5. Breathe one more time and come into an awareness of your heart, beating non-stop with almost perfect precision for your whole, entire lifetime. This alone should be enough to flood your system with gratitude. A heart that does its amazing work without hardly ever a thought from you, the "owner" of your body? That's awe-inspiring.
6. Take one more slow, deep breath and open your eyes. What looks, feels, or sounds different to you through this lens of heightened gratitude?

You are a marvelous biological, spiritual, intellectual, emotional, relational being. Please find a sense of gratitude for who and what you are. Your body is a good body; it works. It may not work as well as it once did. It may now have its constant little aches and pains, or its big ones. Yet, it works well enough. Most mornings, you can get up and get moving and go about living. Some days, you may feel strong and fit and healthy.

Wherever you are on the continuum from perfect health to no evidence of health, you and your body are capable of great change. Let in a little ray of light, a tiny speck of hope, and tell yourself that you can and you will move in a positive direction today. Just for today. Manageable. Small steps. Do-able steps.

And tomorrow you can do it again. And then again the next day. Remember those rabbits? Before you know it, you will be approaching near-perfect health and well-being.

Or, for you, you may experience a simple yet profound 3% increase toward a positive mood, or taking positive perspective, or even just exhaling and settling into the present moment, aligned with your own understanding and experience of "It's like this now." Again, there is no right or wrong way to this. You can't do it wrong. It's your life and your experience. More and more you are trusting yourself and your inner knowing and wisdom. You are gaining confidence in the accuracy of your self-awareness. And probably by now, you are beginning to see yourself through a kind and forgiving lens, appreciating that you are becoming a good friend to yourself.

Befriending Yourself

Those in the world who befriend themselves radiate a different kind of energy and presence. They are unfazed by the drama of others; they don't easily take offense; they can see other, if not all sides, of a situation and navigate the varying opinions with ease and grace. They are often peacemakers, but not at the expense of their own peace. When we are in the presence of those who are kind and compassionate to themselves, we want to be friends with them, for we want their kindness and compassion to get on us, to get in us. We want goodness and we can recognize it in others.

When we begin to see this goodness in others, we stand in a holy place—moved to admiration and respect of the inner beauty that makes its way to the outer world. If we can see it *out there*, it must be *in here* too. In those moments of recognition of the goodness of another, and then in turn, the goodness of self, we have reason to rejoice. We have crossed a threshold into a deep inner dimension where we, even just for a microsecond, touch our own inherent beauty and perfection.

If it's a stretch to believe that even in your messy imperfection you are perfect, at the very least you can honor the truth of your general OK-ness as a human being. And that too is holy ground. And a marvelous place to feel and express gratitude, even a whispered "Yes!" to the sky above.

Your experience might happen on aisle 14 of the local grocery, there among the spices, salts, and olive oils. Aisle 14 will forever be a sacred space for you. Of maybe your *sanctus terra* is found on the rocky trail of Sugarloaf Mountain in the Blue Ridge chain, or on the side of a volcano in some Central American country. Or an actual church where you've been unfolded by the light of divinity shining into and through your heart, mind, and soul. Wherever and whatever your befriending of the self looks and feels like, it is a landmark moment on your path. You can visit it time and time again when you need positive reinforcements to cover the left flank.

Being a good friend to yourself allows you to travel the globe by yourself without ever getting sick of your traveling companion. And that goes for every other event, experience, or moment of life.

And remember, when we're happy with who we are, we're nice. We're not mean to our friends. We're nice to ourself when we're a friend to ourself.

We can always have a friend with us and in us. So maybe it doesn't really matter that *no one is coming.*

CHAPTER 6

Making Personal Meaning

Humans are meaning-makers. We are not only responsible for but also find it necessary to make personal meaning from the events that happen in our lives. Each of us, individually and uniquely, creates the connection between the events we experience, the emotions that arise around those experiences, our interpretation of both the experiences and the emotions, and the meaning we layer over the entire situation.

In the theater of the mind, our consciousness narrates itself into reality and into personal identity. Our perspective of the events that we witness, as well as those we experience as active participants, is a critical component in the design and creation of our personal narrative. It informs the meaning we assign to phenomena that occur.

We create personal meaning of our life's experiences through a combination of inputs: our deductive reasoning, our past experiences, our longings and desires, and our goals. Personal meaning becomes our personal history, which is then cemented into the consciousness as identity.

Taking Perspective: It's My Story

Sherri tells of her experience with the many bicyclists who ride the roads in her neighborhood and of becoming a road cyclist herself.

This particular neighborhood is off the beaten path and includes crossroads that send drivers and riders in four directions, each with equally breathtaking panoramas. The streets are narrow with not much of a shoulder, but are very popular with cyclists for the views and the terrain. However, local residents are impatient with the hordes of bike-riding tourists.

Sherri became increasingly frustrated with these self-important cyclists. They would not get over to the side of the road. They would not stay in the narrow bike lane, causing traffic backups several cars deep, in places where there was no room to move slightly across the double yellow line to pass on a hill or a curve.

The onslaught of bicycles and their inconsiderate riders blocking the roads and causing traffic delays became a topic of heated discussion at the community mailbox, during community picnics, and with neighbors enjoying their evening walks.

One weekend Sherri was invited by several colleagues to go for a bike ride. They drove about an hour's distance to a lake surrounded by a paved hiking/biking trail. It was a popular spot with no vehicle traffic and superb views of the valley. It wound beautifully through the lower hillside forests.

Sherri was hooked.

At her local bike shop, Sherri purchased her first Bianchi and all the necessary *accoutrements*. She wondered where she might go for her introductory ride. Being brand new with no experience she thought the shop owner would have a good recommendation. She would like something close to home, fairly easy, with not too many hills, a nice short ride to get used to the new bike.

Enthusiastically he told of a great ride for beginners—all levels, in fact. There were four options you could take from this particular neighborhood. As he offered descriptions of the location, she cocked her head and narrowed her eyes. Was this guy responsible for the increased bike traffic in her neighborhood? Was this the guy who told the whole world about this little-known, secluded group of houses tucked back against the hill, quiet and friendly, no big trucks, no traffic hazards for cyclists?

"Are you the one who's been encouraging cyclists to ride in our neighborhood?" queried Sherri.

"It's such a beautiful place to ride, with several options depending on skill level and desired incline. Don't you think it's got some of the most impressive views around?" He evaded her question.

She thought about asking him to please stop sending cyclists out to the neighborhood. But would it do any good? People in the cycling community knew about it and spread the word. The cat was out of the bag.

She paid for her purchases with a warm "thank you" and headed home to test out the Bianchi. She would start from her house and turn north at the central intersection, then head through the low, rolling hills.

Being on the bike revealed an entirely new perspective to Sherri.

First of all, it was scary. She was unfamiliar with the bicycle itself, having yet to figure out the intricacies of the gears, when to use the lever on the left handlebar or the lever on the right without losing her balance, keeping her speed steady, and not wobbling off the short cliff-edge of the asphalt. The road was rough and a rugged precipice dropped off to sand and rocks on the side of the road. The shoulder was narrow-to-nonexistent.

She had to pay attention to many things she had never considered before. Rocks, gravel, broken glass, and sticks were hazards she had to keep an eye out for. If she ran over a sharp stone, or piece of glass, she could end up with a flat tire. She had not yet mastered the art of changing a bicycle tire and hoped she wouldn't have to learn the hard way, out on the road.

And then there were the creatures. There were large bugs, lizards, and the occasional snake to watch out for. Trash was also a concern; broken carpenter's pencils, busted side mirrors from cars, even a mangled pair of scissors, with one blade pointed ominously right at her.

How the heck did these things end up here on the side of the road? I've never noticed any of this crap before, she thought, as she nervously avoided the hazardous items littering the narrow edge of road that she was forced to call a bike lane.

And then of course, there were the cars. They would not scoot over and give her the required three-foot buffer zone. They flew by at terrifying speed. The monster trucks revved their engines and sent black exhaust from their gigantic tail pipes as they passed her. Some rudely blared their horns, long and hard.

Sherri's first bike ride was not pleasant. It was nothing like her outing with her colleagues, riding around the pristine lake trail with no road traffic.

She finally made it home and hung the bike in her garage. Exhausted, more from paying attention than from pedaling, she sat on the back porch with a glass of iced tea and considered this new adventure.

Becoming a cyclist was going to require much more than simply learning to ride a road bike. It would demand a change of perspective.

You see, when we are the driver of the car, we don't know the experience of the person on the bicycle. We think they're just in our way and wonder in frustration, *why won't they ride in the darn bike lane?* We have no idea of their skill level. We don't know to what degree they're paying attention to riding and the road, or if they're taking in the view, or listening to music or a podcast on their headphones. What we do know is that they're over there on the side of the road, a road built for cars, and that they're in the way.

When we become the cyclist, oh how things change!

It's like this with almost everything in life. We process our experience through our own subjective filter. Our deductive reasoning and our past experiences create for us a story that we believe is certainly true. How could it be otherwise? This is what I see, this is what is happening, and this is what it all means. *This is what's real.*

But this is only one person's perspective, based on and formed around what they have experienced and paid attention to during the course of their life. Never having been the bicyclist, Sherri was annoyed with the riders who clogged her quiet neighborhood streets and was frustrated that they caused traffic slowdowns and were in the way. They were a hazard.

Then she became the bicyclist, and the drivers were the hazard. Not to mention all the previously unnoticed objects and creatures on the side of the road that could mean major disaster.

How many times have you found yourself in a similar situation—where you had to take perspective, and realized you had become the very person who had once been the source of your agitation, annoyance, or animosity?

Our perspective is a critical element of how we make personal meaning of life. Meaning-making is an integral part of the human condition. We all do it. In fact, it is how we create our sense of self, our identity.

Sculpting Your Quality of Mind

More than twenty-five years ago, one of my professors said, "Society is scared of itself." That's probably true now more than ever. I wonder if it's because we don't know ourselves very well—that we aren't friends with ourselves just yet? Or is it that we haven't taken the time to sculpt the quality of our mind, our internal narrative, our sense of self, or our presence?

Through the exponential growth of technology, social media, and always being connected and "on," we have lost the sense of connection with ourselves. And if we aren't connected to ourselves, it can be tricky to stay connected, in healthy ways, to others.

Knowing ourselves comes partly through listening to, and knowing the flavor of our internal narrative. Our internal narrative is shaped by the experiences we have. So, if our experiences are always focused outward, and we spend very little time cultivating our inner lives, what then comprises the vocabulary and phraseology of our internal narrator?

The words of others. As those words fill my mind, the ideas and theories, perspectives, and philosophies of others build my inner story. But is it really *my* story? Is it *my* truth?

Maybe not.

Perhaps I have just become so used to their words, to their voices, that my own becomes hushed, and eventually falls silent. Perhaps *their* ideas, never carefully considered through the lens of my own experience, become my reality. What I allow myself to be exposed to and don't thoughtfully evaluate and filter, becomes the language I use to shape my internal narrative. And this, in turn, becomes the quality of my character.

We all can fall prey to this. We can allow others to create the story of the life we live. Maybe it's time to consider writing your own story, to consider creating your own inner narrative. Perhaps it's time to throw out the squatters who have fabricated a tale that does not describe the life you want to live.

Vocabulary Creates Your Life

Imagine for just a moment, the course of your average day. Imagine that day without words.

Now, bring to mind the phrases you use most. Do any of these sound familiar?

"Hurry up."

"I'm too busy."

"I don't have enough time."

"I wish things would just slow down."

"I'm so tired."

"I'm not happy."

"I'm hungry."

"This sucks."

"Not again."

"Here we go again . . ."

What are your most-used phrases? How many times during the day is your internal narrative constantly telling stories of lack, not enough, or offering a negative interpretation of events? How did these come to be the phrases that run through your mind?

These negative narratives end up being experienced as stress in the sympathetic nervous system, which then moves you through life in a state of mild to excessive fight-or-flight. The never-ending neurochemistry of survival eventually builds to chronic levels of stress. This then eventually causes a pattern in your physical body, in your biology, of disease and illness.

Your internal narrative is created primarily by the depth and breadth of the vocabulary you use to define and label your experiences. Your vocabulary library is in the hippocampus region of your brain. Your mental habits—like self-talk and self-concept—literally shape the physical structure and development of the brain, as well as your neural patterns of thinking and feeling.

When you continually run a narrative of lack, disappointment born from "not enough," and stress, your habituated vocabulary keeps your system in a pattern of negative emotions—aggression and anger, fear or sadness, and others. These negative thoughts become dominant, and may completely take over. They don't allow for perspective-taking, compassion, forgiveness, or empathy. They darken and narrow your point of view, eliminating from your reality any possibility, any potential. You become serious and somber.

Change your vocabulary and you can begin to change your life. This is not an oversimplification; it is the way your mind works.

You can shift from a negatively structured internal narrative to a more positive one by intentionally selecting positive and constructive rather than negative and destructive vocabulary and phrases. In so doing, you will become very familiar with your own positive internal meaning of self and life. As you are able to deepen and broaden that meaning and sense of self, you are better able to establish the ethical meaning and significance of your behaviors and interactions with others and with the world.

You are also laying down constructive patterns of well-integrated and beneficial long-term memories. Thus, you are able to apply your knowledge and experience from context-specific events and occurrences in a way that transcends "local" context. This enables you to understand how you (through your thoughts, words, actions, and presence) create not only your identity, but also your life experiences, beyond the boundaries of self.

The way that you have and demonstrate emotional *reactions* or emotional *responses* shows you who you are as a person: your identity, what you value, what you care about, what you give your time and attention to. When you learn to interpret your own reactions, both *as* feelings and *to* feelings, and understand that interpretation, you can begin to see clearly what beneficial changes you would like to make. As you begin to work on making those changes and establishing new habits, you lay down a firm foundation of your best self.

A familiar and safe context (maybe the one you create with the accountability buddy you identified in Chapter 2) supports us in enacting our emotional resilience skills. As we gain greater skill and competency, we can move out of a familiar context and transcend the bounds of what has hitherto been our safe practice arena. As we successfully move beyond the familiar context and are able to skillfully manage ourselves across all areas of life, we become experts, artists—able to use even the darkest colors of our palette to create beauty and harmony.

Artistic expertise is indeed required to weave together the ideas, concepts, knowledge, and practices from a wide range of topics and experiences. It is not a body of knowledge, of techniques and strategies, but rather a *process of integration* that manifests in the artwork created. And for us as artists of emotional resilience, it manifests in the way we show up to life; it is our presence.

You are becoming not only the production manager for your internal narrative, but its artist as well. You are creating a high quality regulation system to filter out what is impure and potentially toxic to your system, while also developing an ability to conduct yourself more fluidly, gracefully, and artistically according to the situation in which you find yourself.

Over time, as you use your tools, you will develop skills that enable you to consciously express your emotional process and selectively determine the words you speak and the behaviors you demonstrate. These skills enable you to create not only the narrative, but the experiences as well.

What are these skills? Language, created from the richness of your vocabulary and the acumen of your Inner Wisdom; symbolic systems, such as archetypes or icons; and numbers, art, and music as representational systems of communication. These are all communications skills we use to depict our experiences, based on what each of us individually witnesses, observes, and lives as the felt-experience. We layer subjective meaning over what we observe and over our internal experience regarding that observation.

Sherri, becoming a cyclist in addition to being a driver, experienced a radical change of perception, then understanding, and ultimately was able to release her fixed view and her aggression.

When we can pull ourselves beyond our personal narrative of whatever situational context we find ourselves in, and begin to understand that each and every person creates their unique narrative, we recognize the complexity of both the internal narrative of each individual, and the situation as a whole. It is through awareness of this complexity that we then develop increasingly nuanced and sophisticated strategies for thinking, acting, and communicating. We can begin to fully appreciate that we are indeed the agent of our own life, and others the agents of theirs.

The personal, internal narrative is based on the quality of mind. The quality of mind is created by the experiences we have had in life and our interpretation of those experiences; interpreted through the lens of vocabulary and felt-emotional experiences. The internal narrative is useful. It is our own inner storytelling, which is a critical way that we create not only meaning, but well-being and connection too. Internal storytelling helps us integrate our experiences, and the feelings associated with those experiences, into who we are and how we show up in our lives.

Close observation, learning to carefully notice details and nuances of our experiences, can help us enrich our vocabularies, thereby allowing us to build a bigger, more complete story. An expansive story allows us to transcend the here and now, allows us to see different sides of every situation, other possible meanings, and offers us the opportunity to practice non-judgment. We can gain skillful mastery in several areas:

- Applying what we have previously learned to future situations
- Transferring knowledge from one situation to a another, whether similar or not
- Understanding the perspectives and behaviors of others
- Optimizing decision-making capacity and skills
- Making emotional meaning of this whole glorious mess that is life
- Appreciating that we don't, and can't ever know everything

Quality of Mind

The quality of your mind determines your experience. Your experience is your life.

Please pause for a moment to let that sink in. It might well be the very crux of this whole book.

The quality of your mind determines your experience.

Your experience is your life.

Can we go so far as to say that our life is determined by the quality of our mind? I think we must.

A busy mind is a busy life, cluttered and non-stop. It is constantly dashing hither and yon, unable to finish a thought or a task before being bombarded by the next thought in the crowded lineup, which stumble over each other to gain admittance into Conscious Awareness and be first up for your attentional focus. A mind that can settle down, can come to stillness and silence, and can take perspective, is reflective of a life that is organized and calm.

A constantly go-go-go life mirrors a non-stop, anxious mind. And a life of ease, peace, and usefulness mirrors a calm and organized mind.

It may be useful to consider that busyness, or what we can call *attentional addition* (you just keeping piling things on), is a form of emotional avoidance. Depression may be a way of numbing ourselves to our emotions, especially the ones that need our prompt and undivided attention. And anxiety can be a distraction as well, keeping the mind occupied as another avoidance mechanism. For some, being depressed or being anxious seem to have become subtle, socially acceptable forms of emotional evasion.

It's time to look clearly at your own internal world, to pull back the curtain and examine the quality of your mind and how it has become what it is.

At this advanced point in our journey together, it can be very beneficial to stop for a moment and remember that you love yourself, that you believe in your general OK-ness as a human being, that you are trying, and that you are a good person.

To claim emotional resilience for yourself, you'll need to take a deep, radically honest look inside, moving into the very core of your personal narrative. You have to delve into the quality of your mind to do that. This is a very intimate aspect of our time together. And *you* must do it. These words will guide you and support you. But the work here is for you to do on your own.

We'll dive in and explore several ideas, the first being: *Who creates the quality of your mind?*

You know . . . *you* do. You create the quality of your own mind.

We cannot shirk our responsibility here. We cannot blame others, our situation and circumstances, our upbringing or childhood. As mature adults, we each have to claim our mind as our own. We each have to go inside ourselves and find our inner strength to do this work.

You can do it. You have what it takes.

Remember the fairy tale of the Princess and the Pea? One single, tiny pea under several stacked mattresses made for a highly uncomfortable bed, so uncomfortable in fact that the princess could neither rest nor sleep. She could feel that little pea no matter which way she lay upon those mattresses. She could not situate herself comfortably no matter what she did. Finally, the stack of mattresses had to be disassembled and the pea plucked from bottom of that stack for her to be at ease.

You, dear friend, are a little bit like that princess.

We all have little rumples and bumps and lumps—peas, as it were—in the quality of our minds. Our pea, gigantic or microscopic, will not let us rest, will not leave us in peace. We try smoothing over the hurts, the bumps, the bruises, but still, there can be a big uncomfortable wrinkle in the quality of our mind that colors the entire experience of life.

To find peace, you'll have to excavate some of the layers of your own mind. You can then uncover the offending thing, remove it, and throw it out.

Next, you'll want to explore *how* you create the quality of your mind.

You must take personal responsibility for situating yourself to ease and comfort. You and only you can pluck out the pea and smooth out the wrinkles in order to find happiness and contentment in life.

Some of the wrinkles and lumps you are now experiencing began very small; they were first laid down when you were too young to process the events or feelings, so you might not know where to look to find those troublesome peas that are creating the current wrinkles in your life. During the teenage and early young adult periods of life when you were more carefree, you may not have been paying too much attention, so you let things in that might not have been useful or healthy for the quality of your mind. You were also more susceptible to following the examples of others.

But now, as a fully functioning, rational adult, it's time to self-explore and take ownership. As scary or daunting as it might be, through the process of taking ownership, you will increase your capacity for positive self-concept, for self-efficacy, for optimism, for emotional resilience and emotional intelligence. All of this can lead to the creation of an empowered, autonomous, sovereign self.

Maybe you cannot get past something someone said or did to you many years ago. Maybe you just cannot find it in your heart to forgive. You might have fears that were laid down long ago that still color the quality of your mind. Perhaps you carry fear from your childhood that there will never be enough money, enough time, enough food, or enough love. You may carry the fear that you will never find the right partner, that you're doomed to live life alone. Whatever it is that you fear, it's OK. It's not wrong. And you're not bad.

It's simply time to look at it, name it, realize how much power you've given it, and take back your power.

And so, we find ourselves looking inside, trying to ascertain the cause of the lumps and bumps in the quality of mind. Sometimes, we will not be able to find that cause. We must then ask ourselves if we are able to simply allow that there *is* a bump and if we are now willing and ready to move on.

There might be times when we know exactly what it is. It may be an event that has been seared into our conscious memory. And in those situations, we must ask ourselves, "Am I willing to move past this? Am I willing to reclaim my trust in myself, to reclaim my peace of mind? Am I willing to let bygones be bygones and to forgive? And am I willing to live with the outcome?"

Practice Self-Compassion

At this point in your journey to emotional resilience, you are in the place requiring the highest level of self-honesty, and that requires ample reserves of self-compassion. If you do take it upon yourself to do this deep inquiry work and you get to an uncomfortable place, or even a scary place, this tried and true self-compassion practice may make it easier.

1. Place your right hand over your heart.
2. Find your breath, smooth and gentle.
3. Soften your face, especially your jaw. Relax inside the mouth.
4. Now simply and sweetly breathe into the space of your heart, just under your hand.
5. Stay as long as you want, breathing kindness and peace toward yourself.

You can do this anywhere to settle anxiety and uncertainty. Biochemically, it mimics a hug from your favorite person on the planet. It dilutes stress hormones and chemicals and sends out oxytocin, the bonding, feel-good, and trust-inspiring hormone.

Be easy on yourself. Be kind to yourself. Give yourself time.

Refining Our Mind

And finally, we must look at refining the quality of our mind. How do we refine ourselves?

Healing, clarity, and refinement take time. We might use the phrase, "It takes the time it takes." Because it, whatever you'd like *it* to be, does take time. Healing takes the time it takes. Learning to read takes the time it takes. The sunset takes the time it takes. Tomatoes on the vine take the time they take. Eggs only hatch in the time they take to do so. A storm takes the time it takes.

Allow yourself some time. Be patient. Don't rush the process. You might end up with flawed or incomplete results.

Time. Time is a very big and major part of our lives; some might say time is our lives. Most of us feel like we don't have enough of it, that it goes too fast, that we would like to control it just a wee bit more. We sometimes feel like a slave to time, rather than its master.

An interesting perspective about time is that we actually do have enough. A powerful quote from Seneca, over two thousand years ago, helps us understand this perspective.

> It is not that we have a short space of time, but that we waste much of it. Life is long enough, and it has been given in sufficiently generous measure to allow the accomplishment of the very greatest things if the whole of it is well invested. But when it is squandered in luxury and carelessness, when it is devoted to no good end, forced at last by the ultimate necessity we perceive that it has passed away before we were aware that it was passing. So it is—the life we receive is not short, but we make it so, nor do we have any lack of it, but are wasteful of it.

Again, things take the time they take. Emotional resilience doesn't happen overnight. But we have a "sufficiently generous measure" of time in which to tend to the "good end" of creating a happy and harmonious life through emotional self-responsibility.

A wise teacher, at the beginning of every class, used to say, "Time is only time if you have somewhere else to be." That's right, isn't it? If there's nowhere else to be, if there's nothing else to do, if there's nothing else to think about, you are in the ever-present moment of Now, engaged in current time. You are enjoying an unmediated experience of reality, free of the contrasts and comparisons of the past and unhindered by hoping and wishing about the future.

How often are you there, in that place where you can honestly say that there is nowhere else to be, that there's nowhere else you *want* to be?

Let's go back to the quality of mind. We know who creates quality of mind. Now consider, what *is* the quality of your mind?

Take a moment and look back over the course of the last week to ten days of your life. How were things in your mind? Did chaos and overwhelm reign supreme? Did you flounder in megawhelm? Were you able to pause at various times during your day to come into current time? Were you too busy making sure you and everyone in your charge got to where they were going on time and with everything they needed? Were you just barely keeping all the plates in the air? Did some of them crash to the ground and shatter at your running feet? Were you steady and calm, able to sweetly manage life, to calmly handle strong emotions that flared up?

Back to your personal self-exploration: jot down a couple of notes here about the quality of your mind for the last ten days. And no, you are not too busy right now.

Now, connect the dots of this personal reflection:

- How did the quality of your mind affect the quality of your days?
- How much of the time were you present and available?
- How did you express kindness and compassion?
- How much time did you make for others?
- How much time did you spend taking care of yourself?
- What do you remember most during this period? (Or was it simply a whirlwind?)
- How would you describe the quality of your relationships?
- How would you describe the quality of your sleep during this time?
- Describe your general emotionset:

At this point, the way your quality of mind is created may feel a bit like a no-brainer (no pun intended!). It is a shifting blend of your physical, mental, and emotional states; your perspective and perception; your beliefs; your social groups and relationships; the current events in your life; and your news and social media intake. All of these play into creating the quality of your mind.

If you need to, jot down your thoughts on how you create your own quality of mind:

- What are your habits, both action/behavior and thinking, that affect that quality?
- What is your self-talk like? How would you describe the tone of your "obsessive-compulsive-delusional narrator"? (My meditation teacher used that phrase to describe the voice in our heads that continually narrates our lives.)
- How often do you pause to come into current time and just be present, able to release the need to be somewhere else or to be doing something else?

Pause, Check In

Please come into current time with yourself now. How are you doing with all of this?

Can you allow yourself the perspective right now that you are broadening your self-understanding, but do not have to feel overwhelmed? How can you hold this expansive perspective, this deep level of self-honesty, and at the same time, keep a sense of this being doable?

Remembering *what is within your power to control* can help. What are you responsible for taking care of? What is your duty to yourself? Where can you put your efforts to affect the change you desire?

Now, here's a pretty useful point to remember at this juncture. *There is no right answer.* This is *your* personal inquiry and exploration. As mentioned earlier, this is your inside work, and no one can tell you you're doing it wrong. This is your process.

Can you find simplicity within the complexity of this process? Can you breathe through the big things, the things you haven't yet felt strong enough, or ready enough, to look at?

Can you find a sense of hope during this inquiry phase? Think back to the previous words about hope. In Chapter 5, we read, "with hope, we may be anxious that the worst could happen, but still we have faith that something better will happen in the end, or at least in the long run." As we see around us the strength and resilience of human nature to overcome adversity and struggles, as we see this in our self, hope can inspire us.

Hope unlocks our potential. It broadens our thinking and creativity, it fuels our persistence, and it is a dynamic motivation system to get us moving in a good direction. It is a key factor in emotional resilience, allowing us to be nimble in the ever-changing experiences that happen in the eternal moment of Now.

Please consider:

- How can you harness the power of hope to help you take ownership of the quality of your mind?
- How can you use hope to reconnect to a sense of who you are, your infinite goodness and light?
- How can a sense of hope encourage you to positively engage in life, with the quality of a clear mind and an open heart?
- How can hope help you become aware of, know intimately, and then blossom into your true potential?

Deep Knowing

As human beings, we have a deep-seated need to establish personal meaning and purpose in order to experience thriving and flourishing. We want to understand our true potential; to learn how to make our dreams into realities; we want to know how to live the good life. At times we are unsure of how to do this. And at other times we feel like the champions of the world, strong in our sense of self-differentiation and personal integrity, living life big and intentionally.

Some of these abilities come naturally to some of us. Others will need to spend years in training to develop them. And still others will make it all the way to the end without ever having the opportunity to consider these ideas at all.

Unlike the teenagers in today's education system who are being taught social and emotional skills and practices, most adults did not receive these teachings when we were growing up. Social Emotional Learning (SEL) didn't become part of the public education system until the early to mid-2000s. It's possible that some of us got a bit of character education at school. Maybe our English teachers were so skilled at teaching literature as human nature that we did gain some understanding of behavior, motivation, outcomes, and unexpected consequences and could apply that to our own lives. Maybe some of us absorbed these skills and insights through religious instruction or an optimal family life.

But the level of depression, anxiety, confusion, anger, and alienation that many adults feel today speaks to our desperate need for greater emotional resilience. One glance at most social media feeds and you could easily believe we've descended into an epidemic of emotional illiteracy and regression, fueling the fires of chronic stress and anxiety that disrupt sound emotional processing and logical thinking.

This is not a judgment. Wherever you currently are in your ability to self-manage, to be self-responsible, and to claim ownership of self, is right where you are. You might have a better vantage point than others, able to enjoy a fifty thousand-foot view of the bigger picture. You might be starting at the end of a very long tunnel of self-doubt, insecurity, or fear. You are at your own unique point; and from there, you must choose which direction to head.

And since no one is coming, it might be a very good idea for you to have as many tools as possible at your disposal—all the brushes, paints, and canvases you may need. You will need to practice and become proficient in the use of your new skills in order to be emotionally resilient.

You will also need to observe yourself as you practice. During your observations, take notes. Then make adjustments and try again the next time you're up against a powerful emotion.

Let's return to the intention that you set in Chapter 2. Does it still resonate with you? Do you still find it useful? Or is it time to revise or compose an entirely new one? Do you have, or need, another, more personal Why?

You might now ask yourself, from a new perspective and with a deeper understanding:

- Why am I reading this?
- What do I hope to gain, or understand, or achieve?
- What is my own definition, in my own words, of emotional resilience?
- What would it be like to be emotionally resilient as a way of life?

As you check in and reevaluate, capture your thoughts by writing them here. Bring them into the material world by making them visible. The written word has more power and your chances of satisfying your Why are better when you write it down and look at those beautiful words written in your own hand.

Art Class: Stream of Consciousness

"Happiness and freedom begin with one principle. Some things are within your control and some are not." ~ Epictetus

This exercise is open-ended. It might be beneficial, even enjoyable, to give your thinking mind as much freedom as you can. Try this as a free write, a stream of consciousness where you turn your mind loose and let it flow. Give yourself plenty of time so you don't feel rushed to be somewhere else. Get a notebook if you need more space.

What is your self-talk like?

- How do you talk to yourself?
- What are your most-used phrases?
- When do you talk to yourself the most—under what circumstances, and in what settings?

What is the current story of your life?

- What meaning, or meanings, have you given your personal life story?

What would a new and more personalized story look like?

What would it be like if you let others create their own stories of their own lives, without the need to lay your narration over the top?

- What might this sound and/or look like, both to you and to the other person(s)?

Shaped by Use

Your mind is shaped by how you use it. And so is your life. If you can use it (either your mind, or your life) for beneficial activities and undertakings, it will be good. If you misuse it or are careless or even reckless, it won't be. If you fill it full of junk and toxic thoughts, images, and words, it will mirror its contents. The encouraging part is that it's up to you!

The mind, like the physical body, is shaped by how it is used. If we compare a weight-lifter to a ballet dancer, we will see obvious differences in the physical appearance, in the carriage, in the length and strength of the muscles, even in the lightness of the step. Muscles develop distinctly, based on how they are trained—what they do over, and over, and over. That training eventually becomes the habit of how those muscles are used as well as the structure and form they take.

The weight-lifter is bulky and thick, with muscles that are extremely strong. The muscle fibers are short to provide explosive power, for short periods of time. A weight-lifter probably wouldn't have the endurance or balance to hold a power-lift for more than a few seconds.

The ballet dancer is light and lithe, with muscles that are longer and leaner, allowing for a more graceful appearance. These muscles are better suited to endurance activities, working for extended periods of time. But the ballet dancer also needs strength, for majestic and dramatic leaps such as the *jete* or *grand jete*, or the *pas de chat*.

The mind will develop based on how it is trained, based on what it thinks over, and over, and over. That mind training, unconscious though it may be, eventually shapes the patterns of use and the quality of mind. As you work toward refining your mind by changing up your training routine, it will eventually take on the characteristics of purity. And in so doing, your mind will become a valuable tool helping you to craft the art of your life.

CHAPTER 7

Love

Moving yourself into a more positive frame of mind for more of your time each day takes work and effort. Our work and effort are our feelings of love made manifest, made tangible, made visible in the world. Don't be afraid of hard work. And don't be afraid of love.

As you work toward greater contentment, happiness, and joy, your inner rewards will be the ability to find, cultivate, and live in love. Real love. Sincere love. Not the stuff of romance novels or TV sitcoms. Not "cupboard love," like a pet when it's feeding time. But a lasting love that is unconditional and independent of circumstance and situation. This love survives hurt feelings, differing viewpoints, loss of loved ones, and the anguish of grief. It is the love that overcomes setbacks and tribulations that knock us to our knees.

To what, or to whom, is this deep and abiding love directed?

To all: to everything and to everyone, ever.

In the second year of my master's degree program (all of us students were already teachers in our own classrooms, with our own students), my professor Dr. Brusch taught that in order to be good teachers, we needed to love our students.

He explained that in addition to the challenges with our individual students, we would also face the challenges of parents and community. We would be confronted by many struggles with administration and fellow teachers, some disputes with district level administration, and a few difficulties straggling in from federal-level policy makers. As classroom teachers, we were not just teaching our subject matter, according to guidelines created by non-educators, but we were also teaching character and presence.

As a class, led by his expert guidance, we discussed early in the semester the challenges we faced and how to best overcome them. We discussed how to "stay in the trenches" and how to continue to show up with a happy attitude and an ability to focus on our students. We explored how to let the non-essentials sit quietly on the side.

One afternoon in class, Dr. Brusch must have been feeling his oats. He preached to us! It was the best university class I had ever taken part in. I never did find out what had pushed his buttons, but boy, he let us know just exactly what we were doing as educators and why we needed to do it.

He grew ever more ardent and passionate, in his professorial way, his comb-over lifting and bouncing as he vigorously punctuated the air with his index finger. His eyes flashing behind his thick glasses, his countenance radiant with intense fervor, Dr. Brusch expounded on the importance of love.

If we were to be worth our salt at all in the classroom, he insisted, we must love our students. We must see them for who they really are. We must not let our vision be clouded by the perceptions of other teachers who may not have liked a particular child, or not gotten along well with that child's parents. We were to open our hearts to each and every child in our care and learn to see them, to give them every opportunity to shine, and to move out from under the horrible burden of a label or previous designation.

"There is not one child in your school who does not deserve your love!" he boomed, serious and devoted.

Like a preacher who has just made his glorious, incontrovertible point and brought it all home in a moment of inspired splendor, Dr. Brusch landed back on his heels and exhaled. He smoothed his hair and his suit jacket, and then quietly, calmly, told us, "You must love your students or leave the teaching profession."

As he looked at each of us, his gaze moving around the room, meeting ours, and looking right into our hearts, Professor Brusch conveyed to us his love. We all felt it. Some cried. Some teared up. We got it. We understood what it meant to love others. Yet more profoundly, we felt what it was to be loved by our teacher, the one who shaped us and guided us in our being.

He loved us, and so it was easy for us to go out and love our own students. Each week after that, until the end of the semester, we rejoiced together as classmates, sharing stories about our students. We talked of their goodness and their accomplishments, their progress and their mistakes. We took his exhortation seriously. We started seeing our students for the unique individuals they were. And it was so much fun!

I already liked being a teacher. I liked the kids and my fellow teachers. I liked the school where I was, and the guiding philosophy and principles it espoused. I was content. But loving my students profoundly changed the way I taught and the way I interacted with them. I saw them as real people— capable and creative, smart and interested. I began to teach *students*—real, living, breathing people—not Spanish. And they flourished, in so many wonderful ways. We were having a great semester together.

And then, oh boy, Dr. Brusch had a wild hair. About February, he dropped the hammer on us. He knew that we were now seeing our students in a different light, that we were loving them, and that we, as his students, were happier and more engaged. He must have decided the time was right.

He created an assignment for us: we had to actually tell our students that we loved them. This might not sound like a big deal to most, but to us, as a class of Educational Leadership students, this felt like crossing the line. We all agreed that the Professor had gone too far. We needed to maintain a degree of authority with our students. We could not let them see us as real and vulnerable people.

From my perspective, it was one thing to know in my heart that I loved my students. If any of them were paying attention, they would see it in my behavior. I was doing just fine as things were, thank you very much.

But no. Professor Brusch actually required "I love you" as a graded assignment. Oh, he had some nerve! Because he *knew*.

So, as a good student, I did my assignment.

At the end of one class a few days later, I said to my students, "Thanks guys, you did a great job today. *Luvyou.*" I smashed together these two words, wiping my hand across my lips. I did it so quickly and casually that it was hardly noticeable at all. I had managed to make my very first vocal offering of love to my students.

Whew! Done. Not so bad. But I had to do it again, because the assignment was to reflectively journal my experience, watch my own growth and progress, document it, and then turn it in for the grade.

So I determined that I would say it again with my next class, the after-lunch class. *That* class. Every teacher has one—the class that is just not cooperative. The class full of kids who love to push buttons, who know just which buttons to push. And they know they are "that group," so they push—hard. On purpose. Often. My button-pushers and I had come to a kind of stand-off—we were all just trying to do our best, to get by without any major upsets.

This was going to be a challenge. I thought about leaving this class for last, but then word might get out that I had told all the other classes I loved them, and they would know for certain that they were my "that" class. Nope, that would not be good. Mutiny would certainly result. My only option was to just go for it.

I took a different tactic this time. I decided I would say it first, right at the beginning of class and just get it out of the way. I took my courage in hand and opened the door to welcome my students in to *Español Dos*. As they got settled and I pulled my teaching notes together, I walked to the front of the room and welcomed them with the standard "*Buenas tardes, amigos.*" I gave them my full attention, not shyly, not covert ops, but looking at each student across the room from left to right, just as Dr. Brusch had. Then, panning out to take them all into my vision, I said in English, to make sure they understood me, "I'm glad you're here. I love you."

I smiled and took a deep breath. "Now, let's get to work."

It was the best day I had with that group of rebels all year long. There was an exchange, unspoken yet felt by all of us, of deep appreciation for and recognition of who they were. Yes, we all knew they were the "those" kids, the ones every teacher struggled with, the ones who got calls home to parents and trash pick-up after school. And I saw them, and loved them, and told them. And it impacted them. Enormously. A couple of them came up after class and expressed that they'd felt like none of their teachers liked them. They were open and kind, grateful that I told them I loved them.

One young lady told me how genuine it felt to hear that I loved her, that one of her school teachers, one of the cool ones, could actually love her, even though she was a major "screw-up." She had little tears in her eyes. She was so sweet and so happy. I dipped my chin to get closer to her level, looked right into her eyes, and told her again. "I love you. You are a good person." We bonded forever in that hallway, just outside my classroom door.

My love of my students grew continually over the years. It became my habit to finish my academic instruction a couple of minutes early each day so I could connect with my students on a very real, non-teacher/student level, a level of vulnerability that became my strength as an educator. I would tell them how much I loved them, how grateful I was that they were there every day, and how much I needed to see them again tomorrow. On Fridays, I would encourage them to be safe, to take care of themselves, take care of each other, and to "make sure you're here on Monday."

The love I felt and could convey to my students made my classroom and my school a place of joy and positivity. During the last eight years of teaching, I had perhaps two upsets with any of my students. One of these was when a young lady in the back row exploded at me because I called on her to answer a question. She lost it and screamed at me, the big nasty B-word in front of the entire class. I bit my back teeth, breathed big and deep, and with all the love in my heart and a fierce glint in my eye, asked her to step into the hallway with me.

We closed the door behind us to many *oohs*, *ahhhs*, and *oh boys*, stood face-to-face and stared each other down. Finally, I asked, "Grace, what's happening?"

She broke. She held her tears back with admirable strength, but her words came out in a massive tumble: how she didn't know anything in Spanish and felt stupid every time I called on her, and I kept calling on her, and she kept not knowing the answer, so she felt even more stupid. She was embarrassed to talk to me because she really liked the class, but had barely mastered *hola* by Year 3 of Spanish, and on and on.

We decided that she was simply in the wrong class, and that we would sort it out for her. She moved to a Spanish 1 class where she found success. Every time we passed in the hallway from then on, she said "*¡Hola, Señora! ¿Qué tal, Guapa?!*" I didn't have the heart to tell her it was probably not appropriate for her to call teacher "good looking." Some things are better left unsaid.

Love: The Essential Ingredient of Emotional Resilience

As a result of the love in my heart, in my words, in my tone, in my actions, and in my expression, my students thrived. Sure, we had our emotional struggles and academically frustrating challenges, but because we were all on the same page together, we always overcame the trials and were able to enjoy ourselves in the learning environment. We had a blast together. We laughed a lot. We learned even more.

My last two years of teaching, when I poured all my positive psychology research and practices into the mix, were the best two years of my whole teaching life. And things in the teaching world were crazy then. Our district was doing some startling and disruptive things—I had more students than I ever had before and saw all 208 of them every single day. There were many other things that would have sent me over the edge had I not been solidly established in my own life upon a secure foundation of love.

Love is the seed, the sprout, and the flower of emotional resilience. If we love life, love ourselves, love our neighbor, love the planet and all living creatures, we somehow have within us the power to be resilient. We somehow have within us the ability to take perspective and to see another's viewpoint, and even when we don't agree, we can still be civil and kind. We don't lose it and start a social media war, or join in an ongoing one, because someone likes or loves a certain political figure, or Hollywood star, that we do not.

I feel a little like Dr. Brusch when he preached to us. I guess that's what love does to a person. It makes them so certain of the goodness and happiness that come from loving self and others that they can't help but be an advocate, a very strong voice in the darkness urging us all to just love each other.

Why is it that love does this to us and in us? And for us? What *is* it about love?

Maybe, just maybe, teasing out the why removes some of the mystery and the magic. Maybe it's better to simply *know* in our heart of hearts, without the analysis and evaluation.

Are we always going to be able to love others, unconditionally? No, probably not. I had a unique situation in my classroom where I was mostly calling the shots. It was a pretty specific environment, with the same players every day, though situationally different every day—we might consider it a closed system. I felt like I had a considerable degree of control, certainly not forced, but when you love and respect others—amazing thing!—others love and respect you. Love creates a delightful, reciprocal energy between people and in life. I consider it pretty good proof of the Golden Rule: treat others as you would like to be treated, and they reciprocate.

So in our everyday lives, out in the busyness of the world, on the subway, in the office, in traffic, in line for a table at a busy restaurant or crowded into a packed elevator, (or as I write this, waiting your turn in a line to allow for social spacing), wherever your life takes you, and especially at home, how can we, on most days, love life, love others, and love ourselves?

Like all the other stuff that works, that has proven results, love requires practice. We have to actually *do* it. We can't just read about it, watch videos about it, talk about it. Although those are all great first steps, we have to love.

It's easy to love "my people." It's easy to love people who think like we do. It's easy to love those who support our ideas and goals. It's like that for squirrels too. Squirrels protect their own; they fight off predators to keep their babies safe and protect their little squirrel tribe. Deer do the same. And birds. Probably the whole natural world.

How different from a squirrel are you? Can you love those who disagree with you, those who are mean to you, perhaps even those who try to destroy you? Can you love the classroom full of "those" kids? A boardroom full of "those" advisors?

I think you probably can. Again, that work-and-effort thing pops up right into our faces with this kind of love. And when we master loving the tricky people, we become the Masters. (I think Professor Brusch knew a thing or two about a master's degree. And life. And love, for sure.)

When we have love running through us as our habit, (remember, a habit is thought, word, or action that is frequent, repeated, and automatic) it becomes our character. When we come up against an upset, we respond according to habit. By learning to love, we can counteract the survival mechanisms in the brain and body. We can more easily settle our amygdala and move into our thinking mind, and even more powerful, into our feeling heart.

We can learn to see the true emotion behind the behavior, both our own and that of others. We can learn to see the possibilities: that outrage might actually be maladapted fear, sadness might be the manifestation of loneliness, and stress might be a deep caring to get things done and done well. Love creates in us a nimble ability to take perspective, to move beyond *my* idea of what's happening and to consider the viewpoint and circumstances of the other.

A skilled painter, or sculptor, or poet has much training, many tools, and high quality materials—paint and brushes and canvas; chisels and hammers and the finest marble; a rich and living vocabulary. They can take perspective, they have patience, they have hope that what they create will beautify the world. The great masters have become masters only through years of time, effort, and work they have given to further develop their natural talent.

We too can develop the skills, acquire the tools, and cultivate the qualities that create a bright, luminous, and clear mind and loving heart. Wherever we begin our journey toward becoming an artist of emotional resilience, we can move from muddled, murky thinking clouded with negative input and busyness, to a clear, insightful, loving presence of being.

Pure Form

Refinement is the process of making something clear and pure. Love makes your mind clear and your heart pure, both of them taking on the qualities of radiance and luminosity. As your heart and mind become radiant and luminous, you're able to give and receive love in all that you do.

Developing emotional resilience in a process of self-refinement. As we learn to control the breath, making it slow and smooth and steady in order to calm an upset nervous system, we are laying down the prerequisites for gracefully managing ourselves. When we control our mind, this power enables us to make a conscious choice to respond from love, rather than reacting out of habitual patterns of fear or anger.

Self-refinement is a purification process that brings us to a clear and uncorrupted state of being, free of the coarse and the vulgar, the dark and the mean, the stressful and the sludgy. This process is a continuum, without specific, delineated stages or phases that can be broken into segments, pulled out and analyzed and evaluated. The different points of progress along the way are an inter-relational process of becoming, of maturation, of balance, of steadiness, of resilience. And mostly, of love.

By refining ourselves, we come to see, in due time, the relationship between the breath and the mind. As we can intentionally calm and steady the breath, we calm and steady the mind. As we intentionally calm and steady the mind, the breath becomes calm and steady. It might be that it is easier for us to first work on the breath. We are so used to our physical selves and being able to move the body as we wish. It can seem almost impossible for us to control the mind.

So we start with what we can do. We breathe. And as we do, we realize the quieting effect on strong emotions. We can settle these strong emotions, quiet the beast, and transmute the overwhelming and overpowering negative emotions into love.

It is through love that we become the artist of our own emotional resilience.

Love Yourself

Loving yourself might be the most important of all our practices—for some. Wherever it does fall on your list of personal importance, let it be genuine, authentic love of self.

Please love all the parts of you: the dark parts, the flobbly parts, the ugly parts, the soft parts, the shapely parts, the pretty or handsome parts—all of them. There is no part of yourself that is not worth loving. If you feel like a bit of physical housekeeping for your body is necessary, set aside a little time most days to move, to get some exercise. If it's mental housekeeping that's needed, find some quiet time and let your mind focus on beauty, which might turn to awe and wonder, which might turn to gratitude, which can help alleviate busy-mind syndrome as you sink into the luxurious expanse of the current moment. (You're getting a three for the price of one, here: love of self, heart-felt positive experiences, and current time!)

Here's a simple practice you can begin tomorrow morning: when you wake up every morning, let your first thought be, "I love myself." Begin with a nice long inhalation, and say it several times before you get out of bed:

> *I love myself.*
> *I love myself.*
> *I love myself.*

If that's too much of a stretch, please remember the idea of your general OK-ness as a human being. Please start with this if it feels good and right to you. You might simply say, "I'm OK today," a couple of times. Eventually, please progress to "I love myself."

Say it as often as you need throughout the day. Check your attitude often. Look in the mirror as you wash your hands, and remind yourself "I love myself." When you open the fridge door for a snack, say, "I love myself." (That love may just spill over into a little bit of self-restraint and nurturing, enabling you to set down that box of leftover pizza.) You get the idea: make it a habit—frequent and repeated.

Pretty soon, you will like yourself. And eventually, you will love yourself.

This is not some narcissistic ritual to build a false or superficial sense of self-esteem. It is being able to see yourself for who you are, remembering that you are not here to earn your worth and value. Genuine love of self is honoring and recognizing your *inherent* worth. And it is by seeing the good in ourselves that we are able to see and enjoy the goodness in others.

Equanimity

Equanimity is a potent change agent, right up at the top of the list of powerful skills for ensuring the growth of emotional resilience. We're going to examine equanimity through two lenses: the first reveals the relationship to the self and the second, the interconnected experience of all beings who share this earthly existence.

Considered through our first lens, equanimity is the personal ability to maintain serene composure in the face of challenges and ruffled feathers. We can think of someone who possesses equanimity as a person who is mentally and emotionally stable and balanced, who demonstrates equilibrium in the face of complications, and has a calm, thoughtful demeanor.

This is such a beneficial and essential quality to develop. Holding yourself to your own high standard of self-responsibility requires this type of equanimity. We'll designate this as *e*quanimity, with a small *e*.

The other lens we use to take perspective on equanimity comes from the same teacher who wisely started each class by reminding us that time is malleable and doesn't always behave in a fixed fashion. This insightful teacher explains that equanimity is understanding that we all have the same desires and wants, regardless of everything physical about us, regardless of where we were born and how we were raised, regardless of tradition and belief: we all want to be happy and we all want to avoid unhappiness. Unfolding this a little more, allowing us to peek deeper into the well of wisdom, he makes clear that we all grasp at the good and crave the pleasant and we all push away the painful and unpleasant. What we like, we want more of and what we don't like, we want less of. (We actually want what we don't like to go away, forever.)

Let's remember the behavioral psychology language that explains it this way: "all *untrained* human behavior is to seek rewards and to avoid punishment." (Italics added for emphasis.)

This *flavor* of equanimity takes us well beyond a sense of composure and calm during upset. It takes us into the hopes and dreams, the wishes and desires of ourselves and all our fellow beings on this planet. We all want to be happy. We each have a unique and personal understanding of what we think will make us happy. And we each go along our own path, trying to lay hold of that happiness. Just so, we all try to avoid unhappiness—each of us with our own interpretation of what we think will make us suffer, and doing all we can to avoid that.

We'll designate this as *E*quanimity, capital *E*.

Our Equanimity can help soften the edges of blame and accusation, of denial and justification. We have to be great-big of heart and expansive of mind to find the first form of equanimity—the calm, serene composure. This in turn allows our innate compassion, guided by our experiential wisdom, to reveal to our awareness in the moment of upset, "Oh! This person is just like me. He just wants to be happy," or, "Her behavior is a patterned reaction that tricks her, just like my own reactions trick me, into thinking that this action and performance is going to get her what she wants."

We are then able to see how many times we've acted in a similar manner. At that point judgement dissolves, bringing us into the same boat, at the same moment.

As we enter a difficult moment with another person, this Equanimity, born of equanimity, will bring to our awareness a beneficial cascade of deep, shared truths:

> *He doesn't want to suffer. This behavior may have worked for him in the past and he is simply importing a script because some of the variables are the same and his survival brain has just kicked into high gear. That's right. I remember now that none of us want to be unhappy or suffer. So, we behave in ways that we mistakenly think will help us swerve away from the pain onto the path of happiness.*

But no, it doesn't work that way. If I give anger as a reaction to his anger, I'm activating that principle of ethical reciprocity that says that whatever I give out, I am sure to get back. I will not be angry in this situation. In fact, how can I be, when I understand this man's plight because I, myself, have been there? I too have acted out in ways that I thought would get me more of what I want and less of what I don't want.

So, I now consciously choose to be kind and compassionate, knowing that we are the same. This man and I are the same, deep in the space of our respective Sacred Hearts. And so I see him, and I know him, and I can love him. And I will.

And you do. Your face softens. Your posture relaxes into the posture of a person in whom he can see love, giving him a sense of confidence that you are not going to yell, that you are not going to berate him, which would make him feel a deeper need to defend himself in the survival mode he is in. Your openness and non-judgement can create a shift in his awareness and allow him to sense that he is not under threat. His rational and intelligent mind will come back online. His nervous system will do a little tap dance of reversal and he will move away from fight-or-flight into rest-and-respond. His countenance will change, as did yours.

The volatile energy that could have escalated doesn't, and you both begin to feel a sense of ease and companionship. Maybe as you look into each other's eyes, you will both simply nod and turn away, back to your own tasks. Maybe there will be a vocal exchange of mutual understanding, possibly an apology. Maybe you will decide to go out for a coffee and talk things over like reasonable adults.

Or just maybe, a new understanding and compassion will have created a bond between you that deepens your sense of shared humanity.

And possibly, nothing will happen. Maybe you will simply turn and walk back to what you were doing with a lingering sense of your own self-worth, from having had enough presence of mind to manage your response so skillfully and so beautifully, with authentic compassion and understanding.

Equanimity is easier to practice in person, when we can use our tone of voice and body language to help express our good intentions toward the other person. It can be harder to effectively express our intentions in an email, a text, or on social media. If you know you may have a difficult exchange with someone else, whenever possible, do it in person; second-best is over the phone. Likewise, don't get too wound up around emails or texts you receive. It can be difficult for you to know the other person's intention when you can't see their facial expression or feel their energy. Be cautious when interpreting others' intentions when communicating through electronic means.

Equanimity, the flower that springs from the bud of equanimity, makes life easy and joyful. With practice, and careful tending and nurturing, it can blossom into a beautiful, fragrant orchard where you will want to spend much more time!

Love Others

When Equanimity becomes real for us, through our felt-experience, we will be able to love others. As we have practiced and come to an authentic love and appreciation for the self, as Equanimity becomes the thread in our mind that connects us to all humanity, how can we help but love others?

It might take some time to cultivate your own authentic Equanimity, but it can be done. When you can, on most days, look at life through the lens of Equanimity, you will be looking at life through the lens of love. As you love yourself, and realize that all others are just like you, you will naturally love them.

Please remember to allow yourself the time that it takes. Some of us will get this pretty quickly. Others of us will be working on unwinding our habitual reactions to others until our last days. And some of us will go in fits and starts, being able to have Equanimity on some days and not others, with some people but not others. It's a process. Keep at it—consistently, over time, without ceasing. It's not necessarily the achievement you're after, but the journey to the top of the mountain. Your intention matters!

As you do develop Equanimity, and begin to see others as just like you, it doesn't mean you will want to bring them home, like an adorable new puppy. It doesn't necessarily mean you will want to take care of their every need, or that you should, or must. It doesn't mean that you will talk to every person in the waiting room or at the gas station. You might! What you *will* feel is less judgement, less social disgust, less contempt. You will feel more compassion, more understanding, more softness.

Please know that softness does not equal weakness. In fact, quite the opposite. Look at the person who, in the face of threat, verbal abuse, or emotional shrapnel, can hold their equanimity in order to display Equanimity. There is nothing weak about that individual. It requires nothing less that every ounce of determination and will, every bit of inner strength, to be soft and not to break, and not to play into the drama of the one who is losing their cool.

If you have yet to experience the power of love in your life, either by loving others or being loved by others, please do not give up hope. Reciprocity tells us that you must get back what you give out. As you begin to practice loving others, even by simply waving in traffic or saying "Hi" on the sidewalk, you are planting seeds that *must* grow and bear fruit.

Once I heard a powerful question that shifted the earth under my feet and made new stars blossom in the heavens. I had been in the same study group for many years with Leela, a woman created and birthed from Equanimity. She was advancing from student to teacher and had an opportunity to spread her wings and find her voice during a summer Dharma and Meditation retreat. She held the small audience captive with her noble presence, each of us mesmerized in doe-eyed adoration. She asked us, "How do you live when you know that you are loved?"

"Yes! I know how being loved changes you." I shouted in inner victory, "You do, you really do live differently!" I was so excited to comprehend on the deepest level what she was asking. I had recently enjoyed an occurrence in my life that changed the very core of who I was. I experienced and recognized unconditional love for the first time in my adult life. I think it re-wired my DNA with stardust, something cosmic and galactic—not in a "woo-woo" sense, but through a very real and profound transformation that I felt in every cell of my being.

Her question made perfect and delicious sense to me. I wanted to proclaim my joy and my agreement with her and all that I felt around and because of her inquiry. But it was neither the scene nor the correct setting, so my joy had to do its fireworks inside my own heart. And what a display it was.

She knew the power that question held, so she paused for several moments as the energy of realization spread over us and through us. And then, she let loose the *pièce de résistance* that burst like a shock wave of radiant light through the audience. "How do you live when you know that you *are* love?"

Pause...then a cosmic expansion of my mind, as sparkles of light rained down from my conscious awareness into the spacious expanse of my Sacred Heart. I felt the peace that overshadows understanding. The spontaneous arisal of joy. A depth of truth transcending all imaginable and explainable phenomena.

I had heard in my many years of study and learning that sometimes a person can have such a blissfully profound experience that words will not, in fact, cannot even come close to capturing it. Being a lover of words and a reader of the dictionary, I had my doubts—until that magnificent moment of truth, of sublime radiance, of awakening. Words do not suffice. Words don't even exist.

You live differently when you *know* that you are love. Explanation is impossible. Understanding springs only from the felt-experience of Being Love.

So, love others. Love yourself. And discover what it is to truly live because you know that you *are* love.

Rejoicing in the Goodness of Others

Because of and thanks to this love, you will rejoice in the goodness of others. It will be so much fun, and feel so playful, to delight in the good that others are, and the good that they do.

Until it's not. It seems, and maybe it is, difficult for us maintain that outlook and attitude for a sustained length of time. So, let's come back down to Earth here. Love can take us up-up-and-away to heights that some of us are afraid of. Let's breathe and settle back down to the real task, the heavy lifting of love: trying to rejoice in the goodness of someone we really despise, are jealous of, or feel disdain toward—someone who's not part of our squirrel family. These unfortunate emotions can arise as our feelings of love diminish.

While we may have many experiences that make it possible to bask or frolic and play in the pleasant circumstances and conditions of unconditional love, it is hard to always be there. The glow fades, people reclaim their annoying habits. Our vision clouds and we again see the blemishes on their character. Reminding ourselves that others are "just like me," and that we do have deep compassion for all of them, can help us find our way back when we slip out of love.

Here's the good news: rejoicing in the goodness of others is a reliable way for us to slip right back into love. The mention of this practice can often cause eye-rolling and deep huffs or sighs, but it works. By hitting pause on our gruntings and grumblings about another and looking at them from a different angle, focusing specifically on the good, we can indeed begin to see that maybe, just maybe, this is not a person that only a mother could love. Possibly, if we turn our head just so, we can see a tiny glimmer of goodness in her, in him.

Rather than holding malice and jealousy in my heart because James got that job promotion that I was sure was mine, I can look at the qualifications that proved James the better candidate than I. He has more experience.

And yes, in fact, I can acknowledge that he does turn in his reports more promptly than I.

*But still...*begins your obsessive, compulsive, delusional narrator.

Nope. Don't let yourself get to "But still." Everybody's got a big *but*. Don't get carried away by yours.

Stay the course! Be true to your desire to be mature, to be emotionally resilient, to see the good. Maybe today, you can only get as far as seeing the good. OK. Then tomorrow, you can work on actually rejoicing in that goodness.

But don't hold off, waiting for another tomorrow to come and go, thinking it will be easier, later. All that does is ensure that you will miss out on the good and joy of life today. Holding a grudge is the response of an emotional kindergartener. Grudges are of no use to anyone. Ever. Don't do it. Don't stoop. If you have mastered even the tiniest degree of self-like and self-worth, you will not. It is beneath you to trample on your high regard for yourself by grudge-holding.

Rejoicing in the goodness of others is the antidote for seeing them with anything less than love and Equanimity. I wish I could simply ask you to take my word for it, but you'll just have to commit to trying this practice for yourself. What do you have to lose?

Try this practice enough that you gather solid data to work with. One time is probably not going to make you buy in. Several times, over several days, or weeks will give you some pretty good odds that you'll feel the uplifting results. If you really get the hang of it, you will feel invigorated, refreshed, and renewed by the release of competition and scarcity, worrying that there is not enough to go around or that others might discover that you are not always right (which they know anyway).

There is enough, of everything, for everyone. How can we know, for sure? Because what we give is what we get. If you give praise to others, there will be enough praise for you. If you give the benefit of the doubt to others, you will also be given the benefit of the doubt. If you rejoice in the goodness of others...yep. You get the recognition that will feel good and right to you.

Rejoice. It's fun. It will make you feel really good on the inside. Radiant, and cosmic, and maybe even glittery. Or simply, light and bright and full of joy. You decide the degree of woo-woo you're comfortable with.

So That . . . We Are Available to Others

Friends, all of these practices are tried and true, many of them proven by generations of practitioners, those who know best what will help us become artists of emotional resilience. We begin with and work on the self. It is in the becoming of a certain characteristic or quality, that we are able to see it in others. As we are able to see it in others, our motivation is strengthened and our intentions firmed.

If we are unwilling to work on our own emotional processes, we will languish. If we languish, we cannot be available to others. We cannot love and serve them.

We exist in relationship and we bring our quality of mind to every relationship we enjoy and to every relationship we hate. If my mind is beset with mental afflictions or I am emotionally impaired, then there is no way that I can create a pleasant situation for myself, let alone for anyone else. For the quality of my mind determines my experience. As Grandpa Dahl used to say, "You can't do wrong and live right."

In the whirlwinds of emotional frenzy, can you employ the skills you've learned here, and practiced, to come into a state of equanimity—calm, cool, and collected? Achieving equanimity enables you to objectively examine the contents of your mind and identify afflicting emotions or thoughts. If you cannot develop and practice equanimity you will continue to blame others—justifying yourself, demanding to be heard, and reinforcing the habits of the emotionally immature. You will continue to wreak havoc on your relationships, and maybe even worse, on your own self-worth and value.

These positive practices can become your allies in your quest for self-mastery. They will instill within your heart the ability to turn your back on anger, on bitterness, on jealousy, and on being annoyed. You will even be empowered to turn away from busyness, which robs you of your precious patience. These allies can release the latent power of the mind to heal itself. You have to do the work, but you are not alone in there.

Nothing becomes real until it is experienced. So give yourself every opportunity to lean on the steadying arm of your intention, your breath, your love of self and others, and do these practices so you can enjoy the felt-experience that leads to ownership and sovereignty.

As you do, you become a strength to others. You become an example to the world of the possibility of goodness. We learn best by example and the world is desperately in need of good examples of right living. The world needs kindness and compassion, self-discipline and self-responsibility, and generosity of spirit and love.

Please remember, it is by *being* good that we *become* good, by *being* kind that we *become* kind. It is by loving others that we become loving. And by so being, we become loveable.

When you do all of this work, all of this good for yourself, it necessarily becomes your character. It becomes the way you show up. It becomes your presence, gracefully managing your way through life, especially when things don't go your way.

Art Class: I Love You

> *"If you would be loved, love and be lovable."*
> ~ Benjamin Franklin

This one is short and sweet.

Who in your life needs to hear you say, "I love you"?

It might be the tricky person. Or the person who has not yet forgiven you. Or the one that you stubbornly refuse to forgive. Or even a group of people.

Pick your person.

And then find some time to have a little one-on-one and tell them you love them. Don't be shy about using those very words. They carry enormous power to create beautiful relationships. You can also add any words of appreciation and gratitude that feel good and right to you.

Love and gratitude may well win the title of Best All-Around Virtues for creating the good life.

CHAPTER 8

Composing Your Masterwork

The notion of contemplation as a tool for discovering solutions is almost an anathema to our modern brains. One of the greatest challenges to our budding resilience is the fact that when we're too busy, too consumed by multitasking, too inundated by stuff, by information, and by data, it's all too easy to believe that we don't have the time to sit around and think. We feel we don't have time to "work the program" and cultivate our inner character, which shows up as our demonstrated behavior. We crave solutions. *Now.*

To become an artist of emotional resilience, we must be willing to trust that, yes, we have the mental and psychological capacity to sort through our challenges and be effective problem solvers. And that we can create the time to do so.

Does the idea of being more productive light the fires of excitement or anxiety in you? Do you subscribe to the information age notion that more data and more inputs always lead to better outcomes? Do you feel less than competent when the spinning plates of your multitasking come crashing to the floor?

Somewhere along the recent timeline of life and human consciousness, we lost our ability to say no. We seem powerless against the excessive demands or requests of others. Many of us feel that we're already at or beyond maximum capacity, but can't deny those requests. What demands pull you out of center? What requests cause you to lose your footing, forgetting your values, intentions, or goals? What impositions interfere with your personal power, forcing you to lose yourself?

Saying "No" may sound like a strange concept for a chapter about moving past stuckness and reclaiming ownership over your life. But we can envision our culture's stuckness as the stuckness of a hamster on a wheel: moving furiously while staying in one place, chasing the elusive finish line and being unable to figure out how to get off. When you're chasing something that is eternally un-catchable, like "being caught up" or "clearing your inbox" you're not in current time. Do you ever feel like that little hamster, running for all your worth with nothing to show for it at the end of the day?

You can step off your wheel, take perspective, and begin to compose your masterwork whenever you choose. Learning a couple of potent techniques and strategies can help. This chapter can be a place where you move forward from all your contemplation and consideration of the changes you'd like to make, and actually begin your own wonderful change process.

How can we reclaim our power to say no? How can we know when saying no is the best option? How can we establish a more effective filter through which we can clearly distinguish what to say no to?

As an artist of emotional resilience, one of your most valuable tools can be the word *no*. When confronted with that endlessly-accruing list of activities and obligations, this single syllable can be a powerful way to protect your limited time and energy. And those people you're afraid to disappoint? Sometimes, saying no is for the highest good of all involved. And sometimes, you will discover, you were asked to do something simply because it's known that you always say yes. When you say no, the world doesn't end. Other solutions miraculously appear. Other people step up.

Before we learn the *art of no* we may feel like we are locked in a cage. But once we discover no, we realize that there is no lock on the door, and there never was. All we have to do is push open the door and we're free.

Saying no also includes disallowing the negative emotional reactions that for so long have crowded your inner world. By saying no to patterns of negative emotions, you begin to recognize that these take up much more of your mental bandwidth than you are willing to give. You can acknowledge, that like the busy work, they serve no beneficial purpose. Be willing to say no to those powerful, potentially destructive emotions and again, you push open the door to your emotional freedom.

Sometimes saying no, especially as you find your footing and begin the practice, can feel like a battleground. Others might become upset. You might feel guilty. You might feel a strong pull to get sucked back in.

Stand your ground. Stay firm in your resolution.

Let's look at how we can re-engage with valor in the contest (or the battle, if that's what's happening for you) to regain sovereignty over ourselves and own lives. We might consider being more selective about what we allow in. We live in an era of overload: overloaded with tasks, duties, and pseudo- as well as real responsibilities; overloaded by information and data; overloaded by social media competition, comparisons, and kitty-cat posts; overloaded by algorithmic suggestions on what we *need*, and what we must have or do that will make our life easier and better.

When we're spread too thin, we lose track of our values, strengths, and priorities. When we're off kilter, it can be easy to say yes to everything, removing us further from what we truly feel is important in our lives.

A good way to get clear on what it is you value is to ask yourself where and how you spend your time.

If you say that you value family, but you spend much more time working or engrossed in activities that take you away from your family, you will probably experience a bit of cognitive dissonance. Cognitive dissonance is having a belief or thought about yourself, but acting in contradiction to that belief. This causes inner turmoil (i.e. stress), because your actions don't match the beliefs you hold about yourself.

When you bring your ideas, beliefs, and actions into alignment, you prove to yourself that you really do value what you *say* you value. And as you reconnect with your values, you will feel empowered to say no when you need to.

One potential way to ease our burdens a little bit is to subtract from, (saying no) rather than add to, our lives:

- Can we shut down our technological input for one day a week, turning off all screens and speakers?
- Can we go through our social media friends and make changes, keeping only those that nurture our sense of self, relationship, and life?
- Can we enhance the filter between us and the data and information we think we need to know, and simply not spend our precious time in ways that don't uplift us?
- Can we reduce the number of priorities on our daily to-do list to the "Big Three"?
- Can we remove the things from our to-do list that have lingered there for months?
- Can we have the courage to release toxic relationships and move on, or create relationships of trust that add to the enjoyment of life?

As we consider these questions for ourselves and create practices around them that fit our own life, we can realign ourselves with our values and our desired quality of mind and being.

Return on Investment

In the business world, return on investment is of paramount importance. Why shouldn't it be for our personal lives as well? Are you spending your resources in ways that positively increase your bottom line of mental, emotional, physical, relational, and spiritual well-being?

Return on investment is determined by certain criteria: cost, efficiency, value of the investment(s), and net profit. Looking at your personal life, what is the net profit you gain from all you invest in? What do you invest in? How much of your limited assets are you willing to invest?

In the realm of personal life, our precious and limited assets include:

- Time
- Attentional awareness or focus
- Physical Energy
- Mental energy
- Emotional energy

Just as in financial investment, we do best when we engage in a conscious and informed risk/reward thought process. How much time do you have to spend, and where is it being spent? Where or to what/whom does your energy go? Do the activities that you engage in provide benefit? What kinds of benefits? How *much* benefit? Are these benefits aligned with your stated priorities and values?

If your personal ROI is in the red, it might well be time for an analysis, a comprehensive and exhaustive evaluation. Carefully assess the activities that are a drain on your resources, tangible and well as intangible. Sit down and pencil out the things that can be scaled back or eliminated altogether. Balance the budget of your time, energy, and desires so that you are not dragged down by the debt of saying yes—too often, out of duty, or without a burning, passionate fire behind the yes.

One interesting way to do this is to add the personally significant things to your to-do list that normally don't make it:

- Movie night with kids
- Art class
- Family dinner
- Bike ride
- Campout with the grandkids
- Spa, or self-care day

And then, along with your work to-dos, your honey-do's, and other obligations, schedule these into your calendar. If time with family is truly your top priority it deserves the real estate in your calendar, not the leftovers after you accomplish everything else. Steven Covey, author of *The Seven Habits of Highly Effective People* and *First Things First*, calls these the "big rocks," the important ones that must go into your bucket first. If you wait until later to find room for the big rocks, there won't be any.

And then, watch your personal ROI increase. The process of subtracting what does not serve your progress toward your intention, your why, or your self-concordant goals can help you reorganize your priorities. Subtraction and elimination can open your mind to the possibilities of living your unique genius and to letting the best of you bubble to the surface.

Less Is More

We are drowning in material and information, in data and numbers, in opinions, in science, news, fake-science, and fake-news. We struggle to know what to believe. This creates in us a deep and far-reaching anxiety. We don't know who to trust. We don't know *what* to trust. We don't know if we're safe, either physically or psychologically, in this day and age. And then we spiral into fear.

As we've seen, fear sends us into protective mode, on super-high alert to threat, danger, and potentially life-ending situations. When we end up there, we circle back around to lack of trust. When we don't trust, either the self or others, we cannot love.

Becoming self-aware through personal observation and reflection, regularly monitoring and assessing your inner work, and then using that self-awareness to dial in your level of self-management, directly influences your relationships and social interactions. This introspective process can reveal that the power to create the changes you seek is love. We just went through that process in our last chapter.

Where fear exists, love cannot. Where anger exists, love cannot. Where doubt exists, we lack trust, and so are left without room in the equation for love. When we listen so much more on the outside than we do on the inside, we turn away from the inherent love and compassion that are the compositional elements of our Sacred Heart, of our deepest wisdom, and of our highest good.

When we can shush the maddening noise of *out there* and come to the stillness and expansiveness of *in here*, we can begin to see, and to feel, the liberation of letting go, the absolution (or exoneration) of subtraction. Less is more. And we can only know this through our own unique, individual, felt-experiences. When we unchain ourselves from that which no longer serves our highest good and push open the gate, we step into freedom.

The Illusion of FOMO

According to the German proverb, "Those who taste, know."

The rest of us must scramble around reading reviews and critiques from others. We must take others' word for it, and then we rush on to the next thing, eager not to be left out, not to miss out.

Around the time that the acronym FOMO (Fear of Missing Out) came into popular use, I was at a weekend retreat with a very perceptive teacher. We were deep in the texts of the ancient wisdom traditions that teach the causes of suffering and how we can eliminate those and create, instead, the causes for happiness and well-being.

The retreat began with a group-circle check-in. I grew increasingly annoyed as many of my friends lamented that they were missing out on other exciting things that were happening that weekend.

My turn had already passed. I had mentioned how grateful I was to be there, how nice it was to escape the cold of where I lived, and come down into the warmth of the valley. I was happy to see all of them. As I sat listening to the lengthy status updates of my fellow travelers on this journey, I decided it was a perfect place for me to practice non-judgment.

As I let go of the critical perspective that had been causing my annoyance, I was able to hear their check-ins as the desire to be involved, to partake fully of life and relationships, and to live abundant and active lives. I smiled as I thought about how I, too, love living big—going and doing and experiencing.

I also recognized that things were definitely shifting inside me. I realized that the older I had become, the less I needed to share all the stories of the countries I'd visited, the historic world sites I'd seen, the amazing meals I'd eaten. I no longer felt such an overpowering drive to tour more places, see more sights, sample more exotic foods. I did not need to catalogue more stories that recounted the events of a very cool life. A sense of contentment permeated me.

My teacher's loud "Let's stop here!" interrupted my reverie. I was lost in my thoughts, reminiscing on what a really great life I'd had. I was far, far away from that circle of friends sitting on cushions on the hardwood floor.

"Thank you for sharing where you are," she continued. "We all appreciate the safe space in which we can be vulnerable and authentically bring our story to the table."

She paused. I could see she was making an effort to find the right words. She looked down at her feet crossed in front of her. She stroked the tassel on the edge of the blanket under her.

Time passed.

We all grew even more still, and a little concerned. One older gentleman cleared his throat, clearly uncomfortable with the whole situation.

Still looking down, she held up her hand, palm out: "Wait," it said. "Just wait."

So we waited. Legs uncrossed, stretched, and re-crossed. Lungs loudly released their air. Meditation cushions stopped rustling. I peeked around the circle. Most people now had their eyes closed, the softness of patience visible in their countenance. My heart was still and open, my wandering mind now attentive to the new and different energy in the group.

I traveled my gaze around the circle to the teacher. Her chin was still dipped, her long blonde hair with threads of sparkling silver hung in curtains against both cheeks. Her closed eyelids were soft and wide, mirroring the set of her mouth. A peace and deep wisdom emanated from her.

I watched her take a deep breath, lift her chin, and open her eyes. She looked across the circle, straight into my eyes. I felt like a child, caught with my hand in the cookie jar. My eyes widened ever-so-slightly in a flash of surprise. But my still and available Ms. Inner Wisdom ever-so-gently took the reins of that moment, hushed the surprise, and whispered, "Isn't she beautiful?"

And yes, she most certainly was. In that shared gaze, I felt the potential of all goodness and love as real and fully possible as my own reality. In that single moment of eternity, I experienced a rush of trust and truth that went through me like a shockwave of tenderness, warm and luxurious and sumptuous. And I was so grateful that my whole, entire life had conspired to bring me to this very moment of connection with a woman who clearly knew and *was* truth, light, and love.

She smiled, and the moment shattered like a thousand rays of sun bursting over the eastern horizon.

As she inhaled, she drew our attention out from our inner stillness. She drew our attention to her. All the others took deep breaths and opened their eyes, expectant and hopeful.

She smiled, a mix of calm joy and teacherly authority. "You are not missing anything. Whatever is happening out there, all those many activities and events that you've all mentioned, are meant to happen just like they will happen, just like they are happening—*without you.* You are exactly where you need to be, doing exactly what you need to be doing."

I glanced around. Some heads were nodding. Others were stiffly erect and attentive, clearly having to work hard to absorb this perspective, to allow that it might be true.

"You are not. Missing. A single thing." she reiterated. "This FOMO, this lie that you've allowed to so deeply color your own truth is the cause of your distress and anxiety—your stress, during the last hour we've been sharing together. Why would you believe a lie that someone else is trying to force onto you as reality? Have you considered that you have lived your entire life to be here, exactly at this moment, at this time, with these people?"

Whoa! Not two minutes ago, I had had this very thought. It was like I had read her thoughts. Or she had read mine, which was more probable. It was so supportive to have the confirmation that I was on the right track.

"There are no mistakes. You are supposed to be here, *right here*, right now," she finished.

A collective exhale of relief was heard around the room.

Can you trust that there are no mistakes, that you are not missing out, that where you are is exactly where you need to be, at exactly the right time? With exactly the right people?

It's radical. For sure.

But what if it were true? How would that change your life? How would that change you? What burdens of stress, anxiety, and fear could you lay down at the feet of "No More FOMO"? Which ones are you ready to let go of? Which one will you relinquish?

Life Hacks Defined

It all comes down to your intentions, which you established in Chapter 1: *Why am I here? What I am doing?*

If you love your life, then honor it, and work on it. Work for it.

If you don't yet love your life, begin to honor it, begin to work on it by working for it, and in due course, you will.

It bears repeating here that your work and your effort are your love made manifest.

The Merriam Webster dictionary defines "life hack" as "a usually simple and clever tip or technique for accomplishing some familiar task more easily and efficiently." Why have we become a society that wants, or even feels that we need, life hacks?

If you want to "hack" your life rather than work on it, you'll find it lying in "clumsy or sloppy"[49] pieces at your feet.

Don't get sucked in by this mindset. It's not possible to hack your way to emotional resilience. You're not making a better cup of coffee, you're making a better life. Short cuts to personal refinement, ownership of yourself, your quality of mind, your emotions, and your behaviors—your life—do not exist. This process takes the time it takes. And it can be so much fun—a joyful way to spend your time.

Take pride in yourself and your abilities. Have some confidence in yourself! Put your shoulder to the wheel and your nose to the grindstone, as they used to say in the same era that the word *hack* meant many things that had nothing to do with the unfortunate, ever-more common and illusory definition of current times.

So please be patient. Take one step each day. You have an inner reservoir of strength to draw from. There is no rush. You now have permission to slow down, to go at your own pace. You cannot rush the process anyway. Relax into current time and just do what you can; do it well, be intentional, be filled with love as you approach your practices; don't "behave foolishly or idly waste your time"[50] in these precious, life-changing efforts.

We'll go section by section through several easy yet potent practices that will allow you to hone your skills as an artist of emotional resilience. Feel free to try them all, one by one; do a little personal reflection on each one, and then choose the one or two, maybe three, that really work for you. Remember, we are creatures of habit and we are looking to develop new, positive habits—so don't overwhelm yourself by trying to do every practice shared here. Short and sweet, easy and manageable, OK?

Exploring the Practices

Emotional Resilience as Praxis

When I took the Praxis Exam to get my teaching license, I found myself intrigued by the term. *Praxis* is a Greek word meaning "action, to do." The *Webster's Dictionary* also defines it as the "practical application or exercise of a branch of learning."

Emotional resilience is a practice, and at its best, a habit. Mastering the art of emotional resilience requires hard work, as does any practice. The practices herein don't trumpet a gimmicky quick fix, but within each of them you'll find opportunities for some quick relief, along with the promise of long-term change. There are simply no short cuts to becoming an artist of your emotional resilience.

Take a look, for a moment, at some of the greatest artists the world has ever known; in the West, we are amazed by the genius of the Masters of the Italian Renaissance, the Spanish Masters—da Vinci, Michelangelo, Velazquez, Goya, and Rembrandt, Picasso, and Monet—insert your own favorite artist here. Did they simply pick up a brush or a chisel one day, and *voila!* masterpiece accomplished?

No. Most great artists must learn to use their tool, their instrument. Painters learn skills like composition, color theory, and how to handle materials properly. Many great artists had teachers to whom they were apprenticed. They studied and practiced.

It's no different for your personal cultivation of emotional balance and resilience, and its ultimate blossoming. It will probably require even more work than any aspiring sculptor or portraitist puts in because you never get to leave the "studio" when you practice the art of emotional resilience. The studio is your life.

And while artists work with stone, clay, paint and canvas, or musical notes, materials that can feel like they have a life of their own, compared to the life of your emotions, those materials are pretty inert. Some days your emotions will seem like they're operating independently of you, despite your best efforts. Your "composition" may be torn to pieces by one thoughtless word. Or someone may stand up and heckle your symphony, and suddenly the harmony is gone.

You are a living, changing, dynamic being. Your needs change from day to day, as do your moods and attitudes. The inner work you do requires an extreme flexibility and nimbleness. It requires strength too, enabling you to stick with it and push through the challenging barriers you come up against on your quest for resilience. You become resilient by being resilient.

You can think about your intentions, your Why, your self-concordant goals, even your action plan. You can read all about How-To's. You can write and re-write all the steps along the path of your action plan, but you cannot stall out. Like the great artists, you must strike chisel with hammer, chipping away at the marble of your emotional life. You must put brush to canvas to begin to create the masterpiece of yourself, in all your emotionally resilient glory.

You must do the practices, the work of clearing out the emotional clutter, debris, and pollution. You must face whatever internal toxicity is clouding your awareness, obstructing your potential vitality and relaxation, your originality and creativity.

Please believe in yourself and your capacity for change, inner renewal, and heightened enthusiasm for a life well-lived. You are powerful beyond your knowing. You have a strength within you greater than any challenge you will face. How can this be said with any sense of truth? Because you are here. Still.

You survived your own birth! Birth is traumatic and painful—and not just for you but your mother as well. You have overcome and soundly defeated your previous challenges and obstacles. So far, you've made it.

So, yes. You can do it again. And you will.

You're Always OK in Current Time

The importance of current time cannot be over-emphasized. It's where life happens. It's where you live your unique genius. It's where relationship happens. Current time is where you will cultivate integrity, dignity, and self-worth through demonstrating emotional resilience.

One day, I decided to have the Current Time Discussion with a group of high school students. Together we decided that yes, mostly, we are all OK in current time. Then one young man who had previously shared some of life's challenges that he was experiencing, slowly raised his hand and asked, "What if you're not?"

I stopped. Dead in my tracks, in my mind, and even in my breath. Every teacher these days is on high alert for students who might be "at risk" in one way or another. My mind kicked into high gear, "Do I ask him if he needs to go to the counselor? Do I open this up for a whole class discussion? Do *I* answer? What should I say?" I got nervous. (All of this happened in a nanosecond.) Then I remembered, *"Current Time!* We're here together having a discussion on current time!"

I did what I had just instructed my students to do. I came into current time in myself. I took a deep breath. I surveyed the students. No one was uncomfortable or disengaged. No one was snickering, or taunting this young man who so vulnerably and honestly asked this powerful question.

My current time evaluation of the situation confirmed that yes, indeed, we were all OK right now. And so, we discussed together the reality of being OK in current time. We narrowed it down to three exceptions: if you are bleeding, if you are about to die (in whatever sort of situation), or if you are dying, then you might not be OK.

After a bit more consideration, several students shared the opinion that even if you were bleeding, and came into current time, you would have a clear presence of mind and could make a better assessment as to whether you were *actually* OK, or if, as one Monty Python-loving class clown laughed, it were a "mere flesh wound," or if you really did need to get help.

Being in current time, with a clear mind, they concluded, we would be more likely to think rationally about who we could reach out to that could and would help us.

I encourage you to experiment for yourself. Come into current time often. Establish it as much as you can as a solid habit. Then, the next time you find yourself in one of those questioning moments, your anguished face asking your reflection in the mirror "Why?!", try to come into current time and find a sense of OK-ness.

The next time you find yourself on the brink of a potential unfortunate emotional incident, stop—and come into current time. Begin with your breath, releasing a long exhale. Let yourself just *be* in the expansive moment of Now. Feel into the physical sensations in your body. See if you can identify the emotional energy coursing through you. Ask yourself your assessment questions, then really listen inside to monitor the internal information you will receive. Am I bleeding? Am I about to die? Am I dying? As you answer each of these, keep in mind your central focusing question: *Am I OK in current time?*

As you conduct this inner reflection, a little time will pass. In this passing of time, maybe the volatile situation will have cooled off just a bit. Maybe you will have had the presence of mind and courage to say, "Excuse me please, I need to go to the restroom," and made your escape.

As you buy yourself time by being in current time, you create space to actually practice the artistic brush strokes of emotional resilience. (The bathroom is always a legitimate excuse. Who's going to say, "No! You can't go."? No one. Ever.)

An escape to the bathroom is *not* an escape from of your responsibility in the communication and relationship. It is an escape so that you *can* be responsible in the communication and relationship. In the bathroom, you can get a hold of yourself by breathing, maybe splashing cool water on your face. You might even imagine that you're throwing all your fear or anger or frustration or hostility right into the toilet and flushing it. You can smooth your skirt or your shirt-front, gather your resiliency and kindness, look yourself in the eye and remember who you are. And then you can return to the person or situation, now ready to thoughtfully and compassionately address the matter.

You just avoided an unfortunate emotional incident. Bravo and congratulations! Smile, and give yourself a little pat on the back—and a big hit of dopamine, as you congratulate yourself for achieving an emotional resilience goal. (Remember, that delicious dopamine is key to laying down a new, solid habit. When you intentionally reward good behavior and progress by giving yourself a dopamine hit, you're strengthening that habit and will have a better chance of repeating that behavior in the future.)

Spend as much of your life as you can in current time. It is a lovely place, full of rich and amazing opportunities and experiences. Don't miss life by continually ruminating about the past and fantasizing about the future. Current time is where it's at!

Most Days

It's possible to get very caught up in trying to be the perfect artist of emotional resilience. Let's not. Being perfect every single second of every single day requires too much energy. Trying to wrangle every flared emotion and minor upset flawlessly might only increase the overwhelm in your life. Adding three, or four, or five of these practices to your everyday living and your already-full calendar may overwhelm you. You do not need one more thing that requires anything close to perfection. Simplify—that's the goal.

Please allow that you are a fallible human being who will, on some days, just lose your cool, or worse. The phrase "most days" can be your saving grace.

My dental hygienist gets the credit for "most days". These trained technicians know that most people rarely floss. They can tell the moment they put that little bib on your chest and fasten the chain around your neck and you say "Thank you." Their keen eyes can spot the buildup with your lips just slightly parted. They know!

Dental hygienists really want to encourage us to do a better job, so our teeth and gums will be healthier, for a longer period of time. We also know that it's a more relaxed time in the chair for both technician and patient if patient flosses—on most days.

And so it goes with emotional resilience. The next time you're in the vortex of an emotional upset, it can be less stressful and reactive for all involved if, during the time before and up to the event, you've been practicing your breathing, your intention, and your love for self and others; in other words, practicing at being your best self. The emotional episode is the game; the way you have been living your life previous to the game is your practice. It's a matter of how you have been conducting yourself *before* and up to the point of the event, your preparation through your practices, that determine how well you self-manage and demonstrate emotional resilience *during* the event. You can see the importance then of "most days."

Doing a self-check-in on your emotional processing at the end of most days can offer you a clear picture of your progress and accomplishments. It can also shed light on areas that might still benefit from more effort. At the end of week, check in from a wider perspective and see if you did indeed, practice even just a little something, most days. Then give yourself a dopamine hit to strengthen your neural pathway of emotional resilience by congratulating yourself. "Way to go, Self! We're making progress!"

Just as dental hygienists encourage their patients, you have people in your life who encourage you to be your best self, to be emotionally healthier and resilient so you can enjoy a greater sense of overall well-being and contentment. Celebrate your progress together.

"Most days" is reasonable, not overwhelming. It's doable.

Monotasking

Ancient sages knew that we are capable of truly focusing on one task at a time. So did your mother, ancient sage that she was. (Or is.) How many times during your childhood did she ask you to slow down and pay attention to what you were doing? All those schoolteachers you had for thirteen long years—they also knew.

Somehow, the deleterious myth of multitasking has trespassed on our desires to do a good work, to do more, to be seen as one who can accomplish any task or job. For years, "multitasking" has been written into job descriptions and job searches, proudly announced on resumes, and lauded as a skill of a highly advanced mental processing system. But multitasking was actually a trend. And luckily, as all trends will, it is quietly exiting the scene.

And none too soon, either. We have lost our collective mind thinking that we can multitask. Have you personally felt the excess of stress and anxiety when you have too many things for any reasonable person to accomplish in a given time frame, with inadequate resources, and you think you have to do them all, and do them all exceedingly well? You might feel that if you don't you'll get fired, or at the very least, the boss will yell at you—so you multitask. Don't forget to add in the kids and the spouse and managing the home life and all that entails. You've seen the frazzled, frenzied, wide-eyed stupor of one who has been sucked into the multitasking death-machine.

Much research has recently been done that explains how the human brain cannot, in fact, multitask. (An online search will yield numerous videos and articles).[51]

Instead, the brain "toggles", splitting its awareness and its energy and moving from task to task, back and forth. Brains are malleable and quick learners, and most of us have trained our brains to toggle very quickly. But at what expense?

The studies show that it's a matter of bandwidth. For example, we may have a total bandwidth of 10 "degrees". If I'm doing one task, typing a report for my end-of-month review, it gets all 10 degrees of my bandwidth. When the dog starts whining to go out, some of that bandwidth, say 1 degree, goes to Dog and I wonder, *when was the last time he went out?*

Then my hungry child starts pestering for me for a snack, and some of my bandwidth goes there as I try to explain that I'll be done in a minute. Child-focus now consumes 2 or 3 degrees of my bandwidth. And not only am I thinking of something else, I've added speaking into the mix—using a separate area of the brain, requiring more of my available bandwidth. So now, with Dog and Child, I'm down to just 6 or 7 degrees on my original task. So if I'm lucky, I'll have roughly 60 percent of my attention on typing up that report.

You probably have auto-correct on your word processing program. How many times does it mistakenly "correct" you? Lots. So if you're not giving your full attention to your report, it will inevitably contain errors. And these are just the minor bandwidth-bandits.

Back to hungry Child who cannot find the box of Teddy Grahams, anywhere, and is shouting at me from the depths of the pantry. *I told Child yesterday that they were gone, and why can't Child remember and let me finish this report in peace?* As I think these thoughts and feel this annoyance, I am now down to about 4 degrees of my attentional bandwidth on my original task. And being frustrated at the situation, and wanting to help Child, I begin to explain, *There are no more Teddy Grahams, can you please be patient?!*

Then I refocus my attention on the screen, picking up where I left off and see the last paragraph I just typed. It reads, "The attached letter of transmittal and required submission is not in the pantry. There are none left! And would you please let that dog out!"

We've all been there. We've bought in to the seductive myth of multitasking. We think we're supposed to do it and that we *can* do it—though we fear that everyone else can probably do it better. But here's the clincher: those of us who think we we're actually good at multitasking are statistically shown to be the worst. (Pause here to snicker quietly at ourselves.)

Our brains aren't built to multitask, and thank heavens, science has officially let us off that hook. Now, happily, a beautiful new word has entered our language: *monotask*. (Cheers and applause in the background.)

Isn't it about time that we cut ourselves some slack and allow that no, we cannot do it all and certainly not all at the same time? Will you rejoice with me and join the monotasking revolution? When the desperate cry for Teddy Grahams comes at the top of Child's lungs, you can take a deep breath, pause, lift your fingers from the keyboard, and say with all the confidence in the world, "Child, I'm monotasking. You'll have to find another snack," and then settle placidly back to your report.

Teach your children, and significant other, this concept so that when you say the above phrase they will know what it means. And you can all be mostly-happy, (most days) together until the report is done and it's dinner time.

And don't forget to let the dog out.

Monotasking Among Multitaskers

Teaching others how to honor your monotasking time can be challenging at work, too, where the cult of multitasking may still rule. The open office design trend (surprise!) has been shown to be pernicious to productivity, so if you work in such a setting, monotasking will be a bigger challenge.

You can use an array of techniques to protect your monotasking time:

- Set the "do not disturb" on your phone for your monotasking time.
- Reduce the number of alerts set on your phone and its apps to the bare minimum.
- Make a little sign that says MONOTASKING, AVAILABLE AT [TIME] and put it at the entrance of your workspace (or on a sticky note on your back!).
- Tell the person who has just interrupted you (if possible) "This sounds (important/urgent/interesting). I'd like to give you my full attention. Can we speak about this at (name a time)?"
- Programmers have long known that headphones enable them to focus, reducing the number of casual interruptions, but headphones are not acceptable in all office environments.
- Monotasking has natural limits. Recognize that humans are most effective working in forty-five to sixty-minute focus periods.
- Set the timer on your phone and take a ten-minute break to get up and move. When your coworker who has seen you at the coffee machine tries to bend your ear about something, he'll hear the timer go off. At that point you can excuse yourself politely, saying, "duty calls" and no feelings are hurt.

Self-Responsibility

Part of the teenage stage of our human development is a wonderful process called *differentiation*. It's the process whereby a teen begins to push off from the family to establish a firm sense of his or her own identity. It can be scary and painful and joyful and extreme for everyone involved. But it is necessary and we want it to happen. It's a tragedy if it doesn't.

For most, it's the time when the reins of personal responsibility are handed over. Teens learn how to more easily and skillfully communicate their own thoughts and beliefs, how to incorporate new ideas into what they are synthesizing as their reality, how to empathize with others and see that "I am not the only one in life that matters." They may learn to drive and get a driver's license, increasing their sense of freedom and independence. Some teenagers get jobs and bank accounts and learn the intricacies of skillful time management and budgeting.

If, for whatever reason, teens do not have the opportunity or are not given responsibility and then held accountable, they often don't become self-responsible. Those children whose parent does their homework for them, brings to school the forgotten backpack left behind at the front door, or writes their college entrance essays, will take longer to develop maturity and responsibility than children who must take care of these tasks their own.

We are not speaking about parenting styles or strategies. We are talking about how the teenage brain matures to adulthood. If a child learns to drive at age eleven in order to help feed the cows in the field before getting onto the school bus, that child's frontal cortices will develop earlier than those of his peers. If a child lives in a city and uses the available public transportation, not learning to drive until later in life, the executive functioning area of that brain develops differently and at a different rate, because of the unique experiences to which it is exposed. A farm child will not develop the useful street savvy of an urban child, and that urban child will certainly have a different perspective of life than a farm child.

Our brains develop according to the experiences we have, and that is part of the unique and magical genius of every individual human being throughout existence.

Whatever the age of your brain, it has the amazing capacity to restore itself—all brains enjoy neuroplasticity. Your brain can become self-responsible; *you* can become self-responsible, no matter how old. Self-responsibility means you cannot leave your life in the hands of another—not another person, not an organization, not a church, not a government. It means that when you're in the thick of it and it hurts, you do not expect anyone to rush to your rescue. We are self-responsible when we understand and live the truth that *no one is coming.*

At the beginning of this book I shared the story of the esteemed professor who began the school year by telling his Freshmen exactly what would be expected of them, and concluded with this very phrase: *No one is coming.* That may sound harsh, at first. But think about it just a bit and it will unfold its truth to you.

If raised by parents who preempt our potential failures by *doing for us*, we enter adulthood with the same expectation. We may even spend our whole lives waiting for someone else to do for us, and being deeply disappointed, angry, or hurt when that doesn't happen.

By never being challenged, or believing that challenges always equal suffering, we lose out on the greatness of what this life is. We miss the wonderful opportunities to step into who we are, to test ourselves and our strengths, to blossom into our unique genius ready to share our special talents and gifts with the world.

We can import this idea into our emotional resilience. How many times, when you get mad and lose your temper, or when you're too afraid to try something new, or too sad to laugh, do people not want to "play" with you? How many times, when you must have things your way, do others politely excuse themselves, bowing out of having to spend time with you? How many times have you struggled to enjoy family events, team meetings, or company trainings due to the lack of maturity and emotional self-responsibility of others?

No blame here, at all. We've all been on both sides of this equation. The questions you must now ask yourself are, "Do I want to be there, on the giving *or* receiving end of emotional immaturity, ever again? How much of my life do I want to waste on a lack of emotional intelligence, or on emotional infancy, or emotional blackmail, perpetrated by myself or others?"

None of those are fun and nobody likes them, yet they still happen. Why? Because somehow, some way, we think it's the other person's fault that we're sad, angry, afraid or annoyed: "She makes me so mad!" "Boy he can sure take the fun right out of things!"

We've all heard and used phrases like these, and worse. And the maddening thing is that we believe them! We actually believe that someone else has power over the way we feel.

Let's reframe that belief right now. No one can determine how you feel, about anything. No one can make your choices for you. No one has the power to keep you from being an emotionally resilient person if you really want to be one—unless you surrender that power to them.

Being self-responsible means claiming ownership over your emotions, your words, your behaviors, your beliefs—in short, over yourself. You are in charge of how you decide to show up. Your emotions are powerful and sometimes they do get the better of you, crossing willfully and belligerently over the line into behavior, and sometimes turning around to point a mocking finger in your face.

You, as the artist of your emotional resilience, are able to hold and contain the latent power of those emotions. You can prevent them from turning madly kinetic on you without your approval. You can stop yourself from defecting to the side of the mean, harmful, vengeful, or abusive. Do not let strong emotions abscond with your free will and your best self. Your sense of well-being and contentment depend on you.

Try, Try Again—But Try Something Different

Sometimes, for the especially tricky and slippery challenges, the ones you just cannot seem to overcome regardless of what you try, you'll need a different perspective, something other than plain old will power and determination.

When you get stuck, you'll need to try, try again—but using a different approach.

Unless you have learned how to live like Dr. Wayne Dyer, where "nothing in (your) life ever goes wrong," you will likely get stuck somewhere along the way. Being stuck is no fun. It hurts. It takes our mojo and slaps it back and forth on the mat until we cry "Uncle!" If we're not careful, being stuck for a long period, or getting stuck over and over, can lead us to learned helplessness. This is a discouraging and disempowering belief that no matter what we do, nothing every goes right—so why should we bother trying anymore?

If you are at the edge of this wasteland of deep misery and darkness, turn back!

You are not powerless. You do not have to be a victim of the emotional turbulence and high seas that sometimes pummel you from all sides. You can right yourself, steady the chaos, recover, and set a new course.

When we think of being pummeled by strong emotions, there's no harder pummeling than the one we receive from anger. Anger is tenacious. Once it gets its hooks in us, it can feel like a ride on a runaway train.

Why is anger so poisonous?

Because we feel *powerful* during moments of anger. The primary survival purpose of anger is to enable us to remove an obstacle on our path toward a goal. If there is something in our way, whether the obstacle is physical or mental, we are going to need a lot of strength to move it. We do not flee the scene in anger. The common sympathetic nervous system response of anger is to fight.

In order to fight, and win (remember, in the survival mechanisms of the brain, losing equals death, and winning means the survival of the species) we need to be big—bigger than our opponent. We need to be strong, stronger than the adversary we face. So anger fills us with power, strength, and passion. All to the detriment of our levelheaded, reasonable mind.

In anger, more so than any other emotion, we lose the ability to take perspective. We cannot hear, let alone process, the differing ideas and opinions of others. When we are immersed in the anger experience, the details of our opponents' side of things, their stories, don't matter. Our perspective becomes extremely narrow, and we can only take in what supports our argument. We can only focus on "me and my way." *I* have to be *right*! Or I lose—and I die. And we buy in to that delusion.

Think back to the last time you were angry. How powerful did it feel? How absolutely clear were you, knowing every last detail and intricacy of your argument? How much could you really hear of what the other person was trying to communicate?

Remember our angry, fit-pitching two year old boy in the grocery cart? Remember when he was rewarded with the candy bar? He got his way, which in his mind meant he was right, which meant he was the winner, which laid down a powerful behavioral pattern, inscribed in a neural pathway: **anger = survival.**

The Anger Cascade

Let's review this important sequence. For the paragraph below, the yield symbol, **=>** indicates that each event or action in the sequence yields (produces) the subsequent reaction.

We can visualize it as a flowing cascade of inner and outer phenomena:

Angry display toward another person (my red face; narrow, ferocious eyes; raised voice; big, threatening posture) **=>**

Scared "obstacle" (other person with widened eyes, lips drawn back with mouth open, hands up and moving away from the threat—me) who crumbles in response to my explosion of power **=>**

I win and get my way **=>**

I survive! **=>**

Huge dopamine hit **=>**

My brain lays down a strong neural pathway of this whole string of events, or cyclical episode.

The win felt so good and received such a big internal reward that it happens again the next time an obstacle presents itself and the anger trigger gets pulled. This initiates a cycle where anger becomes a habit—a really strong one.

This is why it can be so hard to overcome and tame the Anger Demon, and so easy to find yourself at the edge of Stuck. Un-sticking yourself is not easy, but it is doable.

How? By trying something entirely new. And a little radical. You know that old saying, *doing what you've always done will get you what you've always gotten*? It's especially applicable here.

We have to catch anger off guard. To thwart anger, we have to go old school, way back to the Golden Rule, that ancient moral principle of reciprocity: *Do unto others as you would have them do to unto you.* If you give anger, you'll get anger. If you give kindness, you'll get kindness.

While I was a faculty member at that prestigious Catholic academy, I was schooled and had my knowledge deepened around this concept. I learned that it is not advised to "repay evil for evil or abuse for abuse"[52] but that we should rather repay that evil, abuse, or anger, with a blessing, with kindness—and as we do, we will in turn receive a blessing.

What goes around comes around, so the old saying goes. And we know that it does. We've seen enough of life to observe this in action, for ourselves. The emotional "sugar high" of anger rarely yields a positive outcome, unless you are literally facing one of those life-and-death threats that anger is designed to help you overcome—or coming to the rescue of someone similarly threatened. Anger can have a stunning knock-on effect, sometimes echoing in our lives for years.

So, to break the habit of anger, tricky as it is, we simply must not get angry. We must stop empowering anger. This is true for whatever negative habit or practice we're trying to change in our lives.

But can we really just *stop* being angry? I don't think that most of us can. It hasn't worked for me. But maybe you have amazing willpower and it will work for you! Maybe your innate temperament is mild, and you're naturally less inclined to angry reactions. But maybe you had a parent that modeled anger, excusing it as blowing off steam, and you're not aware of the impact your anger has on others.

What has worked for me (and I invite you to experiment for yourself) is remembering that what I send out to the world must return to me.

Soothing the Anger Beast

Maybe you don't like being on the receiving end of someone's anger, where you feel the need to defend yourself, to fight back. If you feel the surge of power that compels you to fight back, please don't concede! Please don't fight back. Don't become a victim of another's anger. Don't play into their emotional drama. And for heaven's sakes, do not take it personally. It's actually not about you anyway.

Collect yourself. Then manage the strong and potent energy running through you. Excuse yourself to the bathroom if needed—which is a powerful step in disengaging and disempowering overwhelming emotional sensations and toxic situations.

As you deepen your emotional self-management effectiveness, you will eventually learn to see behind another's anger and see fear, or grief, or megawhelm from stress—each of these an obstacle on their path toward a happy life. You will be able to find a sense of compassion and love, allowing you to repay their anger with a blessing. Or at least a quiet understanding of the myriad possibilities behind the anger. You might even be able to soothe their Anger Beast by kindly saying, *I hear you. I understand how you could feel that way.*

When you get to this point in your emotional maturity, being able to understand the emotional turmoil of others, *because* you now understand it in yourself, you have become the Artist. The artist can see and hold many perspectives at once. Consider the sculptor, who can see the dimensions and contours under the stone and knows exactly where and how much to chip away to reveal the truth of the beauty that lies hidden from every view but his own.

It is in this way that we, too, can learn to chisel away even the hardest of anger and transform it into beauty. It's done with a soft word and a kind heart. This is the "something different" that we need to try. Both for ourselves when we are in a moment of anger, and when we are experiencing the anger barrage from someone else. We can use our self-talk to alter the patterned narrative by inquiring into the internal state of affairs. "Are you sure you want to yell right now? Are you really feeling anger, or are you afraid?" We can them communicate concern and empathy to our upset partner or child, "Yes, I do hear you. I'd like to understand more. Please tell me without yelling. I'm listening."

So yes, try, try again. But try something different. Be radical, and practice giving what you would like to get in return.

Develop Patience

We're in this for the long haul. Be reassured, it's worth your time and effort. We know the promise of success that awaits because we have seen, in action, the emotionally resilient among us.

We can learn much from the survivors who have surrendered to their grief, allowed it to purify and refine them as it raged its way through their broken heart, pulling fiercely at each tender memory, clawing at the mind to open again the tender, raw wounds of loss. Especially when experiencing grief, emotional work is a slow, non-linear process that eventually brings us to the bright border of resilience, where we can experience the peace that comes from conquering strong and painful emotions. We feel a profound sense of empowerment when we've walked side by side with grief, long enough to see it lose its strength and influence over us—when we've felt it blown away like a wisp of cloud by a gentle breeze of kindness or tenderness. This is true for any strong, tenacious emotion.

Let's be patient with ourselves. Patience is the antidote to anger. When you're angry and trying to remove that obstacle from your path, you want to get to your goal right now. Now!

What if you were to come into current time with yourself, breathe, and take perspective? Whether it be anger or grief or any other strong emotion, what does a little time and space do for that emotion? Is patience also the antidote to fear, to sadness, to anxiety, or to bitterness? Again, there are no right answers. These are questions for you to ask as you're working your process of personal inquiry and exploration.

Play with the idea of giving things more time. And then see for yourself how that works out. If you tend toward skepticism and need a little reinforcement before deciding to clothe yourself in the armor of patience, find someone in your life who is patient and observe them. Watch how they behave. Interview them if you need to, and find out how they really do it. We can learn best from those who do it best.

Traffic: A Practice Field for Patience

If you really want to develop patience, traffic is a wonderful practice field. As we know all too well, it's filled with opportunities. Why? Being inside our four-wheeled bubble prevents us from experiencing the emotions and intentions of others on a personal level. There is little social risk. We're separated, insulated—unless we happen to have an accident. We behave in ways we would never dare to, were we in a similar situation in a grocery store. We project intentions onto other drivers—nearly all of them bad. (When was the last time you thought, "That was a beautifully executed lane change! How thoughtful she is!"?)

How do *you* behave in traffic? In the United States, unless we're in large cities, most of us don't honk, knowing that it rarely does any good and can actually add to stress and upset. But how many of us drive faster than the speed limit? How many of us don't let someone merge because we think they're being pushy? How many of us call other drivers idiots, nitwits, or other colorful and anatomical nouns? How many of us text while driving, putting other drivers at risk and causing them to swear and swerve?

When we observe our own behavior in traffic, we can develop a very clear sense of self-awareness. We can watch ourselves and observe our intention (maybe previously hidden from our awareness). Maybe you're locked on to the idea of not letting that Prius pass you: *I have to be first in line!* Or maybe you're losing patience with the slow-poke driver of that old beater: "Get going, for hellsakes!" You probably believe, *I have somewhere important to be, and you obviously don't!*

Traffic offers us the ultimate simplification, the same script over and over: *you're wrong, I'm right.* And our physical distance encourages us in this illusion. It's almost as if traffic is recess from self-management, when we let our id run free, and abandon any shred of emotional resilience.

Observing ourselves with full cognizance and recognition that we sometimes behave as less than our best self can be a rude awakening. And it can also be a time for rejoicing. As we come to see our actual, demonstrated behavior we are provided with a beautiful opportunity for authentic self-awareness and ownership. Once we *own* it, we empower ourselves to *change* it.

But how often does your self-awareness leap the gap into self-management? Can you catch yourself speeding up to pass some annoying, super-slow car that is totally in your way, pause, then consider another, safer option—and take that option?

Here's how one of these traffic moments might look, broken down, for an emotionally-resilient driver:

- You're heading to work, running the anxious "I'm late" script.

- You call the office to let your assistant know you're running late for the operations meeting, when you suddenly realize that you're going 40 in a 25 mph zone.
- You slow down, come into current time with yourself and take a deep breath.
- You take perspective, observing the homes that line the residential street and noticing some kid's toys in a driveway. You recognize that the needs of others (for safety, in this case) are as important as your own.
- You practice self-responsibility and admit that you did not allow yourself enough time for this drive. And you slow down to 25 mph.
- You decide that you will leave for work ten minutes earlier in the future. You move into a place where you put others' needs first.
- And finally, you pat yourself on the back, giving yourself a big dopamine hit to lay down a neural network of new, positive, considerate behavior.

There are so many wonderful ways to practice your patience in traffic, whether automobile, pedestrian, bus, subway, or air. Start to notice yourself. Take ownership. Then make those subtle changes that will produce dependable and reliable patience.

Art Class: Avoiding the Danger Zones

"We can choose to grow thought pain and suffering.
Or we can choose to grow through joy."
~ Shepherd Hoodwin

This entire chapter is a collection of exercises and practices. You might not be ready for another one. So let's take a moment to identify potential danger zones, where you're more likely to lose yourself and slide into an unfortunate emotional episode.

Lack of sleep

For many, lack of sleep is right at the top of our Danger Zone list. When we are tired, we lose our patience; we have no idea where we set it down. We don't have much mental processing space to consider the needs of others. And our fuse gets short so even a tiny spark might set us off.

Emotional resilience is extremely challenging without adequate sleep. Most working adults need around eight hours a night. (You may have different sleep requirements.) Most of us know this, and many of us know how delicious it feels to wake up fully rested—after a good, long, eight-hour sleep.

Take the time to get to know your optimal number of sleep hours. Find out this way: set your alarm clock for the same time every morning for ten days (weekend included). Whatever time you go to bed, make note of that. After ten days your body should create a pattern of knowing when to wake automatically. On the days you wake up just prior to the alarm, check how many hours of sleep you got. That's probably what your body regularly needs.

Another good way to improve your quality of sleep is to take all electronics out of your bedroom—no TV, no e-reader, no pad, no phone. The blue light disrupts your sleep patterns, wreaking havoc on your melatonin production.[53,54] When melatonin production is low, we are more alert and active, which yields a miserable, restless night.

Treat yourself kindly by getting enough and quality sleep. You'll thank yourself. And so will others!

Hunger

Another easily recognizable Danger Zone is hunger. Most of us are familiar with the recently popular term, *hangry*. Hanger is real! We get cranky when we're hungry. Our brains don't function as effectively. We say things we don't mean to say, or wouldn't say if we had enough fuel to supply the pre-frontal regions of the brain.

When you consume healthy food on a regular schedule, you will maintain the correct blood sugar balance to provide a physical foundation for emotional resilience. Some individuals are more susceptible to blood-sugar swings, so if you're one of them, part of being self-responsible is making sure that you're not ignoring your body's messages about hunger.

A great deal of information exists about what nutrients the brain needs to properly function. Recent literature[55,56] helps us understand that the health of the brain affects the health of the entire body. Surprisingly, it is relatively easy to feed the brain. Prioritizing the health and nutritional needs of the brain allows all other systems of the body to fall in line for optimal functioning as well, since they are each directly influenced by the brain.

Feed your brain the nutrients that it needs and you will be feeding your IQ, your EQ (emotional intelligence quotient), and your HQ (your happiness quotient).[57] You know how it feels to be satisfied after a really nice meal. Your brain experiences that satisfaction too, and shares the contentment with your entire nervous system. A satisfied brain ensures a balanced and calm, cool, collected self.

Too Busy

It's easy to get lost in the geography of Too Busy. Our culture perpetuates the idea that we must have every moment occupied, every day calendared to its fullest, and every month stuffed with deliverables, chores, activities, and play dates. The lost Art of Doing Nothing will help us recover from being too busy. Although it may sound like an easy practice—after all there's nothing for you to do—it can take a while for a brain habituated to always having something to think about, plan, organize, solve, or resolve. And it can take some getting used to.

You will most likely go through a process called the "worsening stage." What happens here can sometimes lead you to believe there's something wrong with you. When I teach mindfulness and meditation classes, this is often one of the big concerns—the mind can't slow down and it's a dreadful mess in there. That's probably right. Minds and brains stuck in the habit of *go-go-go* are like a loaded, three-trailer Mack truck on a 6 percent down-hill grade with hot brakes. They're hard to stop.

When I was about eight years old, I was in the pickup truck pulling a trailer full of horses with Cowboy Joe, coming over Donner Summit in the Sierras. We were headed East, down one of the steep slopes of one of the prettiest mountain ranges in the country. We passed a sign that read "Runaway Truck Lane". Off to the right side of the main travel lane was a gravel road with a long, gentle uphill slope.

Not quite understanding the difference between a "runaway" truck and a "get-away" truck, I said, "I would never take that gravel road."

I received the most perplexed look and a slight harrumph from Cowboy Joe. He turned his eyes back to the road. A few minutes later, he asked "Why not?"

"Well," reasoned my eight-year-old self, "If I was trying to get away from the cops, I sure wouldn't want to get stuck in that gravel."

Cowboy Joe isn't one to laugh easily, but his hearty guffaw made me feel a little embarrassed. He explained to me what a runaway truck lane was for. I had to acquiesce to the sensibleness of that.

Maybe you need your own runaway mind lane? A little help slowing down can go a long way when it comes to settling an over-worked mind.

The Art of Doing Nothing—The Antidote to Too Busy

To master the Art of Doing Nothing, find a quiet place where no one, and nothing (phone, computer, pets, kids, sweetheart, any other human on the planet) will bother you. Maybe your local spa is an excellent place—the massage table in the darkened, perfectly-temperature cocoon-like room is akin to heaven. Others might recharge their batteries in the solitude of nature—a mountain lake or stream, a hiking trail through a rocky outcrop, or simply the beauty of your own backyard lounger. During inclement weather, it may just be your favorite couch, with a view of the falling rain or snow.

- To ensure that you create the magic of settling into the great expanse of *nothing,* "where time asks nothing of you,"[58] put that place *on your calendar.* Block out at least thirty minutes. Leave your electronic devices in the car, or on the kitchen counter.
- Immerse yourself in current time, whether on the massage table, the anti-gravity lounger, the solidity of the Earth, or your couch. Close your eyes. Find your breath. Take three really deep breaths with long, slow exhales.
- Soften inside the mouth, between the teeth. Let there be a little cushion of air between the top teeth and the bottom. Just as Dr. Ekman found that by making the facial signature and the body posture of an emotion we can trigger the brain and nervous system into creating the neurochemistry of that emotion, we can send a physiological signal to our brain to be quiet. As we soften the mouth, and let the bottom jaw release in relaxation, we are sending a powerful message to the mind that it too, can be quiet.
- Of course, the mind is not a push-over. It "abhors a vacuum," as is taught in the Mahayana Buddhist meditation world. The mind doesn't like to do nothing—its survival purpose is to keep you alert and focused on potential threats, real or perceived. So you'll have to gently coax your mind into quiet submission.
- Inhale slowly and steadily through the nose, and even more slowly exhale through the mouth, lightly blowing with very soft lips and no audible sound. Keep at this pattern of breathing until you come to or wake up, wondering where you are. (Doing Nothing is a very soothing tonic for the nervous system, allowing you to move far away from flight-or-flight, right into the cradling arms of rest-and-rejuvenate. It offers a deep biological renewal to all systems.)
- As your delicious half-hour of blissful Nothing comes to its close, please return slowly to your physical, tactile, tangible world. Take

a deep breath and stretch. Wiggle fingers and toes. Roll wrists and ankles, arms and legs side to side. Feel your bones. Feel the temperature of the air on your skin. As you use the breath to come back into current time in your body, thank yourself for practicing this long, lost art. Thank yourself for making the time to take care of yourself. And then "smile on the inside," as they say in the Daoist tradition.

The Inner Smile

A smile on the inside is a simple but profound way to show friendliness to yourself. Being a good friend to yourself nurtures you in myriad ways. Of all of the practices outlined here in this chapter, smiling on the inside is the cherry on top. It makes everything easier, more fun, and more enjoyable. It also makes everything more effective. It's a great positivity booster that can encourage you to stay motivated on your path of living with a beautiful awareness of being.

The Inner Smile can be your little secret. The world doesn't need to know about it, but others will feel it emanate from you. It creates a child-like joy for living life to the fullest. It's also a quick way to connect to Inner Wisdom. Joy and wisdom hold hands on the path of the good life. Let them take you by the hand, too. As you fall into step with them, your practices will be filled with more and more delight and ease.

All of these practices and exercises are useful and beneficial. They work. They serve to develop, cultivate, and produce emotional resilience. They support a happier, more carefree and effortless way of being. But ultimately, you will be drawn to the one or two that will make your own goodness, beauty, and unique genius most known—to yourself and to the world.

Once again, let's remember that *you can't do it wrong*. By this point on your journey to emotional resilience your Inner Wisdom has now become a cherished friend and as you listen, you will know which practices will be the right fit for you.

CHAPTER 9

Flip the Script

We're going to have a little fun in this chapter. The topics and material we're covering in this book are serious, and a bit heavy at times. As we approach the end of this book, let's take a slightly different approach and lighten up.

I will present two "plays," dramatic scripts, of two distinct emotional events. The main character will be the same in both: You. Please imagine yourself in this role, making mental adjustments that resonate with you and your role in your organization or work, as well as yourself at home.

A little disclaimer: I'm not a playwright! Traditional script formatting has been streamlined here to make it easier to read.

As you read through the scripts, you will find stage directions, parentheticals, and dialogue. Your Internal Narrator, or thinking mind/inner critic, is a cast member; so is the voice of Inner Wisdom. You'll find the title and subtitle centered on the page. They will be followed by a Director's Note, the Cast of Characters, and finally the script.

Calm, Cool, and Collected

We tend to presume that others think like we do. This is especially true in our organizations, and in a work environment. We all know the company goals. We're all (supposedly) working toward the same end, and on the same page. So it can be easy to forget, especially for leaders, that we all bring our own personal narrative and perspectives to every situation.

Let's look at YOU, as the Boss, who has the capacity to operate from a knowing that "every mind is a universe," as they say in Spain. You are able to hold many perspectives at once, to remember the details of the lives of your employees and team members, and to stand in another's shoes without losing track of your own truths, values, and presence.

A PARAGON OF EQUANIMITY
A Dramatic Performance to Illustrate
Emotional Balance and Resilience

Director's Note: *This script is written for you. Please imagine yourself playing the role of YOU, the Boss, in a leadership role. Imagine your team in your organization as the OTHERS in this portrayal. And please imagine yourself in a situation that matches your personal reality. Here's your chance to act "as if"...remember that in positive psychology we have a very good chance of actual success if we "fake it 'til we make it."*

Cast of Characters

YOU: The Boss at your Organization, an Emotional Resilience Pro at work, a Novice at home

INTERNAL NARRATOR: Your loquacious, critical, reactionary inner voice, who largely operates on auto-pilot

INNER WISDOM: The kind Voice of Reason who provides internal guidance and direction, helping you self-manage your way toward a life of thriving and flourishing

JILL: The head of the HR department, generally a focused and dedicated team player, but hot-headed and strong-willed

ACT 1

Scene 1

SETTING: A stuffy, windowless conference room. At the long oval table are nine of the most cranky and cantankerous leaders (OTHERS) in your organization, most of them pinched and sour, radiating a deep loathing for anyone who suggests the slightest hint that things can be done differently. JILL is at their helm, providing strict guidance and direction on a big organizational shift happening in order to increase workplace well-being and overall productivity. Jill's department is also in charge of the personal growth program for several team leaders.

A few weeks ago, YOU presented to the whole company an overview of the importance of skillful communication and harmonious working relationships. The focus was on how these impact not only employee production, but leadership well-being and effectiveness. YOU were excited to share this information and eager to see the positive outcomes you were sure would result. Apparently, not everyone enjoyed the experience as much as you did. A little clarification is needed, and team leaders will benefit from re-evaluating perspectives in this session. YOU feel like it is a much-needed and timely workshop.

Conversation among the OTHERS is heating up as tension flares.

INTERNAL NARRATOR: *(a little uneasy, sensing the increasing agitation around the table. Noticing the facial signatures of annoyance and insolence on several of these leaders—pursed lips; eyes narrowed—their resemblance to small, vicious animals ready to ferociously attack and protect their dens and their pack is striking. As the dialogue around the table continues, words become even sharper, more pointed, and more injurious.)* Why are these people in positions of leadership? Surely, these are not the faces of people who instill confidence, or a desire to work hard, let alone collaborate.

INNER WISDOM: Okay, not off to a great start. Let's break out those emotional resilience tools!

YOU come into current time, and take several deep breaths.

INNER WISDOM: That feels a little better. Time to focus on your Why: you are an exceptional leader and you want to help this organization thrive. And let's also focus on the positive: this team is highly skilled. They can do this.

JILL: *(whips her head around in your direction, narrowing her beady eyes at you, rancor hanging heavily on every word.)* Who are *you* and why do you think *you* can tell us what our goal is? Do our perspectives, does our experience not count for anything around this table? What lofty solutions do *you* have to present?

YOU recoil in shock from Jill's nasty tone. You stare in disbelief at your dedicated HR leader, the person in charge of well-being and communication.

INTERNAL NARRATOR: What the heck did I do to deserve that attack? Man, this team has a mean and stingy leader. Jill is driven by competition and scarcity. She just can't allow that others might know as much, or more, or different things than she does.

INNER WISDOM: *(Taking perspective)* Wow, maybe this is just an off day in the HR department. It's a beautiful spring day outside and everyone is stuck in a cramped office under these buzzing, ghastly fluorescent lights. It was such a long winter and we're all missing out on the warm sunshine and radiant blue skies. I wonder if that's the reason everyone seems defensive and hostile. I wonder what came over Jill? She hasn't always been this way.

YOU: May I have your attention please? I'd like for us to refocus our energy on the end goal we all share, as integral members of this organization.

JILL stares daggers at you.

INNER WISDOM: *(with gentle compassion)* Ohhhhh, yes. Jill's mom died a month ago. She's still deep in the grieving process. Grief can so easily slide into anger—anger at losing someone with no chance of ever getting them back. She's probably trying to keep her mind busy so she doesn't get swallowed by the anguish. She feels like she needs to stay busy, needs to be at work, and keep her mind focused on other things. It's not easy to confront such deep loss. Why don't you make it a point to check in with her one-on-one at the end of the day?

YOU: *(in a whisper to Inner Wisdom)* I will. Thank you.

YOU experience feelings of gratitude toward yourself for having applied the practices and demonstrated self-control and perspective-taking in a moment of potential catastrophe. Cue the dopamine hit!

INTERNAL NARRATOR: *(in wide-eyed admiration)* Good idea Inner Wisdom! I wish I would have thought of that.

INNER WISDOM: *(kindly to Internal Narrator)* Well nice observation! You're learning. That's good. Do you see that when you quiet down, you can assess the situation rather than criticize or judge? It's in this suspension of judgment that you can imagine the possible reality of another. That imagining is the seed of perspective taking. You're becoming quite an attentive student.

JILL continues her tirade. The heaviness in the room is oppressive. You feel yourself weary and on the cusp of losing your patience.

INTERNAL NARRATOR: *(to YOU, feeling very defensive and protective)* This is over the top! Jill is out of control. Are you going to just sit there and take this? No one is going to respect you after this.

INNER WISDOM: Breathe! Come into current time. I know this feels like a lot, but you're OK. You're always OK in current time, remember?

YOU: *(Sensing your equilibrium fraying, but realizing that no one is coming and that the success of this meeting depends on you and your own emotional self-management)* Why don't we all take a ten minute bio-break? Please everyone, let's go outside and get a couple of breaths of fresh air. The tension is a bit thick, and we have much yet to accomplish. We are all skilled and knowledgeable. Let's put our combined talents and strengths to work and create something we'll all be proud of. See you all back here in ten minutes.

INNER WISDOM: Great idea! Way to take the reins of your leadership authority and regain control of the situation.

ACT 1

Scene 2

SETTING: The garden behind your office building. A sidewalk meanders through the park-like setting. The early spring blue of the skies overhead and the fresh new growth on the trees reminds you that all nature renews itself in a cyclical rhythm. You wonder if Jill has the ability to find a sense of hope in the constancy of nature. You meander down the path, enjoying the daffodils, the chirps of the birds—just being in current time with nothing else to think about for at least three minutes is a tonic for your soul.

INNER WISDOM: (*stretching into the space around you, feeling expansive and refreshed*) Oh, this feels good. This is a great chance to gather your knowledge and your courage.

YOU: (*addressing Inner Wisdom*) Meh, but I have to go back in there. I'm not looking forward to it.

INTERNAL NARRATOR: (*addressing YOU*) Yeah, you saw that demon—she was shooting the flames of hell at you from the other end of the table!

INNER WISDOM: This is the perfect time to make a choice about how you're going to play this. You have a little time and distance now to exercise your creative thinking.

YOU: (*resolutely*) You know what? I'm going to keep a cool head. I am the boss, and I have to guide this team into an organized consensus about our action plan. We have a lot of work to do.

YOU spot JILL leaning up against a tree ahead of you.

INNER WISDOM: Perfect! Here's a chance to practice seeing Jill through the lens of compassion and Equanimity. Check out her posture—see those slumped shoulders, her caved-in chest, protecting her broken heart? And oh, her expression. She's going through some heavy emotions. She's mourning—really struggling.

YOU: *(in intimate conversation with Inner Wisdom)* I do hope she has someone there for support. The passing of a parent is so difficult. If memory serves, she and her husband have a strong relationship. I hope they do. My heart really goes out to her.

INNER WISDOM: *(with obvious approval)* You should be so proud of yourself! You really are becoming quite the artist of your emotional resilience. I've watched you cultivate your inner awareness to the point where you can sense the warning signs of emotional upset. You're doing remarkably well at coming into current time, breathing, and expanding your awareness to include the perspective of others. Your ability to see others with Equanimity is a testament to your committed practice. Nice job!

YOU: *(humbly proud of your progress)* Well, thanks. It's mostly all a result of learning to be still and listen to you, as you just mentioned to Internal Narrator. Thanks for your patience with me. Thanks for not deserting me when I was still so reactive and hostile. I feel good about myself! OK, let's catch Jill before we need to go back inside.

As you make your way to JILL, she lifts her head and looks right into your eyes. She has surprised herself, and quickly looks away. You draw near enough to speak and kindly inquire as to her well-being.

YOU: *(acting from the depth of love you feel at this moment for all humanity)* Jill, how are holding up?

JILL: *(obviously chagrined, near the verge of tears, looks again right into your eyes. You see her heart break open and the precious jewels of the love she has for her mother shine bright, infusing you with hope and tenderness.)* I'm sorry. I've acted so irresponsibly. *(Tears flood over the edge of her eyes)* I miss my mom so much. I'm so angry that she's gone. It's just not fair. She wasn't even old. She was so alive and so . . . *(Her voice trails off, lost in heartache.)*

INNER WISDOM: *(wisely—even more so than usual)* Does she need a hug? Are you willing to support her in that way?

YOU: *(to Inner Wisdom—with a deep breath and lightning-quick scroll through your role as boss and her role as "subordinate")* Yes. It looks like she does. And yes, I am willing. *(to Jill)* Jill, do you need a hug? Would you be OK with that?

JILL: *(surprised yet grateful)* Oh thank you. I'll be fine. I just needed some fresh air. Should we go back in?

YOU: *(a bit relieved, but still supportive)* Yes, I guess we should. But can I ask you one more question? Jill, do you have support at home? I know that's personal and might be considered none of my business, but I see your suffering. I see your sadness. And it's affecting your working relationships. You have a lot of influence with your team.

INTERNAL NARRATOR: *(Unable to resist)* Use your powers for good, Jill!

YOU: I hope you are not alone in this process.

JILL: *(feeling simultaneously moved by your concern and private)* I do have support. Thank you. I appreciate you asking.

YOU: *(one more thing catches the edge of your mind)* Oh, and Jill? One other thing before I forget. Thank you for being here, for being committed and dedicated. It means a lot. I really appreciate you.

You both fall silent as you walk side-by-side back to the building. You're both swept by a mutual understanding of Jill's situation and realize you have introduced the human element into a situation that could have been very sterile and void of the kindness of a generous heart.

INNER WISDOM: *(who loves to have the last word)* Did you see Jill's relief? It was visible, but very subtle. Her eyes relaxed, her mouth micro-softened. Her demeanor thawed. She was no longer a threatening, angry terror. Were you able to see her as a woman who feels a tremendous amount of pressure to do a good job, to lead her people to success, all while trying to manage the impossibility of devastating grief? Can you see her as a fellow human being who has succumbed to outside pressures, of which there are plenty? She may have forgotten the importance of kind words, and lost her ability to take perspective, but she's good. She's got a good and strong heart. She'll make it through.

ACT 1

Scene 3

SETTING: Interior conference room. Everyone is back in their seats, ready to recommence the meeting. YOU sense a change of energy and a more positive, collaborative mood.

YOU: *(as everyone settles into attention)* That felt good, getting outside. *(You smile sincerely at each person.)* Thank you. I realize this is a charged topic, and I want you to know that I hear your concerns, but I'm confident we are heading in the right direction. You're all very good at what you do.

JILL: *(noticeably different after having taken some time outside. She is relaxed and non-defensive, ready to lead the team in a positive direction)* Thank *you*. These are some new ideas, and there are going to be many challenges, but I think we are up to it.

INNER WISDOM AND INTERNAL NARRATOR *(in unison)*: Good job!

The meeting resumes, with the team thoughtful and engaged.

THE END

The Boss Goes Home

Let's look now at another scenario starring our highly skilled Boss, YOU, who at work demonstrates heroic measures of emotional equilibrium and equanimity. Things are a little different on the home front.

LATE FOR THE PARTY, YET AGAIN
An Unfortunate Emotional Incident in One Act

Director's Note: *Please put yourself in the role of YOU. Imagine your significant other in the role of SWEETIE. You can imagine yourself in a similar situation that matches your personal reality or history.*

Cast of Characters

YOU: The Boss at your Organization, an Emotional Resilience Pro at work, a Novice at home

INTERNAL NARRATOR: Your critical reactionary inner voice, who mostly operates on auto-pilot

INNER WISDOM: The kind Voice of Reason who provides internal guidance and direction, helping you self-manage your way toward a life of thriving and flourishing

SWEETIE: Your Beloved Sweetheart, the person with whom you are spending your life—enjoying it most of the time.

ACT 1

Scene 1

SETTING: Your house, early evening. YOU and SWEETIE are to attend a big party this evening with a group of friends, colleagues, and business associates. You've been looking forward to this for several weeks now. Things have been stressful at work, so you need a night out and are eager to connect on a social level with many of the people you know will be there. You have just the right outfit, one that you know highlights all your best features and makes you feel sexy and powerful.

Imagining that traffic will probably be heavy tonight, YOU want to leave plenty early. You give yourself a nice buffer zone of time to get ready. As you are about halfway through your preparations, you begin to wonder where SWEETIE is.

You go in search of and find SWEETIE lounging comfortably in the backyard, still in grubby clothes from an afternoon spent cleaning the garage. SWEETIE holds a cool refreshing drink in hand, gazing up at the last wisps of sunset coloring the sky, doing nothing.

INTERNAL NARRATOR: *(instantly jumps to reaction-mode)* You've gotta be kidding me. *Nothing*! Sweetie is doing NOTHING and we have less than a half-hour before we leave!

INNER WISDOM: *(gracefully entering stage right)* Uh-oh. This situation looks strikingly similar to the last time you two had a date planned. This doesn't have to end up the way that situation did. You've been really working on your emotional balance. Now is a great time to take a deep breath and then take perspective. You can do this! I've got your back.

Swallowed by the impatience that has already leapt onto the stage, YOU get caught up in the moment, the script of your personal past importing itself into your reasoning mind.

INTERNAL NARRATOR: *(swiftly rushing to drown out the voice of INNER WISDOM)* You should not be late because of Sweetie. In fact, you will *not* be late. You do *not* want to miss out on the opening moments of the party. You do not want to miss important people who never stay out late. Time is ticking. Sweetie is miles away from being ready. You have to speed things up!

YOU: *(as anger kicks in into high gear)* Darned right!

INTERNAL NARRATOR: *(continuing loudly)* Hey! You have a goal! You need to get to the party on time and spend a wonderful and fun evening with your people. There's going to be a sumptuous meal, delicious cocktails, shared jokes, and let's not forget—a couple of carefully planned-out connections with select people you've been waiting for just the right moment to connect with. Don't let Sweetie ruin this evening for you, not even with one tiny hiccup.

YOU: *(refocusing on relaxed, oblivious SWEETIE in the lawn chair)* Seriously?

INTERNAL NARRATOR: *(continuing the rant)* You've been looking forward to this night for weeks. You need the break from all the craziness at work. And you may recall that this has happened numerous times before. So Sweetie's obviously doing it on purpose. How could Sweetie be so inconsiderate?

YOU experience the sensations of fear-mixed-with-fury neurochemicals pouring into your bloodstream. Your amygdala is on fire.

INNER WISDOM: Uh..hello? Are you there? Pick up!

INTERNAL NARRATOR: Oh, puh-lease. Sweetie is asking for it. This is unacceptable!

INNER WISDOM: *(finger to her lips, prancing from foot to foot, anxious about the impending explosion, muscles her way in to center stage, interrupting for a microsecond the onslaught of your automatic pattern)* Shhh. You don't have to do this. You can stop it now.

YOU: *(unable to redirect your attention, ignore INNER WISDOM and let 'er rip, you voice sharp and accusing toward SWEETIE)*: Get up!

SWEETIE: *(nonplussed, jolted to attention, and squeaking innocently)* What?! What's up?

INNER WISDOM: *(beseeching)* You don't have to do this! I haven't given up on you! Try current time!

INTERNAL NARRATOR: *(smug)* YOU can't hear what you're saying, *Inner Wisdom*. YOU is running *my* script right now. Brace yourself for some fireworks, baby! It's about time YOU reads Sweetie the riot act.

YOU: *(nostrils flaring, lips pinching together, brows angling sharply in and down, angry voice in full effect)* **Seriously**? "What's up?"!! Are you kidding? We have a big party to attend tonight. You're lying here doing nothing. You're stinky and dirty and we need to leave this house in less than a half hour. *(with disdain)* You better get ready. I won't wait for you.

YOU turn on your heel and march back into the house. In the heat of anger, you return to the bathroom and your preparations, with your mental afflictions accosting you from every side.

INTERNAL NARRATOR: *(bossy and adamant)* Did you really expect anything different? This is what always happens. Sweetie's always running behind. Sweetie doesn't have a very good grasp of time. Sweetie doesn't really care about others. Someone who is interested in others would sure the hell respect their time and their scheduled events. This is supposed to be a really fun date, for hellsakes!

INNER WISDOM: *(hesitant, but determined to support you on your quest for emotional stability, reminds you of what you have learned and are working on) Always*, you just used the word *always*. Remember that *always* is your red flag, waving you back to current time? Maybe you should pause and take perspective? Now is a good time. You're alone, you can breathe, and you can settle your survival brain, and come back to you senses.

YOU ignore the voice of Inner Wisdom. In your injured and self-righteous state, you're sure that yours is the only valid perspective.

SWEETIE saunters into the bathroom for a shower, slow and easy, seemingly without a care in the world. Glancing at you out of the corner of the eye, your visible frustration feeds Sweetie's desire to needle you.

SWEETIE: I just cleaned out the garage, like you wanted me to. That was quite a "thank you."

INTERNAL NARRATOR: *(seizing the opportunity to fuel your fire and give you more power to prove yourself right)* Oh no, Sweetie did not . . . oh yes. Sweetie *did*. Are you going to stand for that insolence? You don't deserve this crap!

YOU: *(fuming on the lip of rage, no longer yelling, but extremely firm)* We are going to be late! And it's your fault. It's always your fault. Will you hurry? We have less than twenty minutes now. You've known about this party for weeks. What is *wrong* with you?

SWEETIE: *(stepping into the shower)* Calm down. You don't need to be so upset. We'll get there when we get there.

YOU: *(now having completely lost your cool, red in the face, your composure has fled the scene. You are operating on an ancient, reactive pattern that your system imagines will protect you and "save" you from the threat the Sweetie is)* "Calm down!" "Calm DOWN!" How many days ago did I ask you to please pay attention to the time tonight so we wouldn't be late? How many times do we show up late because *you* can't get yourself ready on time? How many times do I have to apologize to the host when we show up late? *Always*! We are *always* late. You cannot get yourself together so we can leave on time. Once. Just *once* it would be such a relief not to have this stupid argument about being on time. You can show up for your work appointments on time. You can show up...

YOU go on and on while Sweetie is humming a sweet little ditty, happily washing the suds down the drain. The water shuts off, the shower door opens.

INNER WISDOM kindly attempts to get your attention.

INNER WISDOM: *(cautious, but resolute)* Hey, Sweetie is done with the shower now. It's going to be OK. You'll have a good time, you'll see the people you want to see. You look amazing! You can pull yourself together, and you'll be fine. OK?

YOU *really want to lean into the soothing words of Inner Wisdom, but your system is still awash in the neuro-stuff of removing the obstacle on the path to your goal. So, you skirt around Inner Wisdom, ignoring the gentle voice of encouragement yet again.*

SWEETIE: *(extending a hand)* Can you hand me a towel please?

YOU: *(thrusting a towel into SWEETIE'S outstretched hand, you hurl another word into the thick, steamy air)* HURRYUP!

ACT 1

Scene 2

SETTING: YOU and SWEETIE are in the car, running twenty minutes late. The silence between the two of you is ragged and unfriendly. Traffic is choked and you still cannot release your need to show up on time. That ship has sailed and its turbulent wake feeds into your anger about not having achieved your goal. The big obstacle to that goal is sitting right over there across the car. You simply cannot let it go.

YOU: *(picking at the scab, your voice crescendos as you lose yourself in frustrated anger)* Why, every single time we go to an event together, *why* are we always late? Why can't we figure that out? Why can't we leave the house on time? Just once! Every single drive to every single event is so horrible. I just want us to have a good time, to enjoy our friends, to relax a little after these long weeks we put in. Why can't you ever be ready on time? Why do we always have this same stupid argument?

SWEETIE: *(in a soothing tone, patiently trying to mollify you)* Look, we're in the car now. We'll be there soon. Take a deep breath. Don't be so angry.

INTERNAL NARRATOR: Ohhhhhh, Sweetie. Duck and cover!

INNER WISDOM, *along with* INTERNAL NARRATOR *both flee the scene, exiting stage left with much pushing and jostling to get out first. Your anger is too much for them and even they are afraid. You're left alone now with no support coming from anywhere.*

YOU: *(exploding)* WHAT?! Don't be so angry? You want to see angry? I'll show you angry!

And then holy hell, you unleash all the anger from every time you've ever been late. On and on you vent, unpacking your list of tardy arrivals, enumerating the many times when you've bit your tongue and said nothing, recounting just how often you have shown patience and benevolence.

INNER WISDOM realizes the destruction you're causing yourself and desperate to stop the carnage, sees one final opportunity to interrupt the chemical cascade of anger rampaging through you, knowing that your sympathetic nervous system has free rein.

INTERNAL NARRATOR: *(venturing a peek)* Uh-oh, we're about two seconds from Sweetie saying, "To hell with it. Let's just go back home."

INNER WISDOM: *(tapping you on your shoulder)* Exhale. Breathe. You need to breathe. You need to take the exit ramp off the anger highway. You need to come back to yourself.

The window on your side goes down, automatically. The sudden burst of air on your face makes you catch your breath, and that startled interruption in your breath pattern interrupts the neuronal fireworks in your limbic system, breaking the spell of your amygdalic madness. You snap back to current time reality. You see the lights out the car window whizzing by. You see that the sky is now dark. You feel the cold air on your skin, your hair moving in the wind.

INNER WISDOM: *(patiently)* There. That's better. Breathe again. Relax a bit and you'll be OK.

YOU deflate, feeling exhausted, insulted, and chagrined.

INTERNAL NARRATOR: *(with wounded pride)* Why is it always you who has bear the brunt of this? Why won't Sweetie take ownership, admitting that it takes two to tango and owning their part in the whole thing? It shouldn't be you who has to apologize. You're always the one doing the apologizing.

SWEETIE: *(aware that you have stopped talking and are now breathing, sounds a little indifferent, a little put out)* We're almost there. Are you OK to go in and have a nice time? Can you compose yourself?

INNER WISDOM: Hang on! You're nearly back on solid ground.

INTERNAL NARRATOR: The *nerve*.

YOU: *(in an aside to INNER WISDOM)* I know. You're right. I need to pull myself together. *(turning to INTERNAL NARRATOR)* I can't exactly show up at the party with a mean, angry look on my face, can I? Everyone will know we've had a fight.

YOU: *(still not looking at SWEETIE, you breathe and tightly spit out)* Yes.

YOU and SWEETIE exit the car. You try to regain as much composure as you can before getting to the front door. You smooth your clothing and wipe the corners of your mouth. Holding hands, stiffly and unnaturally, YOU and SWEETIE approach the door. As you step over the threshold, you're sure everyone can see the tension between the two of you. You smile in that awkward, "Everything will be just fine" way, and, spotting a friend across the room, unlace your fingers from Sweetie's and head in that direction, grabbing a glass of wine from the very convenient tray on your way.

THE END . . . FOR NOW

This little dramatic interpretation of an unfortunate emotional incident may be over the top, for some. For others, it might hit the nail on the head. However you resonate with it, can you relate?

Sometimes, we're so good at consciously and considerately managing ourselves. For many, a regrettable situation like this would never happen at work. The power of other people's impressions and positive peer pressure can be enough for us to mind our manners and demonstrate appropriate behavior. But when we're home, with the people we call family, for some reason, the boundaries dissolve. We can behave in ways that would embarrass us terribly, if made visible to the public eye.

And for some, it's exactly the opposite. We behave well when at home, careful and respectful toward our loved ones. But in the organization or work setting, with other dynamics and scripts at play, it can be a different picture altogether. Perhaps you're comfortable and confident at home, where you feel loved and valued, but insecure and defensive at work, where you feel like you have to constantly prove yourself. Whatever your trained-and-ingrained patterns of behavior with others, you can develop the self-awareness and skills that will enable you to be on your best behavior all the time, regardless of setting and characters.

Breaking the thread of the emotional explosion is a wonderful way to come back to yourself, to get a hold of yourself, and to bring your primary attention to the fact that you have a choice—when you are calm and focused. In the throes of a runaway emotion, you actually don't have the power to choose. Your amygdala is choosing for you, running extreme self-preservation scripts when they are not necessary. And so you behave in ways that are less than desirable.

We must also remind ourselves that in a moment of amygdalic madness, we may say something catastrophic that we can never take back. We must train ourselves and learn to get a hold of ourselves and remember that (if absolutely necessary) we can always say it later. If we must. Usually, by the time we have come to our senses, we realize how grateful we are that we didn't actually say, in a moment of intense and overwhelming emotion, something that might have ruined a relationship forever.

The Saving Grace of the Sensory Check-In

Drawing your awareness back to the physical sensations of the body is a powerful way to snap the chemical chain of events, the onslaught of neurotransmitters and neuromodulators. The blast of fresh air as the car window went down was enough to bring our main character back to current time, out of the grip of the reactive habit.

Moving yourself into what I call a "5+1 = Right Now Awareness Check-in"[59] is a technique that can prove useful. The 5+1 Check-in involves using your physical senses to quiet the emotional storm. You'll have to be in current time in order to move through the inputs of your five senses. So you'll need to have frequently practiced coming into current time with yourself as your habit when you feel the first stirrings of emotional upset. (By this time, you're probably a near-master at bringing yourself into the current moment!)

Let's try it here.

- **Come into current time with yourself.**
- **Focus on what you see in front of you.** Single out one object. What is it? Look at the color. Note the texture. How far away is this object? What variations of color or texture do you notice?
- **Next, listen to the sounds around you.** What do you hear? Can you identify the source of the sound? Is it coming from something near? Or far? Focus on that sound for a few moments.
- **And now, come into awareness of the tactile sensations you can feel.** What is the temperature of the air on your skin? Can you feel the solidity of the floor under your feet? What other sensations can you feel in your body?
- **Now move the awareness to the sense of smell.** (Sometimes we smell more effectively when the eyes are closed. If that seems like a good idea, please close your eyes.) What aromas or odors can you detect? What do you smell? Does the smell remind you of anything?
- **What, if anything, do you taste?** Would a drink of water be refreshing?

As you feel yourself fully present in your physical body, aware of virtually all sensory input, something else has happened: your mind and brain have let go of the strong emotion. Your nervous system has moved out of fight-or-flight and you are settling into a more balanced state.

In our play, Sweetie, knowing that the power of a strong, negative emotion completely overwhelms the rational thinking mind, was able to skillfully employ a version of this technique to interrupt the power supply to your anger—lowering the car window and introducing the sensory input of the wind and cool air. It was just enough to confuse the nervous system of YOU, during the meltdown, providing that necessary opening to begin restoring equilibrium.

While it may not erase the upset completely, the 5+1 Check-in can provide the crucial "runaway truck ramp" as an unfortunate emotional incident hurtles downhill. It can circumvent further damage. And while a runaway truck ramp does stop the truck, this doesn't mean the truck is able to immediately return to the highway. Repairs may be required, and some effort made, to get it back on the road. So too with an unfortunate emotional incident.

You can use the 5+1 Check-in technique at any time and in any location to get a hold of yourself. You can teach it to your significant others, and to your children. It is a beneficial tool for people of all ages. It is especially useful in your efforts to become the artist of your emotional resilience.

Coming Back to Yourself

As YOU went your separate way from SWEETIE after you arrived at the party, your attention shifted radically. You transitioned from the argument at home that continued in the car to the excitement of the party. While at the party, you were not thinking about the past, how the argument could have been different, what you *could* have said, or what Sweetie did or didn't do or say. You were not imagining the future, wondering what the ride home would be like, or who would break the ice and apologize first. You were there at the party, *in* the party, your attention focused on your friends, on the other guests, on the food, on the atmosphere. On having fun.

Enjoying yourself with your people, you were back in yourself, confident and relaxed—displaying your unique genius. Ruminating about the past and fantasizing about the future were as far away from your reality as could be. Being present allowed you to create space between yourself and the emotional incident, as well as the emotions themselves. This distance, and the silence of negative emotions, allowed your brain to process the event, filtering out things that didn't serve a useful purpose and filing away those things that did, or would in the future.

This event, and the processing of it, is a useful example of how we create the quality of our mind, as we discussed in Chapter 6. When we experience episodes of powerful and destructive anger, our mind is flavored with that anger. It places a unique filter over the lens of the subjective apparatus that creates the image of our reality. If anger is our habit, we probably have a filter over our lens that makes us see more possibilities to be angry. Rather than looking through a clear filter and seeing things with a neutral mind, we layer over our reality a haze of distortion.

Coming into current time and centering yourself in the breath allows you to peel off that filter. When the filter and the distortion are removed, you can take perspective, seeing things more clearly, more accurately. And when you are able to move into the *possibilities* of the situation, you are no longer clinging to what you've determined the objective reality must be.

There is no objective reality. We all bring our own personal narrative, which colors each and every experience, situation, and circumstance of life. We simply have to be willing to be wrong once in a while.

And because being right equals winning and winning equals survival, we must override our survival instincts and allow ourselves to be wrong. We must re-train ourselves to think of "winning" as *understanding* a person with whom you may be in conflict, rather than *prevailing* over them.

Be sure to give yourself lots of positive reinforcement and an inner standing ovation when you succeed in doing this, to help lay down that new script!

Another Opportunity for Growth

My best friend and I had an argument last night. I had gotten an email notification about a post on Twitter and I was interested to see the whole post. Even though I do have an account, I don't tweet, so I'm pretty unfamiliar with how it works. Eventually, I found what I was looking for, but by that time I was tired of the screen and searching. What I had found was interesting enough so I decided to show Steve.

I handed him my phone, he tapped the screen, and the image went away. He tried to get that image back, so his attention was focused there. Meanwhile, I was yacking away about what the image was and how it related to this and that and the other thing. Lost in concentration, he didn't hear me, and asked, "What am I supposed to see?"

So a senseless argument ensued and then escalated—over something utterly stupid and unnecessary. I was already frustrated. He was trying to focus on one task and didn't hear me, so I felt that he wasn't listening to me and told him so. He responded by telling me to stop being mean. I got very offended, because he's always telling me how mean I am.

There it was—the red flag a-wavin'. *Always.*

I had gotten to the point in the argument where I was using a word known as a "universal quantifier." These are linguistic generalizations: the offending person *always* says this or *always* does that, or they *never* do this or they *never* do that. I was in very dangerous territory.

At this point, steeped in my universal generalization, I was now creating a reality that did not exist. Yes, we do weird things, bizarre things, when we're upset. We create things that aren't real—and we believe them! Then we hand-pick every possible data point to justify our argument, to gain advantage, to be right.

My inner awareness split itself in two and the wise part, Ms. Inner Wisdom, stood off in the corner of my mind and observed; *You're over the line, Moll.*

You know that he doesn't always say that. It's time to reel it in. Take a deep breath. Stop it.

My learning, my practice, my study, and my meditations had built a friend in my mind who reminded me of what I know and what I needed to do. Becoming aware of my inner friend who knows so much, who has so very many tools at her disposal, embarrassed me. I felt stupid and ignorant, knowing all that I know but still not being able to stop this ridiculous argument. I couldn't admit that I was going overboard. I couldn't just take a deep breath and stop it, not then, not in that heated moment.

The survival part of my brain had kicked into high gear, my self-preserving biological functions ratcheting up my false argument and pressing my point, not being able to take perspective on his point of view. I was not willing to die! (Remember, in the survival brain, if we're wrong, we end up dead. So we really dig in and become relentless.) I was certainly in the relentless stage. My tone *was* mean and my words sharp. Looking at him across the footstool, I saw not my best friend, my beloved husband, but an opponent. I saw someone against whom I had to defend myself and prove myself right—or else I was a goner.

My voice increased in volume, my perspective narrowed, I closed out his words in my efforts to prove my case as legitimate. I reminded him of the *always* and the *never* moments of our interactions. I made my case with mighty self-righteousness.

Ms. Inner Wisdom was leaning back against the guardrail at the dizzying drop-off of "Too Far." Arms crossed on her chest, left ankle crossed over right, slighting shaking her pretty head, she muttered, "Tsk, tsk." I finally took notice of her, saw how very close she was to the edge of Too Far, and I realized where I was.

My perspective panned out. I saw over the left shoulder of the armchair where he was sitting that my philodendron had several dried and curled leaves that needed to be picked and thrown out. The flowers on the counter across the room lined up perfectly over his head and appeared to be a crown, making him appear slightly comical. The lighting on the painting just beyond the flowers was too dim—I should have turned up the switch a bit.

My mind was working a little magic by bringing me back into my physical senses with a 5 + 1 check-in. I came back into the reality of where I was. I looked across the room toward where the front door stood open, allowing the chilly spring breeze to refresh the room, bringing with it the sound of frogs in the neighbor's pond and crickets on the front lawn, the heavenly fragrance of the blossoming lilacs. I noticed the beautiful purple tulips spilling over the edge of the vase on the table where we had just finished a wonderful dinner together.

I came back into current time, back into my life in a beautiful home with a very good man.

And then I exhaled.

I huffed an "I'm sorry," stood up and said, "OK, I'll stop. I'm done," and marched across the room to plug in my phone. I stomped back across the room to go brush my teeth and get in bed. My bewildered husband sat and watched me, a look of sadness on his face.

As I brushed my teeth, scrubbing really hard, taking out my anger on my dental plaque, I thought about who this person was, the man in the chair across from me. I thought about the voice of Inner Wisdom, who appears almost as a persona in my thoughts, and I considered why I got so irrationally upset over something that absolutely did not matter.

The knowledge I had gained in all the coursework I'd done—about emotional balance and intelligence, positive psychology, spiritual and philosophical wisdom traditions—was vying for center stage in my mind. I finished brushing, spat in the sink, and then spat again, to get rid of the meanness left over from my harsh words. I turned on the faucet, rinsed my mouth, and washed that meanness down the drain, clearing my mind of my stubborn survival reaction. I watched the water clean the sink and then run clear for several minutes. (Moving water has an especially soothing effect on the human mind and emotions.)

My mind was now much clearer. I looked up into the mirror, afraid of what I might see. I saw that my forehead was sunburnt. I thought, *I need to take better care of myself.*

Which is just what you're doing now, for your emotional and relationship life, observed Ms. Inner Wisdom. Sadness stained my eyes, and a few tatters of spent anger hung limp from the edges of that sadness. Mostly what I saw was a deep resolution to mend the situation with Steve.

I turned off the water, wiped my mouth, and dried my hands. I shook my head at my reflection in the mirror, wishing I had just kept my mouth shut. But wishing would get me nowhere. I stood up straight, firmly grounding myself into both feet, squared my shoulders, lifted my heart, gathered my courage, and reminded myself that he was not my enemy but my best friend. I was afraid to go talk to him. Then I remembered that courage is being afraid and doing what needs to be done anyway.

It's embarrassing and arduous to own your unfortunate emotional incidents. It's especially humiliating when you're in the middle of writing the book about it!

But it is essential if we're ever going to make any progress at all in this game.

Out I went to the footstool. I sat down knee-to-knee with him and apologized, from the very core of my heart. "I'm sorry for what I said. But what you said was pretty ridiculous."

Ms. Inner Wisdom whispered, "Molly! Take ownership. Stop trying to justify. There is no room for justification. It will be easier if you just own up."

So I started again. "I really am sorry. There is no excuse for me to speak to you that way."

And then we talked. We covered a little ground, and then he asked, "Why do you get so angry?" Suddenly, something that had been just at the edges of my awareness, lightly tugging at the sleeve of my mind, stepped right out from behind the curtain. In a flood of tears, I told him why. I could actually *see* and understand why. My heart broke open, releasing the pain of a long-ago incident that had deeply hurt a tender place of my little-girl heart.

"You're safe here. You don't have to be right all the time. It's OK to *not* know," he soothed. "You now have permission to make mistakes. Not that you need *my* permission, but just permission. It's OK to be wrong. That doesn't mean there's anything wrong with you." He paused and repeated carefully, "There is nothing wrong with you."

You see why I love this man so very much? My heart sighed as it let go of the thorn that had been lodged inside it for over forty years. The permission Steve granted found its way deep, deep into my awareness. This conscious thought released an unconscious pattern, one that had been smashed down and repressed for decades. It had festered and grown over time, creating an emotional pustule that would periodically burst in anger.

Our conversation was a healing balm. I did not let the sun go down on my anger. We did not let that ugly situation sit between us, causing us to ruminate and brood, creating more of a big ugly that would inevitably come to a head later. We sorted it out and went to bed as best friends.

Every time we end up in a place of challenge or struggle, we have a wonderful opportunity to grow. We can take a look inside and see who we are *now*, for we are never the same person we were during our last struggle. Each new and successive challenge meets us where we are right now in current time, with the strengths and the knowledge, and hopefully the wisdom, we have gained from previous trials.

If it weren't for the dark and demanding and sometimes embarrassing experiences we have, we would not grow. We would not acquaint ourselves with the depth of our inner knowing, our fortitude, and our courage. Through the uglies of life, we gain our unique genius. We uncover our potential. We realize the power of the exhortation carved into the Temple of the Oracle at Delphi: *Know thyself.*

If we pay attention. *If* we do something positive about the emotional storms that have so much potential to end up as unfortunate emotional incidents.

Thankfully, in this incident with Steve, I did have enough presence of mind to pay attention, to listen to Ms. Inner Wisdom, and to use my past experiences for present-time growth. It was painful. But I felt, afterward, that I made huge progress.

If You Can, You Must

Such an outcome doesn't always happen for us. For many, we must continually work toward understanding and positive resolution.

So, in those instances when we can apologize, when we can have a considerate conversation, when we can take perspective, we must.

"If you can, you must," says my favorite yoga teacher.

The important part is taking ownership of your emotional reactions. It might be the hardest thing you will ever do. It hurts. It may be completely embarrassing and humiliating. Being truly vulnerable is scary. You have no idea how the other person is going to respond. You will be treading on thin ice, which can easily break, sending you into the frigid depths of who-knows-what tangled emotional web. You can only hope for the best, sending up a prayer that the other person will be responsive, and that you will be able to sort things out in a kind and mature way.

So in you go, to do your best. You may not get the outcome you wish for. Things may not go smoothly. If and when the other person reacts, you may feel confused and uncertain. That's OK. Keep your resolve to be kind and compassionate as you speak your truth. Stay level-headed and focused on just *this* situation. Resist the urge to play lawyer and bring up your list of past wrongs and offenses. Know when it might be time to excuse yourself and resume at a later time. But while you're in it, do your very best.

Even if we try and fail we can usually trust that we have not worsened the situation. Your effort and your intention may not bear immediate fruit. But the law of reciprocity tells us that it *will* bear fruit. But maybe not in the way or on the timeline that we expect.

The Receiving End

When you end up on the other side of the table and someone else is doing their best to remedy an ugly episode, or make an apology, please make it easy for them! Recognize and honor the risk that they are taking. Expand your perspective, soften your heart, open your listening ears and close your judging mouth. Converse kindly, allowing a back-and-forth that isn't determined to make one person the winner and the other the loser.

Key to this, as with any practice here, is coming into current time and breathing as you enter this interaction. Take it slow. Anger is fast-moving, but rebuilding trust is deliberate and slow. Trust that there is ample time to digest their words and thoughtfully respond.

Perhaps the person has begun the conversation in a setting that's not optimal. Gently suggesting a better venue is OK. "Can we sit down for a moment?" Or perhaps a walk-and-talk is best.

Don't be a pushover, allowing them to weasel out of their bad behavior. If necessary, be sweetly confident in reminding them that some behaviors are not OK. That person has just taken a *huge* step by owning up to their contribution to the argument, so they are in a place to recognize and take responsibility, but don't rub their nose in it. When you know they get it and understand your perspective, back off.

Easeful, peaceful, useful, as Swami Satchidananda was fond of saying. As you create a safe space for the apology conversation to happen, you are building an easy, peaceful relationship of deep trust in which much growth can occur. Hold that space for the other, and when you need it in return, they will hold it for you.

As much as you know, through study and learning, through practice, through coming to know yourself by watching yourself, you will still make mistakes on some days. Your Inner Wisdom will remind you of how much you know, that you know better than to say that or behave like this, but you will still say unkind things and act like an ass. On occasion. The exciting part about this work is that those occasions will become fewer and fewer, spaced farther and farther along the timeline of your life. And when they do occur, they will be of lesser intensity and shorter duration. It will become easier for you, less terrifying and embarrassing, to take ownership and to move on, into the presence of your unique genius and best self.

Taking ownership, all the pre-worrying and steeling yourself to go and say what you need to say, the actual moment of speaking your ownership, and the consequential unfolding of your best self, is a life-long practice. Don't be dismayed or disheartened when you have to do it again.

Sitting across that footstool from Steve, watching myself come undone, was so frustrating. The realization that I wasn't behaving as my best self actually fed into my argumentative power. I did not want to be there, in anger, having it out with him. It made me sad that I was there yet again.

Part of my anger was fed by a sadness that I couldn't move beyond something in my past that every once in a while reared its beastly head. The post-episode communication allowed some of that past to come to the surface, and in so doing, to be dissolved into the great expanse of forever. That part is now gone and there is a little empty space in my heart that I can now fill with love, kindness, and hope.

If we can allow, if we can simply hold the perspective of possibility, these regrettable episodes can serve for our good, our growth, our maturity. Remember the Princess and The Pea? She had to remove lots and lots of layers to get to that troublesome pea. These episodes can be like that.

These moments offer us the opportunity to open the gates and let our demons out of the corral. Maybe the fences around your corral are pretty strong and high, so your demons don't get the best of you that often. But they are still in there, ready to kick up a ruckus and disturb your equilibrium when the opportunity arises, when the right button gets pushed.

Can you let the gates open and then watch those bloody demons race across the plain in front of you, disappearing on the winds of forever?

That is freedom. That brings ease. That brings peace.

Seeing the Light at the End of the Tunnel

The whole point of cultivating emotional resilience is your happiness and well-being in life. Happiness and contentment matter. Achieving them is a worthy goal. We can say this and know this with certainty because we know how happy people behave. We have seen them. At times, we have *been* them!

Happy people are nice.

They are not consumed by the self, constantly wondering *Why this?* and *Why that?* about themselves and their lives and trying to make things go their way. Happy people move beyond the perimeter of self and are available to others. This does not mean they dissolve useful boundaries and let themselves be a doormat. It means that they have come to know, through the practices outlined above, especially Equanimity, that we are all trying to live a trouble-free life: we all want to avoid pain and suffering. Happy people know that none of us exist as separate and other, but that we are an integral part of the great whole of humanity.

It can be pretty easy to be emotionally stable and resilient when it's just you. Some of us might get mad at the toaster for burning the toast three days in a row, but when most of us are alone and only have ourselves to think about, we can demonstrate emotional stability because there's no one there to push against. (If you do get mad and have a fit at the toaster, then you might need to look a little deeper and do a little more self-inquiry work. And that's OK too. That damn toaster!)

We unquestionably need emotional resilience with others. Do you see how wonderful this whole process is? You get to do the work all on your own, on the inside, where it's invisible except to you. But you are doing this work specifically so that when you *are* in relationship, when you *are* with others, it becomes fully visible. In fact, it shines.

The work you have done in the hidden, personal corners of your Sacred Heart and mind become visible in your actions and your words, through your demonstrated kindness and your patience. And in this visibility is the recognition and the measure of your growth and sovereignty, your victory over your challenging emotions, and your personal integrity in keeping your commitments to yourself.

In these moments of emotional self-management triumph, you will realize that you are not leaving your happiness to chance. You are not leaving your sense of self in the hands of wild, rampant, and hot-blooded emotions. Nor in the hands of others. You can claim the reward of your inner effort and work, that are your love made manifest in the world. These moments of achievement are evidence of your inner mettle and nerve. This tenacity and pluck has helped you overcome your struggles and move into the unique genius and worth that came with you, part and parcel of who you are, when you arrived as a precious new baby in this world.

You see, we didn't arrive here with the task of acquiring or gaining our worth and value. But during the course of life, with all its challenges and learning opportunities disguised as stress, discontentment, heartache, misery, burnout, woe, misfortune, afflictions, loss, grief, adversity, suffering, and disappointment, our vision gets obscured. It gets blurry and conceals from our inner knowing the truth that we are good, that we are *good enough*. And that good enough is just right. So we harbor a deep need to gain approval, to have others establish our worth.

Because of the tarnish of daily life, which dims our inherent luster and sparkle, we go about wondering if we are good enough, or attractive enough, or smart enough, or fill-in-the-blank enough. It's time to wipe off the tarnish, to clear away the obscuring smudges, and remove the blur from our vision of self. It's time for a polish. It's time to *approve* of yourself, as you live more and more in alignment with your values, your strengths, and the virtues that necessarily result in goodness.

Demonstrated emotional resilience, developed by and through love of self and others, consistently, over time, without ceasing, is the way we can assess the results of our efforts, and to what degree they are working. And how will we measure this? How will we know?

Beauty Is Essential

Fortunately, it's not hard. The well-being and happiness gauge will register on the high side of positive emotions, mood, and attitude; you will be pleased by increased lightness of heart and joy; relaxation will be a more frequent experience in your life, as will mental clarity and focus. Your tasks will seem less of a burden and you will accomplish them more easily, more efficiently and effectively. You will sleep better at night, feeling less tired during the day; moments of feeling on edge, anxious, or burned out will decrease and be of shorter duration and intensity when they do happen. Life will seem less grueling and exhausting. Feelings of self-worth and self-love will increase.

All of this interior goodness will necessarily spill over, flowing out to your relationships, which become more harmonious and enjoyable. You will laugh more and share that laughter with others. You will see beauty at every turn, and in every face. You will enjoy an inner warmth, and your presence will radiate good will and contentment. You will more easily and more often rejoice in the goodness of others and cheer on those who are struggling in their quest to overcome difficulties and challenges. You will reach out a helping hand as you express your deeper desires of wanting to support, encourage, and motivate others to success. You will love more. You might, like Dr. Brusch, be moved to preach.

In short, life will just be better and you will just be happier.

Like the artist whose work captivates its audience with beauty, as you become the artist of your emotional resilience, you can create beauty that will inspire others. These sweet lines from Persian poet Hafiz in his poem *It Tried to Prepare Me*, capture perfectly the idea of you, as Artist, creating your own splendor and beauty:

> *The clear night sky tried to prepare me for*
> *what it knew would someday happen;*
>
> *it began to show me ever deeper aspects of*
> *its splendor, and then one evening just directly*
> *asked, Will you be able to withstand your own magnificence?*

This magnificence, blended with quiet humility, draws us in. We seek the refined and the pure; we want beauty to surround us. We long to be good, to harness the vibrant energy of youth, and to fill our lives with purity. All this can be real, for any of us who want it enough to quit being angered, to let go of being angry, to learn to still the inner stirrings of strong emotions, to breathe, and to get a hold of ourselves. It can be our everyday reality, if we want it to be.

Jordan Peterson, Canadian clinical psychologist and professor at the University of Toronto, reminds us that "beauty is not a luxury. It is essential. It is a portal to the transcendent."[60] Beauty is our access to the Sacred Heart and to all that is good in the world. As we all know, beauty is in the eye of the beholder. So behold it everywhere. Find the beauty in the struggle, in the grief, in the playfulness, and yes, even in the tragedy. And layer over that experience of beauty your own personal significance.

Make it personal. Make it heart-felt. It's your life. And you're creating it to be good, and yourself to be resilient, by recognizing beauty.

Lighten Up

Life isn't just meant to be endured. It's also meant for laughter and dance, song and celebration, joy and merriment. Life is meant to be lived in all its fullness and richness, experiencing goodness with others, being grateful for the blessings we call ours. Life is meant to be shared.

Get curious about your ability to gracefully self-manage when things are not going your way. You might be surprised by the outcome as you try something new, something other than your old, worn-out, patterned reactions. Allow yourself to see what arises, without judgement, without fear, assuming nothing. What unexpected joys might arise for you? What unexpected strengths? Can you be available to what might blossom as your experience? You might really be pleased by your new sense of Self—dignified, self-disciplined, lighthearted, peaceful. You might, in fact, really love the lightness of being that comes from grace.

My hope around all I've shared here, my hope for you, is that you leave these pages empowered, standing in your own shoes, autonomous and sovereign, confident in your power and ability to empower your people—your family, your colleagues, and your teams—to their own unique greatness. You do that only after you have found your own.

I invite you to create a harmonious, dynamic work environment where you and your people thrive and flourish in the bright light of creativity, gratitude, and joy. And I hope that you will do this in your home environment too, transforming it into a haven where your family longs to spend time, where they feel deeply valued and alive with their own potential.

I want you to fall deeply in love with your life and with yourself. I want you to own your greatness, and to know that you are Love, and to experience profound connection as you live from that Love. I would like very much to walk with you for a while, and hear your story.

The art of emotional resilience is as much about you becoming a sovereign, inspired, and inspiring leader as it is about creating inspired, interested, engaged, creative, and productive teams, employees, and future leaders. This is our objective. And it's much more than a personal objective or an organizational goal. It's what you are capable of. It's the potential you hold. It can be your reality as you step onto the pathway of your unique presence.

The promise of emotional resilience may seem to lie out there, in some distant future. Yes, it is there. And it is also right here, in current time. It is available to you in each and every moment. Please exercise your free will and power to choose in ways that will support you in your efforts to be good and do good. I will encourage you, as I encouraged students in my classroom for many years, to first be good. It is by *being* good that we are able to do good, and by *doing* good that we are able to *have* good.

The good life, a life mostly free of worry, stress, and anxiety, is yours for the asking. Tap into your innate goodness, share that with others, and goodness will surely return to you, multiplied into abundance. Smile often. See beauty everywhere. Be kind. Be generous. Express gratitude.

The world is a good place, full of good people, most of us doing our best. We all struggle to find joy and to avoid pain.

Soften around the edges. Listen on the inside. Know that the challenges will create in you a strength that you did not know you had.

Finally, please remember to love each other. And please remember to love yourself.

Endnotes

1   Lama Marut, "Your Real Enemies—A Lama Marut Video Podcast," *Youtube*, sahumarut, https://www.youtube.com/watch?v=ku2LMh6avm0, accessed October 22, 2020.

2   I studied positive psychology in 2014 through the Wholebeing Institute. Dr. Tal Ben-Sharah was the primary professor at that time. This phrase comes from the notes I took as I watched his lectures.

3   This information comes from a very handy chart I have titled "Autonomic Nervous System: Precision Regulation **What To Look For** by Babette Rothschild, copyright 2016. She used as her sources multiple medical and physiology texts; P. Leving 2010 and S. Porges, 2011. I include here the ISBN in case you're interested in finding the chart. ISBN: 13: 9780393712803

4   I was watching a youtube video of Dr. Wayne Dyer presenting at a conference when I heard this wisdom. It is sometimes my habit to take notes when I watch videos, but this time I did not. I do not remember which conference. Neither do I remember the title of the youtube video. What I do remember is the power this phrase had; it stuck in my mind without me needing to write it down.

5   This phrase comes from the yoga philosophy world. I do not remember the author and I cannot find a source, but my most educated guess is that it comes from Patanjali in his Yoga Sutras. I remember the profound impact it had on me when I heard it during my studies in my yoga teacher training program with Swami Satchidananda in 2003. It has become an anchor for me to remind me that this work takes time and continual effort.

6   Dr. Wayne W. Dyer Podcasts on Apple Podcasts. https://podcasts.apple.com/us/podcast/dr-wayne-w-dyer-podcast/id988177838. I do not remember which episode of the podcast I was listening to. I listen to podcasts a lot when I'm cooking and often don't have the presence of mind, or clean hands, to find a pen and write down the episode number.

7   Paul Ekman, *Emotions Revealed: Recognizing Faces and Feelings to Improve Communication and Emotional Life* (New York: St. Martin's Press, 2003).

8   Edwin H. Friedman, *A Failure of Nerve* (New York: Church Publishing Inc., 2007).

9   Dr. Daniel Siegel, https://www.drdansiegel.com/, accessed May 25, 2020.

10 Dr. Tina Payne Bryson, https://www.tinabryson.com/, accessed May 25, 2020.

11 Friedman, *A Failure of Nerve*.

12 David B. Myers, *Myers' Psychology for AP*, Teacher's Edition* (New York: Worth Publishers, 2011). The note on the * is this: AP is a trademark resisted and/or owned by the College Board, which was not involved in the production of, and does not endorse, this product.

13 Daniel Goleman, *Destructive Emotions: How Can We Overcome Them?: A Scientific Dialogue with the Dalai Lama* (New York: Bantam Dell, 2003).

14 Mary Helen Immordino-Yang, Antonio Damasio, et al., *Emotions, Learning, and the Brain* (New York: W.W. Norton & Company, Inc., 2016).

15 Myers, *Myer's Psychology*.

16 Goleman, *Destructive Emotions*.

17 Ekman, *Emotions Revealed*. In studying with Dr. Eve Ekman, Paul's daughter, in 2016 in the Cultivating Emotional Balance Teacher Training course, she unpacked for us the depth of the *emotional alert database*. As a summary in my words, this *database* is a repository of our memories, it contains a wealth of information linking previous emotional episodes—the event, the scene and setting, the emotions experienced, the people involved—to emotional episodes that happen in current time. Much of the current-time episode stems from recycled material that arises from the emotional alert database, triggered by a situation in current time that is similar to or has components of a previous event which has been stored in this *emotional alert database*.

18 Ekman, *Emotions Revealed*.

19 Ibid.

20 In 2011 or 12, a colleague was doing her course work to complete her degree as a behavioral analyst. She presented on emotion and behavior at the high school where I was teaching. This phrase comes from that presentation.

21 Barbara Fredrickson, *Positivity: Top-Notch Research Reveals the 3-to-1 Ratio That Will Change Your Life* (New York: Harmony, 2009).

22 Tal Ben-Shahar, "Tal Ben-Shahar: The Incredible Power of Positivity," *YouTube*, WOBI—World of Business Ideas, https://www.youtube.com/watch?v=fJTpIfXnbTc, accessed May 25, 2020.

23 Scholastic Inc., *Scholastic Dictionary of Synonyms, Antonyms, Homonyms* (New York: Scholastic Reference, 1965).

24 Dictionary.com, "change," accessed July 1, 2020.

25 Harvard Mental Health Letter, "In Praise of Gratitude," *Harvard Health Publishing*, Harvard Medical School, https://www.health.harvard.edu/mind-and-mood/in-praise-of-gratitude, accessed September 1, 2020.

26 Glenn Fox, "What Science Reveals About Gratitude's Impact on the Brain," *Mindful.org*, www.mindful.org/what-the-brain-reveals-about-gratitude, accessed May 22, 2020.

27 Barbara L. Fredrickson, "Positive Emotions Broaden and Build" in *Advances in Experimental Social Psychology*, Vol. 47, eds. Patricia Devine and Ashby Plant (Burlington: Academic Press, 2013), 1-53.

28 Happier Human, "31 Benefits of Gratitude: The Ultimate Science-Backed Guide," *Happier Human*, https://www.happierhuman.com/benefits-of-gratitude, accessed May 22, 2020.

29 Tal Ben-Shahar, *Even Happier: A Gratitude Journal for Daily Joy and Lasting Fulfillment*, (New York: McGraw-Hill, 2010) and *Choose the Life You Want: 101 Ways to Create Your Own Road to Happiness*, (New York: The Experiment, LLC, 2012).

30 Barbara Fredrickson, *Positivity* and *Love 2.0: How Our Supreme Emotion Affects Everything We Feel, Think, Do, and Become* (New York: Penguin Group, 2013).

31 Martin E. P. Seligman, *Flourish: A Visionary New Understanding of Happiness and Well-being* (New York: Free Press, 2011).

32 Shawn Achor, *The Happiness Advantage, The Seven Principles of Positive Psychology That Fuel Success and Performance at Work* (New York: Crown Business, 2010).

33 Ekman, *Emotions Revealed*.

34 https://en.wikipedia.org/wiki/Ac-Cent-Tchu-Ate_the_Positive, accessed October 26, 2020.

35 Fredrickson, "Positive Emotions Build and Broaden."

36 Ben-Shahar, *Choose the Life You Want*.

37 Ben-Shahar, "Tal Ben-Shahar: The Incredible Power of Positivity."

38 These definitions are from my notes of years' worth of study with Lama Marut. You can access his teachings here: http://lamamarut.org/, accessed October 26, 2020.

39 Fredrickson, *Love 2.0*.

40 Robert Emmons, "The Benefits of Gratitude," *Greater Good Magazine*, UC Berkeley, https://greatergood.berkeley.edu/video/item/the_benefits_of_gratitude, accessed May 25, 2020.

41 This is my summary of the study of positive relationships that I explored during my time with the Wholebeing Institute to earn my Certificate in Positive Psychology.

42 The summary of benefits is mine, but the three categories are taken from the work of Dr. Robert Emmons, "The Benefits of Gratitude".

43 David Rock, "SCARF: a brain-based model for collaborating with and influencing others," *NeuroLeadership Journal*, http://web.archive.org/web/20100705024057/http://www.your-brain-at-work.com/files/NLJ_SCARFUS.pdf, accessed May 25, 2020.

44 Linda Roszak Burton, "The Neuroscience of Gratitude: Discovering the Personal and Professional Benefits," *YouTube*, TLDGroup, https://www.youtube.com/watch?v=pC_-FbJJ34U, accessed May 26, 2020.

45 Goleman, *Destructive Emotions*.

46 Nancy Eisenberg and Paul Henry Mussen, *The Roots of Prosocial Behavior in Children* (Cambridge: Cambridge University Press, 1989).

47 In 2011 I really started paying attention in my classroom to how my mood, attitude, and mindset affected my students' engagement and leaning. What I learned at education conferences instilled a deep awareness and personalization of "What you model is what you get." and "You teach who you are." I wanted to verify those two phrases for myself in the laboratory of my own life. As I began studying the work of Dr. Barbara Fredrickson in 2014, I gained confidence that I was on to something. I amped up my action research with a special focus on observable behaviors and was not disappointed by what I observed and learned.

48 This phrase is not mine. Somewhere along the way, I read it and it stuck like glue. I have searched many, many times to find the author. I have yet to be successful in that search.

49 The Free Dictionary by Farlex, "hack," *The Free Dictionary by Farlex*, https://idioms.thefreedictionary.com/hack, accessed April 13, 2020.

50 The Free Dictionary by Farlex, "hack."

51 Sanjay Gupta, "Your Brain on Multitasking," *CNN*, https://www.cnn.com/2015/04/09/health/your-brain-multitasking/index.html, accessed April 14, 2020.

52 1 Pet. 3:9 NRSV.

53 Harvard Mental Health Letter, "Blue light has a dark side," *Harvard Health Publishing*, Harvard Medical School, https://www.health.harvard.edu/staying-healthy/blue-light-has-a-dark-side, accessed July 14, 2020.

54 Waveform lighting, "Blue Light, Melatonin, and Circadian Rhythms," *Human Centric*, waveform lighting, https://www.waveformlighting.com/human-centric/blue-light-melatonin-and-circadian-rhythms, accessed July 14, 2020.

55 Erik Strand, "Fighting Fatigue with Diet," *Psychology Today*, https://www.psychologytoday.com/us/articles/200310/fighting-fatigue-diet?collection=61445, accessed July 14, 2020.

56 Mark Hyman, *Food: What The Heck Should I Eat?* (New York: Little, Brown Spark, 2018).

57 Hugo, "The Happiness Quotient: What is it and how to test yours!," *Tracking Happiness*, https://www.trackinghappiness.com/happiness-quotient/, accessed July 14, 2020.

58 Hafiz, translated by Daniel Ladinsky, "It Is A Holy Woman an A Temple" from *A Year With Hafiz* (New York: Penguin Group, 2011).

59 Molly Dahl, *YOUTH Positive Middle School* (Nevada: YOUTH Positive Publishing, 2016).

60 Jordan B Peterson Podcast. I have no idea which episode I was listening to. https://www.jordanbpeterson.com/podcast/, accesses October 26, 2020.

Acknowledgments

There are so many people to thank and to be thankful for.

First, my sweetheart and best friend, Steve Yochum. This work would simply not be possible without you, for so very many reasons. You are not only a fabulous teacher for me, but also provide an ample training field for my own practice of emotional resilience. Thank you for helping me learn and grow. Thank you for seeing me. And thank you for loving me.

For my mom, Nancy, and my dad, Joe, two of my greatest examples of resilience in action. I would simply not be the Molly Dahl I am without your influences for good. Thank you.

For my family, including Jeannette, and for all we've learned from each other. I cherish the shared history and heritage of growing up in the Dahl House with Rachel, Rebekah, Josiann, Susan, and Harvey. I'm so grateful that as grow-ups, we enjoy such deep friendships. You all inspire me! Thank you.

For the friends and colleagues I have that have supported me in the process, not just of writing, but of my own emotional fortitude: Debb Oliver; friend, confidant, mentor, and business partner extraordinaire. What a blessing and a gift you are in my life. To Peggy Wynn Borgman, an amazing friend and editor. Thank you teaching me the value of story and helping me to honor my own.

To Stephanie Gibbons and Josiann Trainor for being early readers and feedback givers. Your insights are so valuable! And your opinions and suggestions helped craft this work. To my heart-friends Denise and Shelby, for helping me keep the excitement and wonder alive. To all those who have come to the classes I've taught, whatever the subject. Thank you for being willing to listen and to share, to offer feedback and suggestions, and to do the work. I know you did your inner work. I watched you change over time, I saw your changes...happier and healthier and more radiant.

It also feels right to honor and thank all the many teachers and guides I have had along the way. Thank you to my teacher, Lama Marut. I miss him daily. Not a day goes by that I don't hear him in my head, offering a treasured teaching that reminds me why I'm here and how to enjoy my life. It is him to whom I refer when I mention my teacher. Thank you to Cindy for teaching me what love is and how to live from the Heart of Love. Thank you to my early teachers of positive psychology, Dr. Winston McCullough and Dr Tal Ben-Shahar. And thank you all those who have researched, taught, and written on the subject. My library is full to over-flowing with volumes of works dedicated to helping each of us to live a life of thriving and flourishing.

And thank you, Reader, for all your efforts to do your best, for hanging in there day after day after long, tedious day. You are the reason I wrote this. I honor where you are on your path and offer you all the love there is. May your journey be joyful, with many rich experiences along the way. May you have the eyes to see and the ears to hear the beauty that is all around you, all the time. Sometimes, you may have to brush off a bit of a smudge, but the beauty is there, just waiting to grace you with a little touch of magic.